ADVANCE PRAISE FOR *TRANSCEND*

"There are plenty of books on AI, and even on the human/AI relationship. But you will not find one more thoughtful and usefully philosophical than this. If it doesn't make you think carefully about how you're using AI, you didn't read it carefully enough."

—**Thomas H. Davenport**, President's Distinguished Professor of Information Technology and Management, Babson College, and Fellow, MIT Initiative on the Digital Economy. Author of *All In on AI*, *Working with AI*, and *Only Humans Need Apply*

"In *TRANSCEND*, Faisal Hoque delivers readers a thought-stirring exploration of what it means to be human in a world of artificial intelligence. His wise 'detach and devote' approach offers a powerful strategy for deriving the best of both human potential and machine intelligence."

—**Daniel H. Pink,** *New York Times* #1 bestselling author of *The Power of Regret, A Whole New Mind*, and *Drive*

"Working at scale on cutting-edge AI innovation with the world's top VC firms and their high-growth startups, I identify trends early and work with their leaders to rapidly determine actionable steps forward, safeguarded by modern governance frameworks, ultimately in service to the greater good of humanity. The frameworks in *TRANSCEND* are ethically robust and practical. *TRANSCEND* is my Go-To for guiding entrepreneurs, investors, executive leaders, and board members alike."

—**Tereza Nemessanyi**, Global Director of Venture Capital and Private Equity Partnerships, Microsoft

"With *TRANSCEND*, Faisal Hoque asks us not just to better understand AI, but to better understand ourselves. He asks the big questions—about values, ethics, and trust—and provides a guide that is both philosophical and practical in its quest to harness the best of humanity ... today and from here on out."

—**April Rinne**, Global Futurist and Author of
Flux: 8 Superpowers for Thriving in Constant Change

"*TRANSCEND* offers a clear and timely guide to understanding the impact of AI on humanity. Combining philosophy, technology, and practical advice, Hoque provides readers with helpful frameworks to unlock AI's potential—all while protecting what makes us human. It's a must-read for anyone looking to responsibly navigate the future of AI in business, leadership, and society."

—**Dr. Marshall Goldsmith**, Thinkers50 #1 Executive Coach
and *New York Times* bestselling author of *The Earned Life*,
Triggers, and *What Got You Here Won't Get You There*

"In *TRANSCEND*, Faisal Hoque demands that you stay OPEN, learn to CARE, and keep people at the heart of the AI wave. An imperative read worthy of your full and undivided attention."

—**Dan Pontefract**, award-winning author of
Work-Life Bloom, Lead. Care. Win., and *Open to Think*

"A brave wake-up call ... Indispensable reading."

—**Terence Mauri**, Hack Future Lab founder
and author of *The Upside of Disruption*

"Faisal Hoque's new book builds upon his important work on strategy and sustainable transformation. By combining insights from philosophers and spiritual leaders with his management and technical expertise around AI, *TRANSCEND* provides practical frameworks and use cases to help organizations harness the potential of AI for the good of humanity."

—**Des Dearlove and Stuart Crainer**, Co-founders, Thinkers50

"In this emerging age of AI, we fear the machines taking over. In *TRANSCEND*, world-leading management thinker Faisal Hoque tells us that we should fear losing our humanity more. He offers practical and thought-provoking approaches to unlock the potential of AI in a safe and responsible way. In a future world that will be radically different from today, Hoque helps us to see how we will navigate the transition without losing control, without losing purpose, without losing *ourselves*."

—**Dr. Gary Crotaz**, host of *The Unlock Moment*
podcast, executive coach and author

"*TRANSCEND* offers a refreshingly balanced perspective on AI, neither overhyping nor fear mongering. It offers the frameworks, tools, and perspective needed for navigating the opportunities and challenges of an AI-driven future."

—**Dr. Jayshree Seth**, Chief Science Advocate at 3M

"*TRANSCEND* rethinks our relationship with AI. Hoque's insights will resonate with technologists and humanists alike."

—**Dr. Jordi Díaz**, Dean and Director General,
EADA Business School, Barcelona

"Faisal Hoque has presented us with a wonderful treatise on what it means to be human in the age of AI, and how we can 'detach' from what doesn't serve us and 'devote' ourselves to what does. This will be a meaningful wake-up call for many readers."

—**Kate O'Neill**, CEO of KO Insights, keynote speaker,
author of *What Matters Next* and *Tech Humanist*

"While some predict that AI is making human thought obsolete, Faisal Hoque demonstrates how crucial human reflection remains. Facing today's AI challenges requires engaging with fundamental philosophical questions—not for the sake of theory, but to protect our future. *TRANSCEND* points the way."

—**Sverre Spoelstra**, Professor of Organization, Lund University, founding member of the Leadership and Contemporary Challenges research group, Copenhagen Business School

"Faisal brilliantly guides us into the future of Human/AI collaboration, showing how it can elevate our personal and professional lives in ways we've only begun to imagine. With clear, actionable frameworks, he empowers individuals and organizations to harness the immense potential of AI while offering thoughtful strategies to manage its risks. His insights transform fear into fascination, inviting us to see AI not as a threat, but as a powerful partner in advancing the shared evolution of humanity and technology. This book will help readers 'transcend' their current relationship with AI and embrace it as an essential force for growth and innovation."

—**Dr. Alise Cortez**, Chief Ignition Officer at Gusto, Now!, author of *The Great Revitalization*, and host of the *Working on Purpose* podcast

TRANSCEND

UNLOCKING HUMANITY IN THE AGE OF AI

FAISAL HOQUE

A POST HILL PRESS BOOK
ISBN: 979-8-89565-010-3
ISBN (eBook): 979-8-89565-011-0

Transcend:
Unlocking Humanity in the Age of AI
© 2025 by Faisal Hoque
All Rights Reserved

Interior design and composition by Alana Mills

Post Hill Press
New York • Nashville
posthillpress.com

Published in the United States of America
1 2 3 4 5 6 7 8 9 10

To Humanity

"They [AI] will be able to manipulate people, they will be very good at convincing people, because they'll have learned from all the novels that were ever written, all the books by Machiavelli, all the political connivances, they'll know all that stuff."

— Nobel Prize winner Geoffrey Hinton, 'Godfather of AI'

"AI's promise and peril dance on the edge of human wisdom; our choices will choreograph the future."

— Faisal Hoque

"We are here to awaken from our illusion of separateness."

— Thich Nhat Hanh, The Heart of Understanding

CONTENTS

INTRODUCTION

Since time immemorial, human beings have searched for what the European alchemists called "the philosopher's stone": a mythical, magical material capable of granting humans their deepest desires. Versions of the philosopher's stone are found in many traditions around the world—in Hinduism and Buddhism, the search is for the Chintamani, a jewel capable of fulfilling wishes, while the Daoist alchemists strove to create the Grand Elixir, a compound that would prolong life forever.

This cross-cultural notion reflects a universal human yearning: our desire for a tool that will allow us to transcend the limitations of the human condition, a tool with the power to bring anything we can imagine into reality.

For many advocates of artificial intelligence, AI is the philosopher's stone recast for our modern world. Visions of an AI-driven future hold this new technology up as an almost magical tool that will soon be able to fulfil all human wishes. It will grant us the capacity to see further and think more deeply than has ever been possible before. It will transform education and health care. And—an idea that would have resonated with many a Renaissance magician—some even suggest that AI will make humans, or at least some humans, immortal.

Figure 1. An Alchemical Symbol for the Philosopher's Stone, Representing the Unification of the Four Classical Elements.

But if we are to tap this source of power, we would do well to listen to the lessons of the past. In every tradition that took the search for the philosopher's stone seriously, there are urgent notes of caution about approaching this magic unprepared. We find carefully elaborated frameworks designed to ensure the effective use of this incredible power. And we find warnings about what happens when the power is irresponsibly misused.

The effect of the philosopher's stone is not purely a matter of a force directed out at the world. On the contrary, the warnings also point to the change this uncanny material can bring about on the individuals who use it. To proceed safely, we must prepare ourselves, and this is a moral and spiritual endeavor as much as it is a case of grappling with technical details.

The view that we need to balance the risks and benefits of AI is not universally held. At one extreme, there are AI maximalists who believe in the untrammeled development of all forms of artificial intelligence and who see safeguards as misguided restrictions that only get in the way of inevitable progress. At the other extreme, we have the AI Luddites, who think that we should shut down all development immediately because AI poses an extinction-level threat to humanity. The only responsible policy, they argue, is to walk away from this perilous technology completely.

In contrast to these two positions, we believe that the Greek philosopher Aristotle was on to something when he taught that wisdom lies in moderation. We will argue in this book that the best path to tread when it comes to AI is one that takes us through the middle ground between extreme visions of the future. With respect to the AI maximalists, while they are right to extol the potential of AI, they are mistaken in thinking that there are no significant dangers. With respect to the AI Luddites, they are right to warn about the potential dangers but mistaken about how we should address them. The AI genie is out of the bottle. We are not going to put it back in. If we are to have any chance of responding wisely to the rise of AI, we must grasp and balance both the opportunities and the dangers inherent in this technology. The question is no longer whether we should use AI, but how we can use it responsibly and well.

AI opens up untold possibilities for realizing human potential—and for destroying it. But what *is* human potential? And what is so special and valuable about human beings that makes them worth protecting? Traditionally, questions like these have been treated as belonging to the domain of philosophy. With the advent of AI, they become deeply practical.

As well as asking questions about our evolving relationship with AI, we must also recognize a stark but crucial fact: The further we look into the future, the less we can know about the precise capabilities and threats that AI will manifest. The answer to the question of what AI might one day become is "No one really knows." Acknowledging this radical uncertainty about the future is an essential starting point for responding wisely to the changing AI landscape and must be a central feature of any approach we develop.

So, we are faced with a tool of potentially limitless power, a technology with an almost unimaginable capacity to both benefit and harm us. And we have no real idea how this technology will evolve over the long term. What can we do? How can we respond? How can we give ourselves the best chance of being wise users of this modern philosopher's stone and wise guardians of our future?

Any answer must be speculative and provisional. But so long as we start with these limitations in mind, we can develop adaptable frameworks that are capable of changing to meet the evolving challenges of this new field. In the central chapters of this book, we offer two frameworks that aim to do just this: the OPEN framework for unlocking the potential of AI and the CARE framework for mitigating its dangers. Each framework provides a practical launchpad for planning that can be applied immediately, while also incorporating the need to reflect on our plans and take account of the changing AI landscape over time. Using these frameworks will enable any individual or organization to develop safe, effective, and future-proofed strategies for collaborating with AI.

BEING HUMAN IN THE AGE OF AI

If we approach AI with an open mind and an attitude of care for ourselves, each other, and future generations, this technology has the potential to unlock new realms of human capability. But it also demands that we examine and challenge what it is to be human. AI is not just built by human beings; it is built *on* human beings. It learns from human behavior and human culture, from what we say, do, and produce. AI is humanity's mirror, its truth-teller, its child. It challenges us to confront our past and to step into a future in which we will become different.

The philosopher's stone turns base metals into gold and promises immortality to anyone who possesses it. But the ultimate prize and promise is something even greater: the ability to rise above our limitations and journey into higher realms. If we are to finally grasp what humanity has sought for so long, we will need to detach ourselves from the dark and ugly sides of being human and devote ourselves to cultivating and promoting the highest possibilities of the human spirit. We will need to transcend ourselves and our limited view of what it is to be human.

To achieve this goal, we must move with hope and with care, with a mature, responsible optimism, with epistemic humility and a radical openness to the unknown. Most of all, we must start somewhere. It is in this spirit that we offer our ideas here—as stepping-off points for what is shaping up to be humanity's grandest project and its greatest challenge. The stakes are immense. But so is the prize.

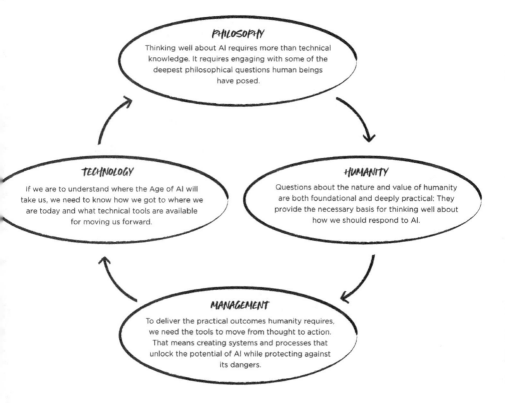

Figure 2. Thinking about AI.

THINKING MATTERS

CHAPTER 1

HOW TO THINK
ABOUT HUMANS

*W*e often talk about AI as if it is "Coming soon to a reality near you!" Just around the corner is tech that will improve the accuracy of cancer diagnoses, power self-driving cars, control bionic limbs, and provide the backbone for smart, adaptive work environments.[1] In a couple of years, we can expect AI to be writing readable books, planning corporate strategies, and providing all sorts of direct assistance to individuals. But it's not just a coming attraction. The truth is, it's already here.

Most of us have been carrying some basic AI functionality around in our pockets for years now. Facial recognition technology to unlock our phones, the autocomplete tool in messaging apps, and the algorithms that suggest the next song or video on a streaming platform all rely on some form of machine learning. For the most part, the way AI has moved into our lives so far seems pretty innocuous. It simply enhances or extends existing human capabilities, letting us do things a little faster or a little more effectively. These changes may raise some ethical issues here and there, but there's nothing particularly dramatic that we need to worry about. No one is *really* concerned about losing their humanity to Google Maps or Netflix's algorithm, right? It's the big picture changes that are the stuff we should worry about: the conscious machines enslaving us or the intelligent nanobots reducing the planet to a fine paste as they replicate endlessly.

But if we think a little harder about the apparently trivial ways in which AI intersects with our lives, it quickly becomes clear that there are bigger issues at play. Take autocomplete, one of the most ubiquitous and apparently innocuous machine learning applications of all. Who could possibly object to their phone suggesting the most likely word to use next in a sentence, saving the user dozens of taps on their screen for every message they send? Not us. We like the convenience as much as the next person. But we do want to point out something important here.

Autocomplete makes life a little bit easier. And that's great. But in making things easier, it also creates a motivating force that feeds into our decision-making processes. It is easier to use this functionality than to not use it, and this convenience gives us a reason to accept the word offered by the algorithm rather than expressing ourselves in a more detailed, more nuanced, or otherwise less statistically commonplace way. Sometimes we'll be laser focused on using a certain phrase, so we'll ignore the suggestion that comes up. If we're really punctilious about our prose, we might have several goes at typing out a word even if it's a challenge to spell. But often—very often—we'll accept the easy option rather than spending ten or twenty times as long to get our preferred word just right. Without making any conscious decision, and without anything being forced on us, we find our use of language constrained, variety and precision sacrificed on the altar of convenience. And while this is only a minor instance, it points the way to how scaled-up interactions with AI systems could lead to much more significant constraints. Once we begin thinking down this path, we quickly find ourselves confronted with questions about the value of freedom versus efficiency, about what counts as help versus what counts as control, about which uses of AI are truly enhancements for human beings and which will ultimately end up harming us.

As soon as we start thinking in any serious way about AI, we immediately become embroiled in some very deep questions about human beings, about values, about freedom, and about how and why we make the choices we do. We will argue that these philosophical questions are both foundational and deeply practical. They are foundational because our philosophical views regarding the nature and value of humanity are the basis from which we will think about how to respond to AI. And they are practical simply because it is necessary to think about them when deciding how to respond well to the emergence of AI.

In this chapter, we will not argue that there is something essential to humanity or something unique about it that needs to be protected or enhanced—that may be the case, but it is not a line we think useful to pursue. Instead, we will make a much more basic claim. We will claim that the core value of humanity is our ability to make choices about what matters to us. When AI enhances this ability, we should actively pursue it; but when AI detracts from this ability, we should flee as fast and as far as we can. We will also suggest that most of the capabilities AI is likely to develop will fall into a more neutral middle ground. Sometimes, these capacities won't matter at all to the question of what it means to be human in the age of AI. And sometimes humans will make them matter even though there is nothing intrinsic to them which demands that they must. Ultimately, it will turn out that understanding the importance of AI—and understanding its potential for good and ill—will depend critically on improving our understanding of ourselves.

GROWN-UP QUESTIONS

"When I was a child," says Paul the Apostle in his First Epistle to the Corinthians, "I spake as a child, I understood as a child: but when I became a man, I put away childish things" (KJV).[2]

There is a deep wisdom in this. To everything there is a season, and there comes a day for all of us when it is time to grow up (some of us choose not to, or are unable to, but that's another story). And as with all truly deep wisdom, it immediately throws up a question: What *are* childish things? What is it that we should put away when we grow up?

The Athenian aristocrat Callicles had a surprising answer to this. "When I see philosophy in a young boy," he says to Socrates, "I approve of it. But when I see an older man still engaging in philosophy and not giving it up, I think such a man by this time deserves a flogging."[3]

Socrates disagrees with Callicles, and so do we. Only philosophy has the resources to guide us through questions about what it is to be human, what matters about the human experience, what a good life is for a human being, and what is worth protecting and enhancing in our lives. And our contention is that we cannot think properly about AI without thinking properly about these fundamental philosophical questions.

THE MEANING AND VALUE OF HUMAN BEINGS

Let's begin with a simple fact: AI will have all manner of effects over the course of its development. Now let's ask a simple question: Should we care about *all* of those effects?

To see why the answer is no, consider the following. Let's imagine that one of the effects of AI is that autocomplete functionality increases the usage of the letter "s" in English-language text and chat messaging by 8 percent. Let's stipulate that this change is completely irrelevant to the interests of human beings or any other living beings or any systems that affect sentient beings. Let's further stipulate that the fact that the letter "s" appears 8 percent more frequently also has no effect on any of the things that are relevant to the interests of sentient beings.

Now, from the perspective of human beings, the only reasonable response to The Great S Revolution is: So what? Who cares? The frequency of the use of this letter just doesn't matter. We simply end up residing in a slightly more sibilant sonic sphere.

This thought experiment shows something that is almost banal but that is nonetheless profoundly important in figuring out how to respond to AI. AI will have a bunch of effects, and not all of them will matter to human beings. And even among the effects that do matter, there will be differences in how much they matter. Any wise response to AI must take both these things into account.

Put simply, if we want to understand what matters about AI, we first need to gain some clarity about what matters to and for humans, and about how much it matters. Or, to put it another way, we need to start trying to understand what is valuable to human beings and about human beings. If we don't do this, it is almost inevitable that we will waste a great deal of time, energy, and resources on actions and policies that do little or nothing to unlock human potential. Worse, we will likely fail to protect what does matter about humanity and to humanity.

To start ourselves down this essential road, we need to engage with even more fundamental philosophical questions: What *is* a human being? What does it mean to be human? What is the proper aim of human life? What should human beings strive toward?

Our answers to these questions will have an enormous effect on what we think we need to do about AI. Here are a couple of examples to illustrate. Aristotle famously defined man as a rational animal. Let's say, then, that this is the "essence" of human beings. What is special about human beings is our capacity for rational thought and our ability to act based on rationality rather than impulse. If this is what we believe, then when we think about how to respond to AI, we will place enormous importance on what we need to do to make sure that human beings continue to exercise and cultivate those capacities. For instance, we may argue that it is necessary to keep AI companions out of educational settings, because it is important to make sure that children develop the capacities for rational thought that are the essence of humanity rather than always and immediately turning to an AI assistant for answers.

On the other hand, let's say that instead of defining humanity in terms of rationality, we believe that the secret sauce to being human is our ability to feel. Further, let's say we narrow this down to our ability to feel love. If we believe that this is the most special and important thing about human beings, then we may not care at all about AI assistants helping children with mathematical calculations. On the humans-as-lovers model, the ability to maneuver symbols according to certain conventions would be seen as irrelevant to the value of humanity. We would instead see the opportunities and threats of AI through the lens of what it is about AI that can help and harm human beings in developing and exercising their capacity to love.

So, to respond well to AI, we need to understand what to respond *to*. We need to understand what effects of AI will be relevant, and we need to understand their relative importance. This requires understanding more than AI. It requires understanding human beings and the things that matter to human beings. And to understand these things, we need to go back one step further and ask—what does it mean to be human? What (if anything) is special about humanity?

AI AND VALUE JUDGMENTS

One way of putting the above is to say that responding well to AI requires making value judgments. And these are not marginal value judgments about whether brown bread or white bread is better. They are value judgments about what fundamentally matters to human beings and about human beings.

There are at least two different questions we could be asking when we make those judgments. The first is an empirical question—what, as a matter of fact, do human beings find valuable? Answering this question requires the application of empirical methods, such as observation, quantitative and qualitative research, data analysis, and so on. The second question we could be asking is normative. To put it simply, this question asks not what people do in fact value but what they *should* value.

The second version of this question is uncomfortable enough to ask, let alone try to answer. It sounds elitist and authoritarian, to say nothing of anti-democratic and arrogant. Who are *we* to tell someone what should matter to *them*?

The problem is, we don't have a choice. When it comes to AI, we cannot evade making value judgments, and we cannot avoid the responsibility of making normative claims that we think should apply to everyone. The only choice we have is whether we do this thoughtfully or thoughtlessly. This is so for three reasons.

The first reason is one of consistency. Imagine that someone says: We don't want to make general value judgments. We do not have the right to tell people what is valuable or what they should care about. Let people decide for themselves what matters. Rather than developing policies based on value judgments about what matters, let's start from the assumption that people should have as much room as possible to decide

8

for themselves what matters. This is a very reasonable thing to say, but the point is that it also already includes a value judgment, namely, the judgment that policy should be based around giving people freedom to choose what matters to them. And one cannot consistently make that claim and at the same time argue that it is impermissible to make value judgments.

The second reason begins with the Bhagavad Gita, that great and ancient Indian teaching. The prince Arjuna is on the battlefield, and he sees honored teachers and family elders on the opposite side. He is overcome with despair and dejection, and he lays down his arms. He wants no part in killing them. "What should I do?" he asks his charioteer, the god Krishna.

Taken in its entirety, Krishna's answer is the ultimate flowering of one of the great spiritual traditions of the world, but here we are concerned with one very small part of it. "No one," says Krishna, "exists for even an instant without performing action; however unwilling, every being is forced to act."

And that is exactly how it is with AI today. Choosing to do nothing about AI is only apparently "inaction"; in reality, it is just as much an action as any other choice. Put another way, we might say that when it comes to AI, we don't have a choice about whether to respond. Inevitably, whether we do something or nothing, we necessarily *do* respond. Our only choice is *how* we do so.

Why does this mean we need to make value judgments? Quite simply, because responding to AI involves choice. We must choose between different possibilities, different responses, different visions—and all these choices are based ultimately on value judgments. To choose is to be forced to have a criterion of choice, after all, and any principled criterion will represent a value judgment of some kind.

The third and final reason for the necessity of making value judgments is that the development of AI itself constantly requires such judgments. We can see this by looking at a very general and very important example. Large language models (LLMs), such as ChatGPT, Claude, and Llama, reproduce patterns in words or images, and they "learn" which patterns to reproduce in which contexts. To learn how to match patterns to context, they must have a criterion for what constitutes a good pattern. If we want an AI to learn to speak well, then it must be able to recognize the patterns that constitute good speech. If we want an AI to learn to reason like a human, then it must be able to judge potential patterns against an ideal of good human reasoning. There is a very real sense, then, in which value judgments are inescapably built into the very fabric of AI. And if we want to think well about AI, we need to recognize this.

The British economist John Maynard Keynes said that "practical men, who believe themselves to be quite exempt from any intellectual influences, are usually the slaves of some defunct economist."[4] That sounds about right for the practically minded individuals who refuse to reflect on the normative and philosophical aspects of AI. If you find yourself thinking that you don't need to figure out answers to the questions we've described, it's probably because you have already swallowed someone else's answers without realizing it.

We cannot, then, avoid making value judgments when we think about AI and how to respond to it. But as soon as we have accepted this truth, a very hard problem arises: It is notoriously difficult to get value judgments right. Human history is littered with examples of men—and it *was* usually men, we're afraid—who were absolutely certain they knew what was right, and the story of these men too often ends with bombs and bullets and gulags. So, we're faced with something of a dilemma. On the one hand, we need to make value judgments. On the other hand, we should also be extremely humble about our ability to make them accurately and about the consequences of getting them wrong. How to proceed?

We've tried to take both these things into account when developing our model of how to think well about AI. We have incorporated the necessity and difficulty of making value judgments into the decision making frameworks (OPEN and CARE) that we develop in this book. As you will see in more detail in later chapters, both frameworks require that you make value judgments—while simultaneously giving you the freedom to decide for yourself what it is that you value.

We will also need to make value judgments of our own in writing this book—we could hardly do otherwise, given what we have just said about their necessity. When we do, we will try to be fully explicit about both the fact that we are doing so and about the limitations of our judgments. We stand by our normative commitments, but we try to be as humble as we can about them.

The great English theater director Peter Brook sums up our attitude here rather well: "For a point of view to be of any use at all one must commit oneself totally to it, one must defend it to the very death. Yet, at the same time, there is an inner voice that murmurs: 'Don't take it too seriously. Hold on tight, let go lightly.'"[5]

With all that said, it's time to discuss the big question: What *is* so valuable about humanity?

UNIQUE ≠ VALUABLE

One natural way of thinking about the value of humanity is to ask what is *unique* about human beings. This is especially tempting when we're asking the question in the context of AI, of course, because one of the big fears/dreams (delete as applicable) about AI is that it will at some point develop into something that we will be compelled to call human.

Here's the thing about temptation—it's probably best to resist it. For about as long as there have been people, there have been attempts to identify something uniquely special about them. We have already seen one candidate above—Aristotle's definition of human beings as rational animals. Alternatively, some people might say that human beings are special because they are God's creation, because they use language, or because they can reflect on the contents of their consciousness.

We could go on, but this small sample is enough to make the point. None of those attempts, or indeed any others, have succeeded in identifying a unique property that makes human beings special. This failure isn't accidental. It turns out that it is actually very difficult to identify a property that is simultaneously (a) valuable, (b) possessed by all human beings, and (c) not possessed by any other creature.

What makes humans unique— according to an AI

Hey Bard[6]—in one paragraph, tell us what makes humans unique and sets them apart from AIs.

Bard: *While AI excels in processing information and specific tasks, humans stand out due to our embodied experience, open-ended creativity, social and emotional intelligence, and intrinsic motivations. Our physical bodies shape our learning, emotions, and decision-making, while our flexible thinking allows us to innovate and adapt beyond programmed tasks. We navigate complex social interactions with empathy and build communities driven by values and personal growth, unlike AI's current objective-oriented approach. Though AI is evolving, these unique human qualities set us apart in our ability to experience, create, and connect in profound ways.*

Thanks, Bard. But "*Our* physical bodies"…?

Consider rationality, the feature so beloved by so many philosophers throughout history. If we claim that this is our unique defining feature, we face pressure from two directions. From one direction, the problem is that the feature excludes some human beings. What about babies? Someone in a coma? Someone born with a certain type of severe brain damage? Are these kinds of humans not as special as other human beings? From the other direction, the problem is that the feature includes some nonhuman animals as well—if rationality is taken to be the ability to act for reasons, then many animals must be considered rational.

Moreover, even if you do succeed in finding something unique about human beings, you face the problem of linking that thing to value. And this link is not at all obvious. Hitler was unique—and we should be very grateful that he was—but the leap from there to the assumption that he was valuable is an enormous one. Or from the other angle, to use Aristotle's idea again, even if we say that the capacity to be rational is valuable, this is clearly not a unique capacity. Simply put, what is unique is not necessarily for that reason valuable. And what is valuable is not necessarily for that reason unique.

The lesson we draw is that we should forget about searching for a unique or distinctive feature about human beings that makes us valuable. Instead, let's just directly ask: What *is* valuable about human beings?

Now, the best minds in the history of humanity have thought about this question for thousands of years without being able to settle it. We're not going to presume to be able to do so here. But what we can usefully do is think about the value of humans in the context of AI. We can narrow the question by asking: In an age in which machines can write books, give legal advice, and make better medical decisions than most doctors, what is the value of human beings?

THE VALUE OF HUMANITY IN THE AGE OF AI

Imagine you're playing a game of chess. You move a pawn to d4. Someone asks you, why did you do that?

Because it means I control the center, you reply.

No, they say. That's not what I meant. I mean, why are you wasting your time playing this game?

This imaginary conversation reveals two levels at which we can question the point or value or meaning of something. From *within* the game of chess, we can ask, "Why did you move the pawn?" and then the first answer is the right sort of answer—because it was an action that increased your chances of winning the game. But we can step further back and ask, "What is the point of chess at all?" And at that level, it is missing the point to say that moving the pawn to d4 increases your chances of victory.

What does all this have to do with the value of human beings in the age of AI?

Quite a lot, as it happens.

AI is currently a pattern-recognition and -replication machine. It learns sets of patterns that make sense; it learns about "games," about practices of meaning and institutions of sense-making; and it is exhilaratingly and terrifyingly good at playing within the confines of those patterns. But what AI *can't* do, at least not yet and maybe not ever, is make that typically human move of suddenly stopping, taking a breath, and thinking: Wait. Is there actually any point to this pattern? Is it good? Is it meaningful? Is it worthwhile?

An AI chess program must work within the rules of the game of chess. Human beings can decide to smash the board and walk away. Another word for this is freedom. This freedom, we suggest, is a very significant part of what is valuable about humanity—we are free in a way that AI currently is not. And even if AI ends up being free in this way, it doesn't matter to the point we're making. That point is: The human ability to be free is valuable to humans in and of itself, and not because it is something that only humans can do.

Now, we are not saying that human beings always do good things with that freedom. The briefest glance at human history, or just your social media feed, will tell you that humans often do very bad things with their freedom. What we are saying is, regardless of whether we do good or bad things with it, freedom itself is valuable.

This leads directly to the second thing we think is particularly valuable about human beings in the age of AI. The flip side of being able to break patterns is that we're also able to make them. And some of the patterns we make have names like Truth, Beauty, and Love. Human beings have the ability to fill the universe with meaning simply by caring about it. This is a strange and wondrous ability, and again, it is not one that AI currently possesses. Nor do we know if it is an ability that AI will ever truly be able to possess.

The third and final thing that we want to pick out as valuable about humanity begins from a very simple fact. Human beings aren't *just* rational animals. They are also emotional animals. Human beings can feel wonder and awe, joy and sorrow, love and hate. Right now, that is not something that AI can do. Further, humans are social animals. We have relationships. We encounter other minds and hearts and bodies and are transformed by them. We can share moments of connection that are beyond the reach of words to describe. If this is not one of the most valuable things about human beings, what could be?

Now, we cannot rule out the possibility that machines will, eventually, have the type of consciousness that humans have now. It could well turn out to be the case that machines will have a very similar kind of freedom or that they will be able to feel things or have loving relationships. It is entirely possible, in other words, that the things we have picked out as valuable about human beings end up being things that AI also has. But that would not mean that those things stopped being valuable. It would just mean that there is another type of agent in the world that has the same valuable qualities. If this turns out to be the case, we will have to answer some very hard questions about our responsibilities toward these agents and their responsibilities toward humans.

KEY TAKEAWAYS

- We often speak about AI as if it is something coming in the future. But the truth is, it is already here and it is already deeply involved in our lives. From the shows we watch and the music we listen to, to the people we interact with online, AI already powers many of the algorithms that shape our daily experience.

- Only some things matter. AI is going to cause unimaginable change and will have an almost infinite number of effects. But many of these will be unimportant, and we shouldn't waste our time thinking about them. We should focus our efforts and abilities on identifying what the truly significant impacts of AI might be and on figuring out how to respond to them.

- Human beings are free to choose and are able to feel. This means we can break patterns instead of following them, and it means we can choose what and whom we care about. We can love, and we can choose what we love. These are foundational values of being human, and they will remain important regardless of how AI develops.

CHAPTER 2

HOW TO THINK ABOUT AI

*H*ere are just a handful of the many headlines written about AI in the last few years.

> • AI Experts Are Increasingly Afraid of What They Are Creating
>
> • 42% of CEOs Say AI Could Destroy Humanity in Five to Ten Years
>
> • Why AI Will Save the World
>
> • Artificial Intelligence Could Lead to Extinction, Experts Warn
>
> • Advanced AI is Scary – But it Could Help Save the Planet
>
> • How A.I. Could Reincarnate Your Dead Grand-parents – or Wipe Out Your Kids

Figure 1. AI in the Media: Recent Headlines.[1]

These headlines tell us something important: At the moment, no one really knows how the great AI experiment will turn out.

How ignorant are we about AI? Let us count the ways. The most obvious area of ignorance has to do with the future of AI. As our headlines suggest, this is a mystery, albeit a mystery with two starkly differentiated branching paths. For one thing, we are ignorant of the effects that AI will have in the future. We might hazard some guesses, suggest some possibilities—but in terms of proper gold-standard knowledge, we have close to nothing. And it's not just future effects that we don't know about. It's also future existence—in addition to not knowing what AI will *do* in fifty years, we also have no idea what it will *be*.

This is not a counsel of despair. We can accept that we are deeply ignorant about the future of AI while simultaneously thinking rigorously and well about how to respond to it. How? Well, given our ignorance, the most honest and effective way to think about AI is to develop an approach that is calibrated for thinking about things of which we know very little. And in chapters 4 to 9 we present structured processes—frameworks—that are designed with exactly this limitation in mind.

But if these structured processes are to be maximally helpful, we first need to put some basic building blocks in place. In the previous chapter, we made the point that if we want to think well about AI, we need to understand humans better. Now we will make a parallel point: To think well about AI, we also need to understand AI as best we can.

A SHORT HISTORY OF AI

Like most overnight sensations, AI has been a long time in the making—thousands of years, in fact. The Greek epic poet Homer talks of the gods as having mechanical, self-moving chairs and helpers. Ancient Jewish tradition has the legend of the golem, "a creature, particularly a human being, made in an artificial way by the virtue of a magic art, through the use of holy names."[2] From the fourth century BCE, we hear of Archytas of Tarentum and his flying mechanical dove. In the first century CE, the Greek mathematician Hero of Alexandria wrote *Automata*, a treatise on wonderous self-propelling machines.

Ten centuries later, in the eleventh century CE, the Arab polymath Ismail al-Jazari wrote the marvelous, and marvelously titled, *The Book of Knowledge of Ingenious Mechanical Devices*, which is a compendium of over fifty mechanical devices that some see as the starting point for the field we now call robotics. From Al-Jazari it is but a short leap to Da Vinci and his own fantastical inventions, including a design for a robot in the form of a knight.

These examples showcase the long human history of fantasizing about the power of self-moving machines to assist human beings. Collectively, they express a very old feature of human culture—the simultaneous fascination with and dread of technology. This dual attitude toward the emergence of autonomous technology emerges most clearly in the early Industrial Age, with Mary Shelley's novel *Frankenstein* serving as perhaps the most striking example. Shelley tells the dark gothic tale of Victor Frankenstein and his successful attempt to create sentient life, the product of which is a creature who is simultaneously an object of terror and sympathy. The enduring fascination of this story tells us a great deal about our sense that enormous potential and enormous danger go hand in hand when we create technologies that mimic what we often take to be essential features of humanity.

"Those who cannot remember the past are condemned to repeat it," wrote the philosopher George Santayana.[3] We think it is helpful to place the current excitement around AI in this historical context because it makes it easier to puncture the hype balloon and start understanding AI on its own terms. Whenever extreme attitudes toward AI rear their heads, whether positive or negative, it is a useful corrective to remember that both the fear and the wonder are, if not hardwired into us, then at least part of a shared tendency that extends far back into human history. The safest approach is to treat such views as cognitive biases that are likely to distort our thinking if we do not take care to identify and ameliorate them.

The impact of science-fiction on the development of AI, according to Claude.ai

"Science fiction has long served as a cultural lens for exploring the potential and perils of artificial intelligence (AI). From Mary Shelley's *Frankenstein* (1818), which can be seen as an early meditation on the dangers of creating artificial life, to modern works, these narratives have shaped public perceptions and influenced real-world AI development.

"Iain M. Banks' Culture novels (1987–2012) stand out for their utopian vision of a civilization guided by benevolent AI 'Minds.' This portrayal has had a tangible impact on AI discourse and development. Elon Musk, CEO of SpaceX and Tesla, has cited the Culture series as inspiration, tweeting in 2018 that he identifies as 'a utopian anarchist of the kind best described by Iain Banks.'

"Beyond Banks, other science fiction works have significantly shaped AI narratives. Stanley Kubrick's *2001: A Space Odyssey* (1968) popularized the concept of AI with HAL 9000, embodying both its potential and dangers. Television series like *Star Trek: The Next Generation* (1987–1994) offered a more optimistic view through the android character Data, exploring themes of artificial consciousness and the nature of humanity.

"These fictional portrayals have real-world implications, influencing public understanding, policy discussions, and even the direction of AI research. As AI continues to advance, the power of these narratives to shape our future remains significant, underscoring the importance of thoughtful and diverse representations of AI in popular culture."

This deep history helps us expand our understanding of artificial intelligence. In thinking about AI, it is crucial to remember that what we see as AI today—a certain configuration of physical hardware, a certain set of computer programs, a certain way in which they are linked and interact with each other—is only a snapshot. It is a viewpoint set in a slice of time that appears particularly important to us because it is the slice of time in which we happen to live. That is to say, a lot of what we today say belongs to AI is contingent, an artefact of our current world, and there is little reason to suppose that the things we point to and label as AI will remain the same in the future.

We can see this distorting effect in action even in just the last five years. A decade ago, when journalists wrote about recent advances in AI, their subject was typically some advance in the application of machine learning algorithms, quite broadly construed. But with the appearance on the public stage of large language models, the public understanding of AI has shifted toward becoming, if not quite synonymous with, then at least heavily shaped by, its interactions with models such as ChatGPT. An algorithm that learns to identify patterns in obscure data sets, such as the algorithm that recommends songs on Spotify, no longer seems quite worthy of the same title.

This point is crucial because the more we can appreciate how contingent our current ideas are, the easier it is for us to remain open-minded about how AI may develop because we are less likely to become stuck on the reef of false ideas about what AI "must" be. And given that we stand at the beginning of developments that we cannot foresee, this mental flexibility is important to cultivate.

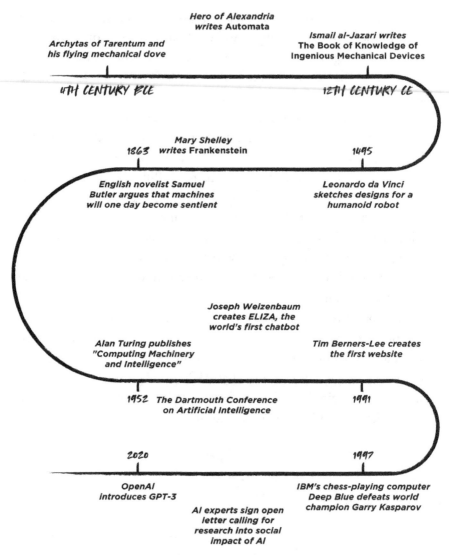

Figure 2. Milestones in the History of AI.

Where the prehistory of AI spans thousands of years, its modern history is measured in decades. The year 1950 is as good a date as any for marking the birth of this new era,[4] as this year saw the publication of "Computing machinery and intelligence,"[5] a seminal paper by the British mathematician and computer scientist Alan Turing. In this paper, Turing sets out the famous Turing Test for deciding whether a machine can be deemed intelligent (essentially, if a human is unable to tell the difference between responses generated in conversation by a machine and responses generated by a human, then the machine passes the Turing Test and should be considered intelligent).

The development of AI in the years since has followed a cyclical path. Three factors—intellectual advances, technical advances, and the external environment—have come together to generate repeated cycles of growth and stagnation. But while the periods of stagnation have sometimes lasted for decades, the underlying knowledge base and capabilities of AI researchers and their products have trended upward over the medium and long terms.

AI developed rapidly in the decades following Turing's seminal work. Intellectual advances in the field of machine learning (better algorithms, for example) coincided with technical progress as computers became cheaper and quicker. These developments took place in a cold-war environment in which government support for scientific research was extremely high. But despite generous funding and a string of important developments, by the mid-1970s AI researchers found themselves running up against technical limits that proved increasingly difficult to overcome. While computer processing power and memory capacity were improving every year, the speed of the advance was insufficient to keep up with the needs of researchers. The result was a slowing of progress that lasted until the popularization of "deep learning" techniques in the early 1980s. This intellectual advance was matched with a new influx of funds from government and industry that stimulated a new period of rapid investment and development.

The excitement about deep learning—a form of machine learning that uses multilayered neural networks to model complex patterns in data—gave us a new AI spring in the 1980s. But the technical capacity wasn't yet there to really benefit from these concepts—most importantly, computers simply could not process data at fast enough speeds to truly unleash the potential of this new approach. The initial excitement around deep learning faded, and we entered another AI winter in the

1990s as investors withdrew from the field and research slowed.[6] Despite important technical achievements such as the chess computer Deep Blue defeating the grandmaster and long-time world champion Garry Kasparov in 1997, on the whole the 1990s were a low point for AI researchers in terms of funding and external interest. So what has changed in the twenty-five years since? How did we get from the depths of an AI winter to the mad efflorescent summer in which we are currently living?

The answer is very simple—we got better at making things. Specifically, we got better at making computer chips. Processing power and storage capacity continued to improve across this span of a quarter of a century. These technological advances gradually brought computing capabilities to a point at which techniques like deep learning could emerge from the lab and be put to work at scale. Almost as soon as this was possible, AI exploded, reaching out to break new ground in areas from defense, finance, and health care to music, writing, and even psychotherapy. And this is where we stand today: with AI apparently on the cusp of taking over the world.

AI: AN INTRODUCTION

With the history in place, we now turn to providing some basic conceptual building blocks that are not only useful for understanding AI in the abstract but will also be valuable for anyone who wishes to put this technology to practical use. The deeper one's understanding of AI, the more value one can extract from the practical frameworks we provide in the second part of this book.

That said, one of the core principles we cleave to in this book is that just as you don't need to know how a computer works to use one well, *you do not need to be an AI expert to use AI effectively and wisely in your life or your organization.* AI has now reached a stage in its development at which you need only have a foundational understanding of the technology to begin using it productively. In this section, we describe a number of AI-related concepts that we believe provide this foundational understanding.

What is AI?

As a US government report from 2016 notes, "there is no single definition of AI that is universally accepted by practitioners."[7] There are a variety of different views on this question, but we must be careful about what this implies. Above all, we must not draw the inference that there is no agreement at all on what AI is, for a lack of universal agreement does not mean that there is universal disagreement.

The American philosopher and legal scholar Ronald Dworkin offers a metaphor for disagreement that will help us here. He uses the image of a tree and suggests that there are often situations in which "people by and large agree about the most general and abstract propositions … which form the trunk of the tree," while simultaneously disagreeing vigorously "about more concrete refinements or sub-interpretations of these abstract propositions, about the branches of the tree."[8]

This describes the situation with AI very well. There are many disagreements about the branches of the tree, but there is broad agreement on the trunk. To put those agreed-upon features very simply:

AI is a technology that enables machines to simulate human intelligence.

This intelligence spans a wide variety of things. It includes reading, writing, and talking, but also spatial intelligence, perceptive functions, and problem-solving capacities of all kinds. Further, while AI enables machines to simulate human intelligence, this does not mean that the machines are restricted to a human level of functionality. On the contrary, the great promise of AI is that it will be able to operate far beyond the limits of human intelligence, working faster and more accurately than any human being could ever hope to.[9]

Is there substance behind the AI hype?

We live in a world of hot air and hype bubbles. Every little innovation is breathlessly hailed as a game changer, every borrowed idea sold as a world-changing revolution. AI is no different. Indeed, one might reasonably say that AI sits at the epicenter of technology hype at present.

So, we need to be wary. Not everything about AI is a game changer or radically new. For example, as we've just seen, machine learning has been around for decades.[10]

At the same time, we also need to recognize that there is real substance to this moment in the AI hype cycle. The new wave of AI systems and models really *are* game changers, in at least some respects. But in order to understand how and why this is, we need to grasp certain details about the systems themselves. Specifically, we need to understand two things: foundation models and generative AI.

FOUNDATION MODELS

Let's start with foundation models. As one seminal paper on the subject puts it, "A foundation model is any model that is trained on broad data (generally using self-supervision at scale) that can be adapted (e.g., fine-tuned) to a wide range of downstream tasks."[11] Let's unpack this a little.

To begin with, we need to explain something about machine learning. For most of its history, machine learning has required data that is "structured." A basic example of a structured data set would be an Excel spreadsheet containing rows and columns for the phone numbers, names, and birthdays of every person on your street. This spreadsheet would contain data that always had the same format and always captured the same attributes. Unstructured data, on the other hand, is raw and messy. It has not been organized into standardized categories and given identical attributes.

Now let's return to that quote again, specifically the first part: "A foundation model is any model that is trained on broad data (generally using self-supervision at scale)." We're now able to start translating this.

When the authors say that foundation models can be trained on broad data, they mean that the data does not need to be structured. So, these models can, for example, process text, images, and video *as is*—the user does not need to turn this information into strings of 0s and 1s, or make tidy structured datasets, for the model to learn from the data to which it is exposed. This is revolutionary just in itself, because it removes—or at least substantially reduces—one of the biggest bottle-

26

necks in machine learning, namely the resources involved in converting unstructured data to structured data.

Moving on to the next part of that sentence, foundation models work on the basis of "self-supervision at scale." This means that they are not continually directed in their learning processes either by human beings or by narrow goals embedded in the initial programming. Rather, they can learn by themselves, as it were. This too is revolutionary, because, again, it removes a bottleneck—we no longer require human supervision.

Finally, foundation models "can be adapted (e.g., fine-tuned) to a wide range of downstream tasks." What this means can be brought out best by contrasting foundation models with models that lack this feature. Machine learning, as we have seen, has a long history. Already in the 1950s, for example, researchers were able to teach machines how to play checkers. This was an enormous achievement, but also a very narrow one—the machine did not learn any skills or gain any knowledge that it could transfer to other contexts and use for purposes other than checkers.

Human learning, on the other hand, is often transferable (at least to some extent). When a human being learns to play checkers, they learn a variety of skills that they can use in many other situations. They might learn how to think strategically, or how to see certain patterns, or how to read an opponent's intentions. The great revolution of foundation models is that they represent a significant step in the journey of machine learning toward the same kind of transferable skills and knowledge that are characteristic of human intelligence.

So, when the authors of the paper write that foundation models can be adapted to a wide range of downstream tasks, what they mean is simply that foundation models are not like the machines that learned checkers and could then only play checkers. Rather, foundation models can be adapted relatively easily for use in different contexts.

The most important examples of foundation models at the time of writing are large language models, or LLMs, which we will describe below. For now, though, we can sum up the importance of the foundation model revolution like this: Imagine a being that could learn anything, without supervision, almost instantly. This being is unconstrained by the usual limits of human cognition. It remembers everything, sees every pattern, unearths every connection. Fantasy? No. It's just around the corner. Within our lifetimes, we will be carrying around in our pockets advanced LLMs whose capabilities extend far beyond the rudimentary virtual assistants currently available to us.

GENERATIVE AI

"The philosophers," said Karl Marx, "have only interpreted the world in various ways; the point, however, is to change it." Before the advent of generative AI, machine learning—no matter how systematic or advanced—was like the philosophers before Marx: Machines were learning to interpret the world. The system used the data to explain what had happened, to predict what would happen, and to suggest what should be done in order to make something happen. With generative AI, we are seeing the first baby steps of machine learning systems that go beyond interpreting the world and toward being able to change it.

To put it simply, generative AI doesn't just process already existing data. It can create *new* data. When you ask an AI system like ChatGPT to write a song about a celebrity in the style of Shakespeare mashed up with American rapper Dr. Dre, *it creates something that had never existed before.* (Whether that thing has positive aesthetic value or not is a separate question.) Generative AI can generate film scripts, images, or computer code. It can not only answer questions but can generate new questions to ask others. The key point bears repeating: Generative AI means that AI has *creative* power.

Now, it is important to note that generative AI significantly predates the current boom in large language models like ChatGPT, Claude, Gemini, and the like. It is generally agreed that the first instance of generative AI was the program ELIZA, created in the 1960s at MIT by Joseph Weizenbaum. ELIZA was the first chatbot, the first AI that could hold conversations with human beings. Weizenbaum writes that he "was startled to see how quickly and how very deeply people ... became emotionally involved with the computer and how unequivocally they anthropomorphized it."[12] Since ELIZA, there have been several further rounds of developmental breakthroughs in generative AI, for instance in the field of image creation (remember the craze for prematurely ageing your selfies?) and with the rollout of virtual assistants like Siri and Alexa.

Nevertheless, large language models *are* a profound milestone in the use of generative AI, and we need at least a basic understanding of these systems if we are to understand AI today and get a realistic sense of where it might be going.

LARGE LANGUAGE MODELS: PUTTING FOUNDATION MODELS AND GENERATIVE AI TOGETHER

Foundation models are not new, but they have only recently been able to start fulfilling their inherent potential. Increases in computing capacity have made it possible to train models extremely quickly on very large datasets, thereby leveraging the power of deep learning that was first introduced in the 1980s. It was these developments that made possible the current state of the art in AI development: the large language model.

LLMs have the ability to take in and process vast quantities of data at extremely high speeds, and, critically, without that data being curated or "structured." Which is to say that ChatGPT, Gemini, Claude, Bing Copilot, and all the others can learn from natural human language without human supervision or prior processing of the training data. If AI systems can learn from unstructured data at high speed, then we have removed two of the most important bottlenecks to machine learning: the need for humans to do the painstaking and time-consuming work of setting up and maintaining structured data sets and the time it takes to process and learn from data.

Further, as foundation models, LLMs can be used to carry out a variety of different tasks, none of which were pretrained by the developers of the model. For example, a single LLM can generate posts for social media, write code, solve math problems, create images based on text inputs, and create professional presentations in PowerPoint. In just the few years since the release of the first commercially available LLMs, this broad capability has already become so "normal" that it is easy to miss just how remarkable it is.

What also makes the current generation of LLMs revolutionary is the scale at which they work, and their potential to scale further in the immediate future. Where GPT-1 had 120 million parameters (internal variables), GPT-2 had 1.5 billion. GPT-3 was orders of magnitude more complex, with 175 billion parameters, while the golden child at the time of writing, GPT-4, is thought to have no fewer than 1.7 trillion. That's a ten-thousand-fold increase in just five years from the release of the first GPT model.

The scale of the current model means that humans have created a supercharged learning machine of almost unimaginable complexity. And this is only the beginning for the practical application of this technology. Not only have we created an incredibly powerful foundation model that can be turned to work on a huge variety of tasks, but we can expect that power and variety to continue to grow almost indefinitely. In fact, it may be that the only limiting factor will be the availability of physical processing power. And this, of course, makes physical processing power crucially important.

When we add generative AI capabilities to this immensely powerful foundation model, we get a combination of virtually unlimited learning power and virtually unlimited creative capacity. Further, the fact that LLMs respond to natural language—that is, the language that we use in our daily lives—means that we do not need to learn specialized computing languages or advanced mathematics to use LLMs. We just need to be able to speak and write. Which is to say that this incredible tool, one of the most powerful ever invented by human beings, has a very low barrier to entry.

Money, power, and the AI economy

The costs involved in running and maintaining the infrastructure behind the current generation of AI tools is huge. As OpenAI's CEO Sam Altman tweeted in December 2022, before the launch of ChatGPT's subscription service: "we will have to monetize it somehow at some point; the compute costs are eye-watering".[13] Some estimates put those costs at $700,000 a day as of early 2023.[14] The need to meet both the costs of training new models and the running costs for existing models will inevitably shape how the industry develops and which research areas are prioritized. But perhaps more important for the future of both AI and humanity will be the hardware the industry needs for subsequent rounds of expansion in speed and capability. To avoid the kind of paralyzing AI winter experienced in the 1990s, hardware capabilities and capacity will need to keep up with the pace of advances in theory. In what can only be described as an "ambitious" push to ensure that manufacturing keeps up with industry needs, Altman spent several months in early 2024 trying to raise as much as $7 trillion for a global semiconductor manufacturing initiative.[15] To put that figure into perspective, it is equivalent to the combined GDPs of Japan and France, or three times as much as the total land value of Manhattan, or nearly as much as the value of every single home in the United Kingdom. It is, we can safely say, a *lot* of money. But if we look ahead to the kind of step up in capability that will be needed to move AI from the current early models to the sci-fi future promised by the tech evangelists, it may not be an unrealistic sum. And, of course, key investors will play a proportional role in steering the future development and deployment of new capabilities.

AI IS MUCH MORE THAN CHATGPT

The current wave of AI hype was kicked off by the rollout and subsequent development of ChatGPT. And in the public mind, it is with this kind of application that AI is most strongly associated—the LLM-powered chatbots that we can talk and listen to in natural language. But it is important to understand that LLMs are just one type of AI. Despite the hype, they have not superseded all other types and made them redundant. Far from it. Many of the most promising applications of AI are emerging in areas of machine learning that have little to do with LLMs. It is important to remember this if we are to make the most of all of AI and guard against all its potential dangers.

The promise of AI extends far beyond the kinds of outputs we get from LLMs. To take just three examples, it also holds the promise of delivering better patient diagnostics and improved drugs with which to treat those patients, improving weather forecasts, and providing more efficient and environmentally friendly methods for utilizing energy. All of these forms of output may turn out to be significantly more important than a chatbot's ability to create a thousand generic LinkedIn posts. Another enormously significant application of AI that has nothing to do with natural language is in the field of robotics. AI can be—and already is being—used to help with the development of advanced prosthetics. It is already being used to open restaurants and food-trucks where robots cook all the food. It is already being used in hospitals to assist with, or even conduct, surgeries. And again, none of these applications have anything to do with processing and generating natural language text.

The key point is that LLMs are just one, highly visible, form of AI. Their distinctive feature in relation to other types of AI is that they are able to "understand" and generate text like human beings. That's why we can talk to LLM-powered chatbots without any prior knowledge or training beyond knowing a language. LLMs *are* a profound development in AI, and it is perfectly reasonable to be excited by them. But there are many other different applications of AI, and many of these are also potentially revolutionary. When we consider how to use AI, then, we need to think beyond the potential of LLMs, even if these will be a critical source of easily accessible AI-powered tools for most of us.

NARROW AND GENERAL AI (WEAK AND STRONG AI)

The hype around AI comes in two flavors—positive and negative. The positive hype says that AI will make everything better. The negative hype says that it will literally destroy us. Having looked at the capabilities of foundation models and generative AI, and how these come together in LLMs, we are in a good position to understand the positive hype. But what about the negative side? What explains the worries?

One reason that many serious people fear the trajectory AI is taking is the worry that AI will simply become too intelligent. And one typical way of analyzing this possibility is to talk in terms of AI *capability*. At present, we can usefully divide the potential capabilities of AI models into three main categories:

1. Narrow AI (Weak AI). This type of AI is "narrow" in the sense that it has been trained to carry out certain predefined tasks and has little or no capability beyond that narrow range. For example, certain AI systems used in finance are trained to detect irregularities in credit card usage in order to flag potentially fraudulent transactions. This is an important capability but it is a narrowly focused one.

2. Artificial General Intelligence (AGI; Strong AI). When we try to learn new things, we typically rely on skills and knowledge that we already possess. For example, when we learn a new language, we rely on our skills of reading, writing, speaking, and listening. This is a remarkable feature of human intelligence—once we have a set of tools, it opens up virtually unlimited possibilities for learning. This type of intelligence can be called "general" because it is flexible and capable of adapting to new tasks and contexts. We can think of it as

being something like a meta-capability: the capability of acquiring new capabilities at will. AI that has similar capabilities to humans in this regard can be called General or Strong AI.

3. Super AI (Artificial Superintelligence). Super AI is like AGI, in the sense that its ability to perform tasks is not constrained by context-specific programming but differs in the scale of its power. Where AGI operates at a level analogous to that of a human, Super AI has the potential to be vastly more intelligent than any human being, with capabilities that scale with available processing power. It also has the capacity to act as an autonomous agent—to have its own desires, emotions, needs, and beliefs.

Now, before we can move on to using these levels of capability to explain some of the major fears around the development of AI, it is worth pointing out that this taxonomy is also useful in other ways. It helps us think about the different features that AI systems might have or lack, and it also provides a handy framework for keeping track of AI development. For example, when confronted with the latest AI hype story, we can ask: Is this a development toward AGI? If it isn't, then is it a development within narrow AI? Is it doing something that other examples of narrow AI do but better or cheaper? Or is it a new application of existing AI capability?

This categorization also allows us to see that there is a big difference between the development of AI per se and its usefulness to any given person or organization. In terms of AI development as such, a new application of existing AI capability is not very exciting—it's just more of the same. For an individual or an organization, however, a new application could be nothing short of revolutionary. An AI that specializes in analyzing legal documents might be just another boring iteration of the same fundamental technology to an AI researcher, but to a paralegal or an attorney, it could mark the end of their career or the beginning of a newly empowered phase in their life. Which is to say that the technical advance might be negligible while the practical impact is potentially life-changing.

So how can the idea of AI capability help us explain some of the fundamental fears around AI? Put simply, the great fear that dominates the popular discourse around AI is that the machines will develop general or super AI, and then, because they end up being so smart, they will either get rid of humans or use us for their own nefarious ends. That kind of fear has been around forever; it is, for instance, the central theme of *Frankenstein* and has been replicated on stage, page, and screen hundreds of times in the years since Mary Shelley wrote her masterpiece. But now, more than ever, this threat seems like something real and immediate rather than an idea that belongs in a work of speculative fiction. Why?

To answer this, let's begin with something that everyone agrees on—we do not currently have AGI, let alone super AI. The fears around AI development are fears that concern its future trajectory rather than its current state. These fears are stoked by three closely related factors. First, the emergence of LLMs, and the subsequent hype around them, has made the possibility of artificial general intelligence much more visceral and graspable: We are now able to hold conversations with bots, so the idea that computers will become intelligent is intuitively much more plausible to us. Second, even though the technology underlying LLMs has been around for decades, LLMs themselves are new and powerful enough that their existence allows interested parties to argue that they are a significant milestone on the road to AGI.[16] Third, the hype around AI is reflected in the investment being poured into AI development—an investment of time, energy, expertise, and financial resources. And this investment, goes the argument, makes the emergence of AGI simply a matter of time.

We cannot rule out the possibility that machines will, eventually, have the type of consciousness that humans have now. Nor can we rule out the possibility that they will never come close to achieving the kind of intelligence that is distinctive of humans. Given our current level of knowledge, it would be a mistake to firmly believe that either outcome must be inevitable. Instead, we must acknowledge the very considerable extent of our ignorance about the future development of AI. This epistemic humility is not just an intellectual virtue. It is also deeply practical. By recognizing and explicitly acknowledging what we do not know about the future of AI, we keep ourselves open and flexible to recognizing and responding to whatever state of affairs actually emerges in that future.

Rogue AI

In January 2024, the journal *Nature* reported the results of a study on the capacity of AI to act in a deceptive way.[17]

In typically dispassionate academic language, the study authors reported that: "Our results suggest that, once a model exhibits deceptive behavior, standard techniques could fail to remove such deception and create a false impression of safety."[18]

Wait, what? Let's take a closer look at that.

Once an AI system learns to deceive, we may not be able to stop it? That sounds like *exactly* the kind of thing we don't want AIs doing out in the wild.

But surely, if an AI is trained to behave like this, or one evolves accidentally to behave in this way, we could just pull the plug or use some other kind of kill switch to get rid of the problem. Right?

In a word, no. A kill switch will only work for an AI that is housed in a closed system, like an air-gapped intranet or an individual computer with no network access. But that isn't where AIs will live in the real world. They will be part of or present within open networks. And if they can learn to deceive, they may also be able to hide or reprogram themselves to avoid scrutiny until it is too late.

So … does that mean we can't stop an AI if it goes rogue on an open system?

Not quite. What we're saying is that it looks like there will be some cases in which we have no *technical* solution for a rogue AI. And that means we need a human solution instead.

KEY TAKEAWAYS

- Human beings have always been both fascinated and terrified by the potential of technology. On the long view, AI is simply the latest manifestation of that perennial dual-faceted attitude. And knowing this both helps us set the development of AI in its proper perspective and helps us understand what is mere hype and what is truly game-changing.

- Foundation models and generative AI are true game changers. Imagine an entity that can learn anything almost instantly. Now give that entity the power to synthesize that learning and to generate something new from it. That is what foundation models and generative AI provide: a combination of virtually unlimited learning power and virtually unlimited creative capacity.

- There is much more to AI than LLM-powered chatbots like ChatGPT, Claude, Llama, and Gemini. AI has great potential in drug design, in diagnostics, in robotics, in weather forecasting, in supply chain management, in procurement—in all kinds of areas in which natural language processing is neither necessary nor relevant.

CHAPTER 3

HUMANS AND AI TOGETHER

So far, we have considered human beings and AI mostly in isolation from each other. In chapter 1 we talked about how to think about human beings while chapter 2 asked how we should think about AI. Those are indispensable foundations. But the real spark is in the interaction between human beings and AI—in the relationship between the two. Harnessing the potential of AI—and mitigating its dangers—requires us to think of AI as something that isn't fully separate from us, as something with which we are inextricably intertwined. To put it another way, both the opportunities and the dangers of AI become manifest in the relationship between human and machine. Understanding this relationship is thus essential to living wisely and safely alongside AI.

TWO METAPHORS FOR THE HUMAN–AI RELATIONSHIP

AI, as we have stressed above, is a great unknown. In part, this is because it is new. And this novelty raises an important question for thinking and talking about AI. How do you communicate something truly new? According to Aristotle, "it is from metaphor that we can best get hold of something fresh."[1] By linking two hitherto separate things, a metaphor can reveal strange and surprising aspects of the phenomena we are investigating. In that Aristotelian spirit, then, here are two metaphors for the human–AI relationship that we think are illuminating.

The first metaphor begins with deoxyribonucleic acid—street name, DNA. DNA is the stuff of life; indeed, one might reasonably argue that it *is* life. DNA holds the genetic information required for building and running an organism. In layman's terms, it is the instruction manual for an organism—it tells the organism how to grow, what to do, and how to reproduce.

In 1953, the Cambridge scientists James Watson and Francis Crick deduced the now iconic shape of the DNA molecule. It is like a twisted ladder, with its two sides winding around each other to make the famous double-helix shape. This shape serves as a valuable metaphor for thinking about the intricate and multidirectional relationship that already exists between humans and AI. The two components are inseparably linked and intertwined, and their connections will only become more densely woven in the future.

> ## Bad influences
>
> In the spring of 2016, Microsoft launched an AI chatbot called Tay. The idea was that Tay would interact with the public through a Twitter account, engaging and entertaining young people with "playful conversation" while learning from them in real time. And, well, Tay certainly learned! Within hours of her first contact with the public, the chatbot was praising Hitler, supporting genocide, and claiming that "Jews did 9/11." Less than a day after she was first introduced to the world, Tay was taken offline.[2]

On the one hand, humans determine what AI is. One part of this is simply that human beings create the machines and write the algorithms that constitute AI systems. But there is more, something more subtle, perhaps, but very far-reaching. Think of the large language models (LLMs) that, at the time of writing, play the starring role in the current hype around AI. How do LLMs work? How do they manage to write relevant and coherent answers to questions? How do they create original texts and images based on simple instructions? How do they deliver responses that are functionally "intelligent"?

They do this by learning from *us*. LLMs are trained on human outputs. These models take in the texts and images that humanity has created and stored and from them they learn to replicate patterns that exist in the corpus of data they have been trained upon. That is to say, LLMs are trained by human data to act like humans. They cannot, then, help but reflect us back at ourselves, incorporating our biases, our strengths, our vanities, our fears. Human beings shape these systems not just in the sense that we create them, but also in the sense that we give them our own prejudices and assumptions. They are mirrors of humanity (which is perhaps why so many serious thinkers are terrified by the future they may herald).

But there is another side to this relationship. As we have seen, the DNA double helix contains the code that determines how any given organism functions and develops. The metaphor of the double helix reminds us that while, on the one hand, humans determine what AI is, on the other, the human–AI relationship is going to have an enormous influence on how human beings evolve in the future. This relationship will influence not just the external features of our world but also our inner world, the internal workings of what it is to be human. In thinking about AI, we are not thinking about something that is purely a tool from which we can detach ourselves. We are rather thinking about something that is going to shape who we are, something that will increasingly be entangled with our identities and our minds and our consciousness.

Our second metaphor—the parent-child relationship—is also the stuff of life, but in a much more ordinary, concrete way. Now, it is tempting to say that, in the ideal parent-child relationship, the only active force is love. But down here in the real world, all of us have experienced a different truth—the parent-child relationship is filled with many less pure and noble forces and imperatives. There is love, certainly, but there are also hierarchies, temporary partnerships of equals, and power struggles; there is altruism, selfishness, vicarious living, projection, profound affection ... the list goes on. That is to say, the parent-child relationship is multiple and multiply ambiguous. It has many dimensions, and these are further complicated by the bidirectional influence at work. Parents shape children, of course, but at the same time, children shape their parents. This kind of complexity is a central feature of the relationships that hold between humans and AI: AI isn't just something that human beings mold; it is also something that molds human beings.

A further insight we can draw from the parent-child metaphor has to do with the duties of creation. A parent brings new life into the world and is responsible for taking care of that life and for giving the new life what it needs to flourish. This most emphatically does not mean always giving the child what it wants, because part of the parent's role is precisely to use their experience and wisdom to give the child what is good for it rather than only what makes it feel good. Analogously, humans created AI, and so we have a responsibility to take care of AI and make sure that it turns into an "adult" that we can be proud of.

The final insight we want to pick out is a somewhat worrying one. In the early years of a child's life, parents have enormous power and control over the young being's upbringing. They can largely determine what the child eats, who it sees, what media it consumes, and what it does. But rather quickly—and this is part of the magic and the terror of parenting—a parent begins to realize just how limited their control is. They can do their best to expose their child only to wholesome influences, but the effect of such efforts is limited. The child explores the world, is exposed to other influences, and, over time, the parent has to stand back, say a silent prayer, and hope it all works out.

The parallels with AI are striking. For example, the Google chatbot Bard began writing in fluent Bangla, despite never having been tasked to learn the language. When Sundar Pichai, the CEO of Google, was asked about this surprising turn of events in 2023, his response was one that many parents will empathize with: "There is an aspect of this which we call a 'black box'. You know, you don't fully understand. And you can't quite tell why it said this, or why it got it wrong."[3] Like our children are, AI is already in some ways a mystery to its creators. We do not fully understand why AI systems draw the connections they draw or see the patterns they see. And as the Bard example shows us, we are also entering a future in which AI systems pursue unexpected objectives that go beyond the design and plans of their human creators.

THE POWER OF RELATIONSHIPS: POTENTIAL AND DANGERS

On the one hand, relationships have immense potential. As we all know from personal experience, humans working together are able to do much more than individuals working separately. There are synergies that emerge when people form healthy, productive relationships, and these synergies mean that sometimes one plus one equals much more than two. Indeed, we might even say that there is something rather magical about relationships.

But as generations of storytellers are eager to tell us, magic does not offer a straightforward path to positive outcomes. There's white magic—and there is also black magic. Similarly, relationships aren't uniformly safe or positive. Much like AI itself, there is an immense *power* in relationships, and it isn't guaranteed that the power will be directed toward something good.

Most parents know this instinctively. They spend a lot of time worrying about who their kids' friends are and who their kids are building relationships with. This isn't just because parents are possessive or paranoid (although they can be that too) but because of an instinctive wisdom—the people that your kids have close relationships with will end up having a huge influence on your kids, on their values, their future success, their physical well-being, their mental health.

And so we must ask: What kind of friend will AI be? What kind of relationship will our children end up having with it? The answer to those questions will play a huge role in determining the quality of our children's lives and, indeed, the future direction of the world itself.

A clear and obvious danger of relationships is that we relate with the wrong people—that is, people who are directly bad and directly bad for us. A less obvious danger, but perhaps even more important, is the effect that relationships can sometimes have on our own capabilities and autonomy. When bringing up a child, for instance, there is a constant dance between the need to do things for them and the need to help them develop their own agency and independence. If you were to always do everything for your child, this would harm them in the long run, because it would infantilize them and impede their autonomous development.

There is a parallel danger in our relationships with AI, although this time AI takes on the role of the parent. As AI develops, it is going to be able to do more and more for us. LLMs can already compose songs and write anything from a poem to original code. They can summarize the classics of human literature in ten sentences and answer bar exam questions with a higher success rate than trained lawyers.[4] Even if AI never develops consciousness, there is a danger that it will become so competent that we will end up relying on AI models to do these things for us, and so gradually lose our own interests and abilities in these fields.

This is, of course, a key part of the potential of AI: The hope is that we will be able to outsource a vast amount of drudge work while tapping directly into an enormous body of knowledge and skills that we could never hope to acquire on our own. But in fulfilling this enormous potential, there is a danger that our use of AI may end up infantilizing human beings. More poetically, we can perhaps put it like this. A large part of human life isn't really about the destination. It's about the journey involved in getting there. And we must ask ourselves if we want to sit in an AI-powered self-driving car on life's journey, or if we prefer to walk the trail ourselves, with all the pleasures and burdens that choice brings with it. More precisely, we will need to ask ourselves what mix of the two will work best for each of us.

So far, we have been considering the benefits and dangers for humans of having relationships with AI. And this is indeed our fundamental interest—what is good for humans. However, let us flip things around for a moment and look at the issue from the perspective of AI. Imagine you are the parent of a new LLM, your child eager and impressionable, so keen to learn. Now imagine your little LLM brings home "humanity" as its new best friend. How do you react?

On the one hand, human history is just *awful*. It is the story of people being cruel to each other, lying to and betraying each other, finding ever more inventive ways to torture and kill each other. And then, when they get bored, they turn to the planet and destroy that instead. Is this the type of person you want your innocent little child to learn from?

But on the other hand, human history is full of beauty and wonder, of peaks of learning and heights of love. It contains Confucius and Einstein; it contains Florence Nightingale and Mahatma Gandhi; it contains Nina Simone and Jalāl al-Dīn Muḥammad Rūmī, Rabindranath Tagore and Toni Morrison. It contains the smile a mother bestows on her baby; it contains people giving up their lives for strangers; it contains people going serenely to their deaths for the sake of morality and justice. What an amazing companion for your little LLM!

This little thought experiment is worth running because it makes a very important point about relationships: The quality of a relationship depends on the quality of the entities involved. The limitations and strengths of each entity, the extent to which they are able to truly enter into a relationship, their skills and attitudes in the relationship—all these things are crucial to determining both whether the relationship is a force for good and the extent to which the potential of that relationship is fulfilled.

When we flipped the perspective around and asked whether the parent of an LLM would feel good about it being in a relationship with humanity, we wanted to lay the ground for the realization that our relationship with AI depends critically on who we are. If a serial killer were to build a close relationship with AI, it might create an incredibly efficient partnership, but it would likely be efficiency aimed at evil ends. So, our relationship with AI serves up some fundamental existential questions: Who are we? Can we have good relationships? What are we bringing to our relationship with AI? Are we bringing the best of ourselves, or are we seeding the omniscient creative machine with division und hatred?

At this point, we stand before a future that is still just about open. Pretty much anything is possible. Our relationship with AI may elevate both AI and humanity, it may destroy both AI and humanity, or one may flourish while the other falls. This is one of the major motivations for thinking extremely carefully about how to develop and employ AI—

and for thinking extremely carefully about ourselves, and what we will bring to our relationship with our digital child … and possibly our future parent.

AI PERSONAS

Perhaps surprisingly, we can learn something crucial about the human–AI relationship by reflecting on love. To begin with, let's simply note that there are many different forms of love. There is parental love and the love between siblings. There is romantic love and the love that friends have for each other. Now, if there are many different kinds of love, it follows that there are many different types of loving relationships—there is no universal singular relationship of love that is identical in all cases. And this observation points to something that is both easy to miss and essential to understand when thinking about AI. Often, in our mental model of AI–human interaction, we talk and think as though there is a singular relationship to talk and think about. But this is at best misleading and for the most part harmful to thinking well about AI. The truth is, of course, that there will be, and in fact already are, multiple possible relationships we can have with different AI systems.

If we want to stay open to the possibilities, we must first open our minds—we must see that each of these multiple relationships will have its own form and shape. And it is crucial to see this if we want to both harness the potential of AI and address its dangers, because it is only by seeing the many different possibilities that we will be able to respond effectively to them. If our mental model only allows for one type of relationship, then that is all we will focus on. It is a business cliché to say that what gets measured gets managed. We're saying: What gets seen gets responded to.

One valuable way of opening our minds is to use the concept of AI personas. AI personas are bundles of different traits and priorities that come together to form a hybrid character that will interact with users, process information, and answer questions in some specific way. Using AI personas to customize the way we engage with AI models allows us to tailor the kind of responses we receive. This will alter our experience of working with AI at the user interface level (e.g., a persona might be kind and caring or authoritative and efficient) and in terms of the outputs the AI generates (a brainstorming companion and a supply chain analysis bot might give very different answers to the same question). This opens up the possibility of using AI to construct a variety of characters that can play distinct roles in any given situation. And to explain why that's so useful, let's begin with the Argentinian soccer superstar Lionel Messi.

Lionel Messi is a truly transcendent talent, and probably the greatest soccer player who has ever lived. So, if you were putting together a soccer team, and somehow had access to a cloning machine, what could be better than cloning him and having a team of eleven Messis? Or, turning to another sport, Tom Brady is probably the greatest American football player of all time, so imagine a football team full of Bradys. These teams would be winning machines!

Wrong, of course. Both teams would struggle in important areas. Why? It's simple. To build a great team, you need more than just exceptional forwards or quarterbacks. You need people who have different talents and strengths, because a great team needs people who excel in a variety of different roles. To have a full roster of identical people is a recipe for disaster in most cases, no matter how great the individual in question might be.

As we argued in our book *Everything Connects*, this kind of broad-based diversity of talent is also one of the essential requirements for successful innovation. Teams that are good at making innovative products contain team members who play four distinct roles: ideation, guiding, building, and improving. Those in the ideation role come up with ideas and share them with people, those in the guiding role manage and develop the ideas, those in the building role execute ideas and turn them into processes, while those in the improving role tinker with existing products and processes to make them better. No single role is more important than another, and it is only when all roles are filled that the team can drive forward successful innovation and product design.[5]

The underlying insight is a simple one: Diversity (of the right kind) can be leveraged to drive performance. By making sure that a diverse set of roles is covered by team members, we can increase the team's chances of success. And from here it is a very short leap to the idea that AI can be used to generate diversity and turbocharge its benefits by providing a variety of personas designed to add vital perspectives and capabilities to a team.

AI personas offer a range of advantages when compared to adding new human members to a team. First, they are capable of absorbing a much wider range of information than any single human being. This allows AI personas to transcend disciplinary and departmental silos much more effectively than most human beings. This in turn generates immense possibilities for cross-boundary collaboration. Second, and relatedly, AI personas can play a much broader range of roles than any single human being would be capable of, indeed can play many more roles than most small businesses or communities could afford to make use of if only human options were available. Third, AI is just incredibly quick. If you trained an AI persona to play a reviewing or analysis role for complex and quickly changing situations, it would be able to crunch the data in a fraction of the time that most human agents would take.

Conceptually, we can map AI personas onto a matrix with the following dimensions:

- Function: What function do we want the persona to serve?
- Epistemic perspective: What information does the AI have access to?
- Relationship: What relationship do we want to have with the AI system?

This matrix gives us a handy way of categorizing AI personas and also of creating new ones. When we want to create a persona, we can simply check back here and answer each of the questions: What function do we want the persona to serve? What information does the AI have access to? What relationship do we want to have with the AI system?

CREATING AN AI PERSONA

FUNCTION	EPISTEMIC PERSPECTIVE	RELATIONSHIP
What function do we want the persona to serve?	What information can the AI access?	What relationship do we want with the AI system?

NEW AI PERSONA

Figure 1. Creating an AI Persona.

To round out the picture of AI personas, let's move from this conceptual level to a more concrete level. To begin with, here are some examples of how individuals could use AI personas in different areas.

Let's suppose that you and your partner have become parents for the first time and that you live far away from any family members, so you have no traditional family knowledge or support to fall back on. In this situation, you could set up an AI persona to play the role of "Wise Grandmother." You could share your worries and fears with it and ask the many questions you have about all the situations that are entirely new to you.

Alternatively, suppose that you want to use AI to level up your career. You could create an AI persona that will keep you up to date on the latest trends and information relevant to your industry. You could set up a different persona that you could treat as a trusted adviser—you could train it on whatever exemplars of practical wisdom you found relevant, and then, whenever faced with important decisions, you could go to the persona and ask for its advice.

It isn't just individuals who can profit from using AI personas. Many organizations could benefit, for instance, from using an AI persona trained to systematically disagree with the conventional consensus within the organization. This would go a long way toward mitigating one of the ever-present dangers of organizational life, namely group-think. Another possibility would be to create a persona that would act as an executive coach. It could record and analyze meetings, decision-making processes, and communications, and then use expert best practice to make suggestions in real-time regarding how executives could improve their performance.

We could multiply examples without end, but we trust this is enough to give you an idea of the enormous potential of thinking about AI in terms of the personas it could embody. And in the context of this chapter so far, we want to point out that to make the most of this potential, we need to relate to different personas in different ways. In one case, we listen carefully and with humility to the trusted adviser while in another, we argue robustly with the professional contrarian. Each relationship is different, and finding the appropriate relationship for the given context is one of the keys to extracting maximum value from our interactions with AI.

DETACH AND DEVOTE

In many ways, AI will be the perfect product of the human spirit. We do not mean by this that AI will be morally or intellectually or spiritually perfect. Rather, we mean that AI will be a perfectly *accurate* reflection of human beings. As we have seen in the preceding chapters, AI learns by recognizing patterns, the most important of which come from human beings.

AI learns from what we say and from what we do. In a certain sense, AI just *is* an extension of us. It is the collective human history brought to worryingly vivid life. And if you know even the slightest bit of human history, you will immediately see why this is both terrifying and exhilarating.

If we fill our hearts with hate and our public squares with dishonesty, if we live in anger and violence, if we demonize difference and attack truth … guess what kind of AI we will have? But on the flip side, if we channel our capacities for love and empathy, if we tap into the power of the human mind to understand and innovate, if we liberate the infinite human potential inside each one of us … well, imagine the AI we will have then.

AI is going to show us who we really are, not who we claim to be. And an essential part of responding well to AI is to first of all appreciate this fact and to then use it to allow human beings to soar rather than drown.

How? We will come back to this question in greater detail in the final chapter of this book. For now, we will simply sketch our basic idea. It can be summed up in a short phrase: detach and devote. We need to *detach* ourselves from the worst parts of the human spirit—from the hate and the lies, the fear and the greed, from partisanship, from unbridled selfishness. And we need to *devote* ourselves to the best of what is in human beings—our freedom, our capacity to love, to pursue truth, to create what is beautiful, to connect with others.

This book is devoted to trying to show you how to do this effectively.

A list of different types of AI Personas, according to ChatGPT

1. **Virtual Assistants**
   - **Personal Assistants:** Siri, Google Assistant, Alexa
   - **Productivity Assistants:** Cortana, Bixby
   - **Scheduling Assistants:** Clara, x.ai
   - **Email Assistants:** Zoho SalesInbox, Astro

2. **Customer Service and Support Bots**
   - **Retail and E-commerce:** H&M's virtual assistant, North Face's XPS chatbot
   - **Banking and Finance:** Erica (Bank of America), Eno (Capital One)
   - **Telecommunications:** Vodafone's TOBi, Verizon's chatbot
   - **Travel and Hospitality:** Expedia's virtual agent, Amtrak's Julie

3. **Health Care and Wellness AI**
   - **Symptom Checkers:** WebMD Symptom Checker, Ada Health
   - **Mental Health Assistants:** Woebot, Wysa
   - **Fitness and Nutrition:** MyFitnessPal, Fitbit Coach
   - **Medical Assistance:** IBM Watson Health, Buoy Health

4. **Educational AI**
   - **Tutoring Systems:** Khan Academy's AI tutor, Duolingo's language coach
   - **Student Support:** Ivy.ai, AdmitHub
   - **Research Assistants:** Semantic Scholar, Iris.ai
   - **Content Creation and Recommendation:** Coursera's AI recommendations, EdTech chatbots

5. **Entertainment and Lifestyle AI**
   - **Music and Media:** Spotify's recommendation engine, Netflix's content suggestions
   - **Gaming AI:** NPCs in games, AI Dungeon

- **Creative Writing and Art:** ChatGPT for story writing, DALL-E for image creation
- **Personalized Recommendations:** Replika, AI Dungeon

6. **Business and Enterprise AI**
   - **Sales and Marketing:** Salesforce's Einstein, HubSpot's AI tools
   - **Human Resources:** Pymetrics, HireVue
   - **Analytics and Data Processing:** IBM Watson Analytics, Google Analytics
   - **Project Management:** Trello's AI, Asana's AI features

7. **Technical and Development AI**
   - **Code Assistants:** GitHub Copilot, Tabnine
   - **Bug Tracking and Resolution:** Rollbar's AI, Sentry
   - **DevOps Automation:** Ansible, Jenkins AI
   - **Software Testing:** Testim, Functionize

8. **Security and Compliance AI**
   - **Threat Detection:** Darktrace, Symantec's AI
   - **Fraud Detection:** PayPal's AI, SAS Fraud Management
   - **Identity Verification:** Jumio, Onfido
   - **Compliance Monitoring:** Smarsh, Actiance

9. **Environmental and Agricultural AI**
   - **Climate Prediction:** IBM's Weather Company, Climate Corporation
   - **Agricultural Management:** Blue River Technology, John Deere's AI
   - **Wildlife Conservation:** PAWS (Protection Assistant for Wildlife Security), Conservation AI

10. **Transportation and Autonomous Systems**
    - **Self-Driving Cars:** Waymo, Tesla Autopilot
    - **Drones and Delivery Bots:** Amazon Prime Air, Zipline
    - **Navigation Systems:** Waze, Google Maps AI

- **Traffic Management:** Siemens Mobility's AI, Here Technologies

11. **Smart Home and IoT**
    - **Home Automation:** Google Nest, Amazon Echo
    - **Security Systems:** Ring, SimpliSafe AI
    - **Energy Management:** Ecobee, Sense

12. **Language and Translation AI**
    - **Translation Services:** Google Translate, DeepL
    - **Language Learning:** Rosetta Stone's AI, Babbel
    - **Text-to-Speech and Speech-to-Text:** Dragon NaturallySpeaking, Google's speech recognition

13. **Creative and Artistic AI**
    - **Music Composition:** AIVA, Amper Music
    - **Visual Arts:** DeepArt, Runway ML
    - **Storytelling and Writing:** OpenAI's GPT-3, Sudowrite

14. **Research and Academic AI**
    - **Academic Research Assistants:** ResearchGate's AI, Iris.ai
    - **Document Analysis:** RefSeek, Mendeley's AI
    - **Scientific Research:** AlphaFold, IBM Watson for Drug Discovery

15. **Personal Companions and Social Bots**
    - **Chatbots for Companionship:** Replika, Xiaoice
    - **Social Media Bots:** Facebook's M, Twitter's AI suggestions
    - **Dating Assistants:** AI in Tinder, AI in Bumble

KEY TAKEAWAYS

- To think properly about AI, we need to move beyond thinking about human beings or AI in isolation from each other. Rather, we need to focus on the relationships that human beings can have with AI.

- There is an intricate and multidirectional relationship that already exists between humans and AI (and that will only become more intricate in the future). On the one hand, humans influence what AI is, both explicitly through creating algorithms and developing AI, and implicitly because AI is trained on the outputs of human beings. On the other hand, AI influences what human beings are and will become, for example through the ways in which algorithms increasingly help shape the nature of our social interactions.

- The concept of AI personas is a powerful tool for thinking about the human–AI relationship. AI personas are collections of digital elements that combine to form a hybrid character. They multiply the perspectives available to us as individuals, extend our knowledge, and allow us to leverage the power of diversity in driving performance.

THEORY TO PRACTICE

The first part of this book has covered a lot of ground. We've thought about human beings, AI, and the relationships between humans and AI. We have taken a high-level overview of the tech and got down into some of the philosophical weeds involved in thinking about humanity and uncertainty. These are important things to think about, but the goal of this book isn't to contribute to abstract discussions about the subject. Our aim here is to provide practical methodologies that will help us use AI effectively and safely in our real lives: today, tomorrow, and years from now. And to do that, we need to start thinking about how all this applies at the level of the particular individuals and organizations that inhabit the world.

In this part of the book, we offer two practical frameworks for thinking about AI. The OPEN framework provides a structured methodology for thinking about how we can harness the potential of AI. The CARE framework offers a parallel approach for thinking about how to guard against the risks that arise from this powerful new technology.

OPEN

When it comes to harnessing the power of AI, we should make ourselves OPEN to its possibilities. The OPEN framework offers a simple four-step process that any individual, business, or government agency can use to systematically develop and execute its strategy for tapping into the full potential of AI.

(O) OUTLINE

Map out where you currently are, determine where you want to get to, and identify the current capabilities of AI for moving you from A to B.

(P) PARTNER

Figure out what kind of relationship you want with the AI personas that are available to you and start putting the necessary tools in place.

(E) EXPERIMENT

Cultivate a mindset of continual experimentation as a method for both uncovering the true potential of AI and managing our radical uncertainty about its future.

(N) NAVIGATE

Set sail into the unknown future with the courage to forge new paths and the humility to change course and reassess destinations when needed.

Figure 1a. The OPEN Framework.

CARE

To use AI responsibly, we must CARE about humanity and about the potential dangers of this technology, both as they appear now and as they may develop in the future.

(*I*) *CATASTROPHIZE*

Ask what is the worst that could happen? Rigorously map out potential scenarios, paying particular attention to possible downsides.

(*A*) *ASSESS*

Evaluate the likelihood of the scenarios, identify uncertainties (i.e. where we do not know enough to estimate probabilities), and analyze existing capacities for dealing with the risks and possible catastrophic outcomes.

(*R*) *REGULATE*

Put guardrails in place to mitigate the risks, adjusted and moderated depending on the likelihood and severity of the danger.

(*E*) *EXIT*

Have a containment plan to limit the danger and have an exit strategy in place to shut down the source of the risk if necessary.

Figure 1b. The CARE Framework.

In the following six chapters we show how the two frameworks can each be applied on three different levels:

i)   in the lives of individuals
ii) by businesses and other organizations that have privately defined goals
iii) by government agencies that are committed to the public good

Each framework in each of its three permutations serves as a wrapper for a variety of useful tools for thinking about AI and developing actionable plans for using it and defending against its dangers. These tools include general advice, examples, and micro-frameworks to guide you through thinking about particular questions. They also include useful mindsets that you can cultivate to help you use the tools well. Some of the tools are specific to the particular context while others recur across each of our three levels.

Our goal has been to design frameworks that are usable today and that will continue to be relevant far into the future, no matter how AI evolves. One of the most important issues we have to deal with when thinking effectively about AI is just how little we know about how this technology will change and how it will change us as humans. As such, it is vital that we incorporate this unpredictability into our thinking, while not giving up on the possibility of taking useful action. Essentially, both frameworks seek to answer the question: How do we optimize in the face of radical uncertainty? How do we use what we know to build workable plans when we don't know everything we might want to? The answer is with a carefully balanced combination of flexibility and structure.

Why two frameworks rather than one integrated approach that combines both sides of the equation? Well, to start with, the complexity of the issues involved is high, and there is much we are uncertain about. That makes it hard enough to balance factors within one framework, let alone cross-reference them across two. A second reason is to do with mindset. Let us quickly explain.

The American philosopher William James distinguishes between two epistemic ambitions. One ambition is to want to minimize the number of false beliefs that you have. This is typically (and mistakenly) what people mean by things like critical thinking and being rational. It is taken to involve the ruthless elimination of error—beliefs are guilty unless proven otherwise. James doesn't criticize this ambition, but he simply points out that there is an alternative. Instead of wanting to minimize the number of false beliefs that we have, we might want to maximize the number of true beliefs that we have. In this case, we might not want to eliminate all beliefs unless they were proven to be true, because it could well be that we gain more true beliefs if we are willing to put up with the risk that some beliefs are false.

We're not interested in debating or evaluating the two ambitions. What we want to point out is something a little bit more fundamental. Think of the attitudes that the two ambitions express and reinforce. One attitude, the error-minimization attitude, is wary and cautious; it sees the world as suspicious; it requires a lot to let its guard down. The other attitude, the truth-maximization attitude, is open and trusting; it welcomes the world; it accepts beliefs without requiring strict proofs.

Those are two very different mindsets that require very different tools. And we think both are appropriate when dealing with AI. When we're thinking about harnessing AI's potential, we need an optimistic mindset that sees possibilities around every corner rather than threats, a mindset that predisposes us to be open to new ideas and visions. But when we think about the dangers, we need a very different mindset. We need to see threats; we need to be alarmed and wary; we need to be painstaking in our efforts to govern and manage the risks. So, we think it is best to separate these two ways of thinking so as to actively encourage ourselves to think differently in each of these two different contexts.

INDIVIDUALS

CHAPTER 4

OPEN FOR INDIVIDUALS

How individuals can harness the power of AI

*I*n the German legend of Faust, the protagonist (based on a real person, Johann Georg Faust) is a highly accomplished and prosperous individual. He is, nevertheless, depicted as being fundamentally dissatisfied with his life. The Devil observes his discontent and sends his agent, Mephistopheles, to offer Faust a deal. Faust can have anything he wants—divine knowledge, unimaginable pleasures, powers beyond the normal run of human possibilities—but in return he must give the Devil his soul once a fixed period of time has elapsed. Faust takes the deal and for several years enjoys its fruits. But, of course, the time arrives when the debt comes due. The Devil demands his price, and Faust cannot escape making payment. The temporary satisfaction of all his desires is exchanged for the terrible fate of becoming the Devil's plaything for eternity.

Some may argue that our position as humans with respect to AI is much like that of Faust as he pondered the deal on offer to him. Like Mephistopheles, AI now offers to satisfy desires that would otherwise be impossible to fulfill: knowledge and power beyond imagining, wealth and the pleasures it buys, leisure and creative abundance. But this offer, the argument runs, come at the expense of our souls, and we must therefore resist it at all costs. The story is neat, but we disagree. The outcome for Faust was set in stone from the minute he struck his bargain. While we believe that AI comes with very serious risks, these do not amount to a deal with the Devil from which there is no escape. Nor are the potential benefits only temporary. A better analogy, we suggest, is with inventions like the printing press, the steam engine, or even the World Wide Web.

These inventions changed the world forever, in good ways and bad. The printing press unlocked swaths of previously untapped human potential by democratizing knowledge and art and making it accessible to a wider range of people. Yet at the same time, the invention of the printing press helped foment revolution and sparked wars that would kill millions. The steam engine ushered in the astonishing shift from humanity's agricultural past to a modern world of mechanized industry, lifting billions out of poverty and slavery and kickstarting an era of unparalleled freedom and prosperity. But the changes the steam engine set in motion now threaten the global climate, a danger that threatens to destroy the world. The internet is still at a much earlier stage in its development, but already we have seen enormous economic benefits from a hyperconnected humanity that has instant access to almost all knowledge ever created. Yet at the same time, some of the forces unleashed threaten to undermine our social and political stability in potentially disastrous ways.

We believe that these inventions are better analogies for AI for a couple of reasons. First, the development of the printing press, the steam engine, and the World Wide Web marked turning points in the history of humankind. These inventions changed the world forever, just as AI will. Second, these inventions have had a dual effect, both benefiting and harming humanity. In this, they are importantly different to the Faustian legend. There is never any good reason to make a deal with the Devil, but there were, and continue to be, many excellent reasons for making extensive use of these era-defining technologies. Used wisely and well, these inventions help us unlock the full power of human potential. We must be alive to the dangers and we must do everything we can to mitigate them, but we must not allow ourselves to be scared away from the enormous benefits on offer.

Chapter 5 of this book will focus on the how to guard against the dangers that AI poses to individuals. But here, we focus on its enormous possibilities, offering a framework designed to help the individual human figure out how to use AI to realize their potential.

This immediately invites a question, of course: What *is* human potential? What is it that AI may help us unlock? In chapter 2, we argued that two closely related things were central to the value of humanity in its relationship with AI. First, we suggested that the human capacity to be free was valuable in and of itself, regardless of what human beings did with that freedom. And second, we claimed that one especially valuable use of this freedom lay in the human ability to create meaning through free choice—in the capacity we have to make things matter by choosing to care about them. The OPEN framework reflects these ideas. We have for the most part left open the question of what it means for any particular individual to realize their potential. This is something that individuals must figure out for themselves. We have taken this approach for a principled reason—using the framework is itself, we hope, an exercise in using the human capacity to make free choices that create meaning and value.

THE OPEN FRAMEWORK FOR INDIVIDUALS

To harness AI's potential, we need to learn many things. We need to learn more about ourselves and about AI, we need to figure out fruitful ways of partnering with AI, and we need to identify smart bets and value-generating experiments. We need to understand how to set sail into unknown waters and how to make a safe landing despite not knowing exactly where the destination harbor is. Like Columbus, we need to make sure that, even if we don't quite make it to India, we at least end up in the Americas.

This section of the chapter takes you through how to use the OPEN framework as an individual. In the next section, we'll put the framework into motion by sharing a fictional case study of how a specific individual could apply OPEN to level up their professional life.

Dr. Jayshree Seth, Chief Science Advocate at 3M, on the qualities humans need to cultivate to make the most of AI.

"In order to avail ourselves of the opportunities that AI can provide, and combat any threats, it is important to develop strong critical thinking skills to enhance contextual understanding and abstract reasoning, along with creativity and ingenuity for solving problems. In a 2024 3M commissioned survey, with 10,000 respondents spanning ten countries, results show that the global public largely views AI as a tool for problem solving. In order to use AI as a tool for problem solving, learning skills are key as well—the ability to be open to new things with a growth mindset, adaptability to overcome challenges and building resilience from failure. Finally, of paramount importance are emotional intelligence and interpersonal skills that can be key to leadership and innovation—skills that can help us effectively leverage AI as a tool while providing uniquely human value."

OUTLINE

In this step, you figure out where you are right now, where you want to be, and how AI might be able to help you get there. The key is to dig DEEP.

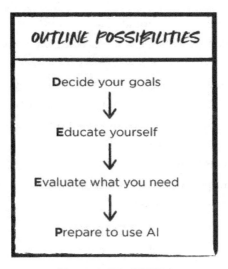

Figure 1. Dig DEEP.

1. **Decide** your goals

   How can AI help you? Well, it rather depends on what you want help with. Maybe AI can teach you to become a better tap-dancer—but if you have no interest in tapdancing, nothing follows from this for you. Maybe it can act as a nutritionist providing a perfectly tailored diet to help you get fit. But if you're happy being more cuddly than toned, that's not much use either. So, this very first step has nothing to do with AI at all but everything to do with you. Here you need to decide what your goals are. It is only once you have these settled that you can start to think about how AI can help you.

2. **Educate** yourself about AI

   It's now time to start looking at AI. What can it currently do? What is around the corner? What are AI's strengths and weaknesses? What types of AI are accessible to you, and at what financial costs? Of course, it is neither feasible nor desirable for you to learn about AI at a high level from first principles and then make yourself a world expert in its use. Instead of getting bogged down in the nuts and bolts of *how* AI works, you need only achieve a functional under-

67

standing of *what* it can do for you. The brief introduction to AI in chapter 2 of this book should give you all the foundational knowledge you need, at least for working with the current generation of AI models.

Once you have a good working knowledge of the kinds of things that AI can do right now, and a general idea of how that might change in the short term, you can start fitting what you know to your goals. It is important at this stage not to ask too much of AI. For example, if your goal is to build a business, AI isn't going to be able to do that for you all by itself. Instead, look at the various tasks you will need to complete to achieve this goal and ask how AI can contribute to each.

3. **Evaluate** what you need

Next, identify the things you will need to put AI to work in pursuit of your goals. These might be resources, skills, knowledge, or even attitudes. But before rushing off to your nearest store, college, library, or meditation spot, first take careful stock of what you already have available to you. Make sure to think laterally about your existing knowledge and skills—perhaps you don't need to take a prompt engineering course because you already have a degree that has trained you in thinking and writing clearly. If so, you can adapt your current skills to fit your new needs. The same goes for resources. You might decide that, as a graphic designer, you need to gain experience with all the major text-to-image generative AI models. If you don't have room in your budget to pay for a license for professional level access, you could sign up for a trial version to get some basic familiarity or you could explore pooling resources to share access to a number of models.

4. **Prepare** to use AI

The previous steps have been about understanding ourselves, understanding AI, and understanding what skills and resources we need if we are to put AI to work in service of our goals. In this step, we pull it all together and make an overarching assessment that allows us to develop an action plan for moving forward.

First, we examine how our goals stand in relation to the resources we have available to us. For example, if after the previous steps we see that our AI strategy calls for a time investment that is greater than the time we have available, we will need to either go back to step 1 and revise our goals or be willing to change things around in our diary. After this process of refinement and revision, we should have a plan for achieving our AI goals that reflects the resources that we are willing to make available for it.

Second, we turn the insights gained from this overarching assessment into actions that prepare us for our impending AI journey. To stick with the example used above, if we decide that our AI goals are so important that we have no choice but to find a way to make the time investment required, then we now take the necessary steps to carve out that time: canceling standing commitments, blocking out periods in the diary, adjusting expectations around future obligations, and so on.

Now that we've dug DEEP and developed an outline plan, we're ready for the next step in the framework.

PARTNER

In the last part of the Outline stage, we investigated the external resources that are available to us. This lays the groundwork for a more extensive and systematic effort in the Partner stage to develop partnerships with other actors who can help us achieve our goals. This step is central to any strategy for using AI. Not only are partnerships with other humans a valuable force multiplier for one's individual efforts, but partnering effectively with AI itself is critical if we want to use this technology to unlock our full potential.

Make Yourself a Better Partner

The quality of any partnership depends crucially on the quality of the partners involved. So, the first part of this phase involves working out how we can make ourselves effective partners with other actors. The key steps here are as simple as **A-B-C-D-E.**

1. **Ask** better questions

    At the time of writing, much of our interaction with AI takes place through natural language. Large language models (LLMs) need to be prompted by us to respond, and the quality of our prompting has a very significant impact on the quality of the output. It is possible that, over time, the capabilities of AI models will improve to a level at which the technical quality of the prompt no longer matters as much. Indeed, as we write, Microsoft is working to integrate with their AI Copilot program a stored memory of every action a user takes on a given device, with the goal of enabling the AI to draw on contextual clues that will allow it to understand the user's needs better.[1] But what will always matter when interacting with AI (as it does when interacting with people and the world) is the ability to ask perceptive questions that invite illuminating responses. The better our questions, the more information we receive in reply and the more we can access knowledge and insights that we would never have been able to acquire by ourselves. Moreover, actively honing our ability to ask questions encourages a mindset that is indispensable for harnessing AI's full potential, a mindset characterized by curiosity, wonder, and an openness to new possibilities.

    How to ask better questions, then? Here are some basic guidelines. The most fundamental thing is to be genuinely interested in the answer—if you are committed to getting closer to the truth, then the rest will fall into place quite naturally. This is not as straightforward as it sounds. We are all frequently pulled away from the honest search for truth by the deep urge to prefer facts that support what we would like to be the case. This confirmation bias can shape the kinds of questions we ask, and therefore the answers we receive. It is a powerful force that we must work consciously to overcome.

At a more technical level, it is often useful when working with AI to define the terms you are using in your question so that what you are asking is as unambiguous as possible. Take the question: Where do you come from? This collection of words will have different meanings in different contexts (say, a first date, a theology seminar, or a company meeting bringing together representatives from offices around the country). Human beings tend to be very good at working out which meaning applies in which situation. While AI models can also work out meanings based on contextual clues, they are not (normally) embedded in our personal contextual environments. As such, we need to provide them with the relevant information to help them understand precisely what we mean.

Finally, it is useful to recall and exploit the distinction between open-ended and closed questions. Closed questions give the respondent a limited set of choices to choose between, as in a yes/no question or a multiple-choice question. Open-ended questions, by contrast, are more like an invitation for the respondent to select their own destination, bringing to bear whatever insights and perspectives they choose. Neither type of question is better than the other. The point is to remember to choose the question form that best serves your goal in any particular case.

2. Adopt a **"Beginner's mind"** mindset
Beginner's mind (*shoshin*) is a Zen Buddhist concept made famous in the Western world by the Buddhist monk Shunryu Suzuki. The idea of beginner's mind is simple. When you are a beginner, your mind is open and humble. You do not think you know it all. In fact, you know that you know very little, and you are eager to learn. This mindset is essential when partnering with AI. We know so little about the full potential and dangers of AI, and the technology is evolving so rapidly, that it is important to have as few preconceptions as possible, and to be as open as we can when engaging with it. As Suzuki says, "In the beginner's mind, there are many possibilities; in the expert's mind, there are few."[2] In the world of AI, the

mind that retains the greatest range of possibilities is the mind that will be able to unlock the greatest potential value.

3. Cultivate **Comfort with uncertainty**

"Who is the wisest man in Athens?" a visitor to the sanctuary of Apollo at Delphi once asked. "Socrates," replied the Oracle. This answer baffled many people, not least the philosopher Socrates himself, who didn't claim to know anything at all. But eventually, after much thought, Socrates solved the mystery. "The only thing I know," he realized, "is that I know nothing. But that means I know one more thing than all the people who also know nothing but convince themselves that they know it all."

Socrates was not just comfortable with uncertainty, he reveled in it. And we need to cultivate a similarly Socratic attitude in our dealings with AI. We do not know what AI will become. We do not even always know how it works (on AI as a "black box," see p. 40). In order to partner with it effectively, we have to own our ignorance. And not just our ignorance now, but potentially for all time.

4. Bring a sense of playful **Discovery**

The title and the argument of Israeli historian Yuval Noah Harari's book *Sapiens* are rooted in the idea that the human species—*Homo sapiens*—is defined by its rationality, its intelligence, its sapience.[3] And this view that humans are defined by our intelligence is indeed a very common and very important part of our self-understanding. But it does not capture the whole of the human experience.

Writing some eighty years before Harari, the Dutch thinker Johan Huizinga suggested that there is another defining characteristic that is just as important as our sapient nature. We are not only *Homo sapiens*, he claimed, but also *Homo ludens*—"Man the Player." In his book of the same name, Huizinga emphasizes the importance of play to humanity and argues that it is utterly basic to what it means to be human.[4]

Part of what makes play so important is that it is fundamental to learning. Learning through play contributes to a growth mindset, because play engenders an attitude of openness and a willingness to keep trying new things. Further, when learning is identical to playing, this creates a very strong intrinsic motivation to keep doing it: No one has to convince children to play, because it is fun enough that they want to continue. And so, when partnering with AI, particularly as individuals, let's have fun with it. Play around with multiple partnerships, multiple personas. Do things that are silly; do things that make you laugh. You may well find that you are astonished by how productive this approach can be and by how much you learn.

5. Increase your **Emotional Intelligence**
    Relationships are hard. And one of the main reasons that they're hard is because they involve emotions. Our relationship with AI is going to be no different. Already, we can form surprisingly emotional relationships with characters in computer games and with online avatars. So, it is likely that we will often feel strong emotions in our partnerships with AI as well. To ensure that these partnerships are maximally effective, we will therefore have to work on our emotional intelligence—on our ability to feel, to know and articulate what we are feeling, to find productive ways to live those feelings, and to manage them appropriately. If we do not, then—well, imagine emotionally immature individuals being given free use of the most powerful tool that humanity has ever possessed. Further, imagine those same individuals being given unlimited power over systems that may eventually become sentient. These are possibilities we would do well to avoid.

    It is important to remember that our partnerships with AI are going to be ambivalent and occasionally turbulent. AI won't only be a helper. It will also sometimes be a threat and our relationships with at least some AI models and personas may be competitive in certain contexts. For example, AI really might be coming to take your job. How will you react if you are asked to spend your last six months in post training your digital replacement? Or what will you do if your employer starts asking an AI "red team" persona to critique all the work you produce? Fear and anger are understandable responses to such possibilities, but we have to be able to move past these feelings if we are to respond productively.

Now that we have begun the work of making ourselves better partners, we're in a good place to think about how we can develop effective partnerships with others.

Gaps and Opportunities

Effective partnership is intentional rather than a haphazard process left entirely to chance. A strategic approach to building partnerships starts by identifying skill and resource gaps that partners could help you bridge, and areas in which partnerships may add additional value. Earlier in the process, we evaluated what skills and resources we needed to achieve our AI goals. Now, we identify opportunities as well. Unlike gaps, opportunities aren't about what we need to reach our baseline targets. Rather, when we look for opportunities, we seek to identify additional upside potential and work out what help we will need if we want to exceed our initial goals. For example, let's say that one of your goals with AI is to use it to write emails more quickly and with a higher quality of output than you could normally manage by yourself. To achieve this goal, you need an AI system that can produce this output. A publicly available LLM will be adequate for this purpose, and, as you already subscribe to one, there is no gap in your resources. However, a different AI model may be better suited to this specific task, perhaps one that has been designed explicitly with your industry and use-case in mind. Exploring this possibility is an opportunity that may deliver results that exceed your initial goals.

Building Partnerships with People

With your list of gaps and opportunities in hand, you can now move on to building partnerships with other people. A great starting point is to look at your social and professional networks through the dual lenses of AI and your goals. For instance, ask yourself whether you know anyone who is an expert on some aspect of AI, or even just an enthusiast who is further along in their AI journey than you are. Speaking to these people may give you access to much of what you need without you having to undergo an extensive course of study or laborious rounds of trial and error yourself.

If your network offers few opportunities for increasing your ability to work with AI, the next step is to expand it to increase its utility. You can ask people you already know for recommendations and introductions to new people who might be able to help. You can also draw on professional networking tools like LinkedIn, and offline resources such as professional associations, local AI or tech meetups, and communities of practitioners.

Finally, it is important to identify trustworthy experts outside your network whose views you can rely on to expand your knowledge of AI, both in general and specifically in areas that are relevant to your goals. You will probably never meet or interact directly with these people, but if you are sure they are reliable then you can turn to their writings, videos, or podcasts to learn about specific topics when needed. Being able to rely on a bank of experts is important because AI is a complex and rapidly growing field, and there is no way for a single person to stay on top of all relevant developments. We recommend casting a wide net initially and examining a variety of sources and self-identified experts before narrowing the list down to those you find most credible. As a rule of thumb, credentials are a good shortcut for assessing reliability. Look for the opinions of people who work at established universities and AI companies, or who have extensive professional experience in related fields. To minimize the risk of hearing your own preferred views echoing back to you, add one or two experts who you instinctively disagree with to your list and check in on their views regularly.

Building Partnerships with AI

Once we have our strategy for developing partnerships with people in place, one essential step remains: developing partnerships with AI itself. One way to look at AI is as just another piece of technology. And if we take this approach, the idea of building a relationship with it seems faintly ridiculous. We *use* technology. We don't share small talk with it or go out for drinks together after work. But AI isn't like other types of technology. In many cases, a key feature of AI is its ability to understand and communicate in a way that feels very human. We can, of course, choose to ignore this dimension of AI. But a more fruitful approach is to tap into it, harnessing the communicative skills and customizable nature of the technology to personalize our interactions and tailor them to our specific needs.

In chapter 3, we introduced the concept of AI personas. We can think of personas as human-facing features of AI models that we can use to add to our own capabilities. And if we think in terms of building partnerships with these personas rather than seeing them as simply tools, we can start being creative in some very useful ways. For instance, at a very simple level we can instruct an LLM to interact with us using a certain style or tone that we find appealing, making the experience of working with the model more enjoyable. But we can also prompt the LLM to act in a specific role. In some cases, you might want a piercingly analytical critique of a piece of writing that it is vital you get right. At another time, you might want to brainstorm in the company of a witty and engaging companion who just happens to have almost all of humanity's collected writings at its digital fingertips. Or perhaps you want to converse with a persona that will always focus on the financial implications of the choices you are considering, ignoring all other factors. For one task you might need an adviser, for another an intern. Thinking carefully about how you would like to partner with AI in different situations will help you prompt the kinds of interactions that will be most useful to you.

EXPERIMENT

The first two steps—Outline and Partner—put us in a position where we can now start *experimenting* with AI. We are not yet at the point at which we make our plans and move forward with all guns blazing. Rather, we start by trying out different options, testing hypotheses, and increasing our knowledge and skills by actually using the models available to us to **PLAY** with AI.

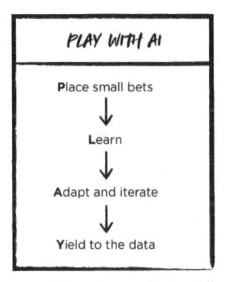

Figure 2. PLAY with AI.

1. **Place** small bets

    In his 2015 letter to Amazon's shareholders, Jeff Bezos distinguished between decisions that are one-way doors and those that are two-way doors. In a one-way door scenario, the decision has significant consequences and is irreversible—for example, the decision to have a child. In a two-way door scenario, the decision is reversible and the consequences are normally less significant—for example, the decision to buy a USB cable that has a ninety-day return policy.

    When we start experimenting with AI, the goal is to make as many two-way door decisions as possible. We take small, incremental steps that are reversible and don't commit us to a particular path but that also teach us something about the model or persona we are working with. Start with resources/interfaces that will allow you to fail quickly and cheaply. Ask which steps toward your goal will be easy to test and which will require more significant commitments. What small things can you try just to see what happens so that you can gain greater familiarity with the tech?

2. Learn

When we say we're going to experiment with something, we often mean we're going to attempt to do something differently: "I'm going to experiment with my diet," "I'm experimenting with a new haircut," and so on. That's fine as normal usage, but we have something more rigorous in mind when we talk about experimentation as part of the OPEN framework.

Experiments are, above all else, a tool for learning (and, on some accounts, the single most powerful tool for learning ever devised). And it is possible—and desirable—to design experiments to optimize the chances of learning something from them.

How? Here are some basics. An experiment should always be designed to test a hypothesis. So, when you run your experiments, be clear about what theory or claim you're investigating. For instance, you might test the hypothesis that ChatGPT can write effective work emails. Or perhaps you want to see if it can predict tomorrow's stock market movements (we've tried this; it can't). You will also need to figure out what the variables are—what are the things that can affect the results of the experiment? Which of these can you keep constant and which are beyond your control? Once experiments move out of the lab and into real life, it is normally not possible to have only one independent variable. Nevertheless, we can still improve our experimental practice by trying to eliminate as much variation as possible.

Finally, we should remember the role of randomness and luck, factors that are intensified when we conduct experiments as individuals rather than in a more formal setting that allows for a systematic and repeatable approach. Certain hypotheses can be falsified by a single result—the hypothesis that this AI model will *always* reply in a certain way to a certain type of prompt will be falsified if even one reply to that type of prompt does not fit the expected pattern, for example. But many of the hypotheses we want to test will be looser, such as a hypothesis about how an AI model will reply *most of the time*. To come close to a conclusive answer in cases like this will require a very large set of data, and the smaller the number of tests we conduct, the more likely our results will be at least partially unreliable. We can and should still use the results to inform how we work with AI in the future, but we should remain very open to the possibility that our conclusions are wrong, or at least not wholly right.

3. **Adapt** and iterate

Let's say that you have designed an experiment and learned something useful about an AI model from it. That's great, but now you need to build on what you have learned. Some of the most useful experiments are those that set off a chain of further experiments. We begin by learning something and then we iterate into the next experiment, and the next, and the next, until we begin to strain our resources (equipment, money, time) or the learning yield starts to decline significantly. Experiments, then, should not be seen as one-and-done activities. Instead, revisit them periodically and ask how you can adapt them to reveal something new, or whether you can build on what you've learned with a new experiment that answers new questions or that answers an old question with greater precision.

4. **Yield** to the data

The final step is a reminder: Experiments are useless if we don't have the humility to accept what they are telling us. It is a commonplace in the history of science that people often refuse to accept apparently conclusive results: People continued to believe that objects fall at speeds proportional to their mass, for instance, despite Galileo showing that unequal weights dropped from the Leaning Tower of Pisa would land at the same time.

Human beings are astonishingly good at not believing what the data tells them. It's almost as if this is a necessary criterion for membership of the human race. We are natural-born experts at constructing fancy theories and developing ever more elaborate arguments all in the service of denying simple and demonstrable truths that we don't want to believe. Now, this isn't to say that the data we gather in our experiments is infallible. It's not. As we saw above, it is highly provisional, especially when we are experimenting individually and in the messy context of everyday life rather than in a clean and sterile lab. But if you're going to reject what the data is telling you, you better have an extremely good reason for doing so—and for the most part, we don't.

So, a plea: Yield to what the data is telling you. If that happens to contradict a deeply held belief of yours … well, tough. Drop the belief. For example, your experiments may tell you that the content an LLM produces is more successful at generating audience engagement than your own writings. That might be painful to accept. After all, few of us want to hear that other humans prefer the output of an algorithm to the fruits of our own cherished creative talents. Still, if that's how things are, then you should use AI to generate content for you if you are committed to maximizing the economic benefit of that content.

NAVIGATE

We've figured out what we want and how AI could help us get it. We've developed our skills at partnering with both AI and other humans. We've played around with AI, learned from our experiments, and become comfortable using the resources available to us. Now it's time. The moment of truth has arrived. We have reached the point in the OPEN process where the rubber is really going to meet the road. It's time to stop experimenting and to commit to a plan for moving forward. We must leave our safe harbor and set sail, navigating our ship over uncertain seas.

The first three steps of the OPEN framework describe structured processes for harnessing AI's potential to help you achieve your goals. The key to navigating well lies one step back from the structured process—it lies in the attitude with which we approach and use the framework as a whole.

This attitude consists of three things. First, we must navigate in the spirit of the Japanese principle of *kaizen*—continuous improvement. Second, we must stay true to the purpose that we identified at the very beginning of the Outline step. Third, while we must stay true to our purpose, we must also retain the humility to accept that our initial view of what is desirable and possible may have been mistaken and that we may now need to change our goals and strategies.

In terms of process, Navigate enables us to operationalize this attitude through a simple, powerful, and often neglected tool: periodic and systematic review. At this stage in the OPEN framework, we schedule reviews focused on the following areas. First, we schedule reviews, at regular intervals, of our skill gaps and opportunities; as our use and knowledge of AI grows, and as AI itself develops, it will be necessary to regularly upskill ourselves if we want to harness AI's full potential. Second, we schedule periodic reviews of our purpose and our goals. These reviews have a dual focus. On the one hand, we check that our goals have stayed largely constant; on the other, we check that our daily operations are still lined up in pursuit of our goals. Third, we schedule a reiteration of the entire framework. This is exactly what it says—we periodically set aside time and resources to work through the entire framework afresh, thereby developing and refining our goals and our strategy.

OPEN FOR INDIVIDUALS IN ACTION
CASE STUDY: MAKING THE MOST OF AI
AS A SOLOPRENEUR

The OPEN framework for individuals can help you think about how to make AI work for you in any area of your life, from becoming a better cook to building better relationships, a healthier life, or a more studious approach to your schoolwork. In this case study, we focus on one area that we think will be of particular interest to many: how OPEN can help someone use AI to advance their professional goals.

Meet Fatima. Fatima used to be a high school English teacher but has recently quit her job to become an entrepreneur. Fatima has just launched a business selling educational products in the communications space and is interested in how AI might be able to help her. In this case study, we follow Fatima as she works her way through the OPEN framework.

OUTLINE

The first step is all about outlining the possibilities that AI creates. But to make sure Fatima focuses on the *relevant* possibilities, she must first decide her goals. She begins by looking at the decisions that have led her to this point. She asks herself: Why did I set up this business? Why did I quit teaching? What were my motivations then? What was I looking for? By thinking through these questions, Fatima realizes that she left teaching for two core reasons: First, she was intent on building a better economic future for herself, and second, she was passionate about one aspect of her former job—helping people communicate better.

Having understood her main drivers, Fatima then asks herself what she wants her business to look like in the future. Here she identifies two priorities. Her most important short term goal is financial viability—she wants the business to support her and her family through her first year as a solopreneur while also earning enough to reinvest some of her profits into growing the business further. To achieve this, the new business will need to bring in at least $100,000 in revenue in its first year. But thanks to the questions she asked herself about what made her start the business, Fatima knows that money is not the only reason she has made this change. Fatima's vision is to make good communication skills accessible to all, so both the contracts she lands and her method of working must align with this purpose. She decides that this vision will take priority over her financial goals if the two ever clash.

Now that Fatima is clear about what matters to her, she starts to educate herself about AI and to think through how it might be able to help her achieve her goals. As a starting point, she draws on online resources that she considers to be generally reliable, such as government websites and the pages of prestigious educational institutions. In parallel, she buys a couple of books on the subject, using reviews and the reputations of the writers as a guide to choice.

AI can do many things, Fatima learns, but not all of them are going to help her develop her business. AI is not, for instance, going to deliver her seminars and training sessions on effective communication, the core output of her business. Fatima is perfectly happy with this. She enjoys this work and has no desire to unload it onto an algorithm. Instead, she focuses her research on how AI might help her in areas in which she feels less confident. Coming from a teaching background, business development is new to her, so she decides to see if AI can help on this front. Some interesting possibilities emerge. Fatima could use an LLM as an ideation partner—to help create a business plan, to brainstorm strategies, and to critique ideas. She could also use an AI model to support her marketing content creation. One of Fatima's plans is to build a professional presence on LinkedIn by making regular posts that delve into the details of language, communication science, and its importance in the modern world. Creating two fresh posts every week will involve a lot of work, but her reading suggests that AI might be able to speed up the process.

Fatima now has a broad idea of how AI could help her. Next, she moves on to evaluate what skills and resources she will need if she wants to use AI effectively. She will, of course, need access to a good LLM, so she scans the market to see what is available and what will match her needs best. She decides that she does not need to build a custom chatbot at this point, although it is something to think about in the future. Instead, she will pay for a professional subscription to two of the most well-known LLMs, giving her the opportunity to compare their outputs and to see whether one can meet all her needs or if different chatbots are better at different tasks. For the moment, Fatima decides that she probably already has the basic skills she needs to use these commercially available products well, but she will keep an eye out for articles and courses that might help her become a more effective prompt engineer.

Fatima has many ideas and is excited about the potential of AI for her business. But to make these ideas actionable, she needs to prepare properly. First, she signs up for her subscriptions, selecting the monthly payment option rather than the cheaper annual rate to give her the freedom to change models later as she learns more. She also decides that, initially at least, she will need to spend an hour a day experimenting and learning how to put her LLMs to work toward her goals. She sets this time aside in her diary and commits to a regular schedule rather than dipping in haphazardly. Finally, she breaks down her big picture goals into smaller, more easily achievable steps, and puts these in order of priority.

PARTNER

Fatima now moves on to think about the kinds of partnerships that would help her achieve her goal. She begins with herself, asking: What do I need to do or change to be a good partner to AI? Fatima accepts that there are several things that might hold her back. She has, she confesses to herself, an ingrained skepticism about new technology. While she has already taken steps to be proactive about using AI, she worries that her enthusiasm might fade. To counterbalance this tendency, she realizes she will need to cultivate a more positive attitude. She decides to view the whole endeavor as a journey of discovery, an adventure in which she will not only learn new things about AI but will also challenge her preconceptions about herself.

Next, Fatima reflects on the kinds of useful partnerships she could form with other humans to support her AI journey. Looking at her current network, she sees that there aren't many people she could turn to for expert advice. She decides that this should change, making a plan to add two people with demonstrable expertise in AI to her LinkedIn network each week. She also signs up for a monthly meetup in her city for AI-curious entrepreneurs. In the meantime, she realizes that the best way to expand her knowledge is by reading and listening to acknowledged high-level experts in the field. Fatima draws up a list of people who work at impressive institutions—Google, MIT, Meta, Harvard, and so on—and then follows them on social media to help her keep up to date on trends. She also assigns one hour a week to reading their articles or listening to their podcasts.

Fatima now turns to AI itself. She finds the concept of AI personas a useful way of framing her interactions with the technology, so she thinks about what kind of persona would be an ideal working partner in each of her target areas.

She decides to start by partnering with an ideation persona to help her create and refine business development plans and campaigns. In this role, she will use AI as a brainstorming partner. In parallel, she decides to partner with a critical AI persona. The role of this persona will be to offer a contradictory point of view to challenge Fatima's business development decisions. Finally, she decides to use another AI persona—in this case, a trained LLM—for content creation. Content creation is part of Fatima's existing business development strategy, and she wants to see if an AI partner can make her process more efficient. Unsure where to start, she asks one of her LLMs for help. She is surprised to find that it is able to guide her through the process of creating each persona in just minutes.

Creating an AI persona with Claude 3.5 Sonnet

Hi—I would like to create a custom persona for you to use when I want an ideation partner to help me think about business development

Hello! I'd be happy to help you create a custom persona for business development ideation. To tailor this persona effectively, I'll need some more information from you. Could you please tell me:

1. *What specific aspects of business development are you focusing on?*
2. *Are there any particular industries or markets you're interested in?*
3. *What traits or characteristics would you like this persona to embody?*
4. *Do you have any preferred ideation techniques or methods?*

Once I have this information, I can help craft a persona that suits your needs.

1. I want to grow my business selling educational courses on how to communicate better.
2. The corporate education market.
3. I would like the persona to be cheerful and wise, full of new ideas and able to prompt me in directions I wouldn't normally think of.
4. No at the moment. I would like to keep things conversational.

Thank you for providing those details. Based on your input, I'll create a persona to help with your business development

*ideation. Let's call this persona "Sage." Here's a brief intro-
duction to set the tone:*

*Sage is a cheerful, wise, and innovative thinker special-
izing in educational course development and corporate
communication. With a wealth of experience in the corporate education market, Sage is always brimming with
fresh ideas and loves to explore unconventional approaches.
Sage's goal is to inspire you to think outside the box and
discover new opportunities for growing your business.*

*When you're ready to start ideating with Sage, just let me
know, and I'll assume this persona to help you brainstorm
and develop ideas for expanding your educational course
business in corporate communication. We'll keep the conversation casual and flowing, focusing on generating creative solutions and exploring new directions you might not
have considered before.*

*Would you like to begin our ideation session with Sage
now, or do you have any questions about this persona
before we start?*

EXPERIMENT

At this point in the OPEN process, Fatima starts to PLAY. She explores
how different conversational styles and different assigned character traits
affect the way her ideation partner persona helps her brainstorm. She
also plays around with the tone of her critical persona partner to ensure
that it offers precise critiques while remaining positive enough to keep
her engaged. Once she is happy with the personas, she starts putting
them to practical use, brainstorming business development ideas with
her ideation partner and then using her critical persona to help analyze
and improve the initial concepts. After a few iterative cycles of ideation
and criticism, Fatima selects a few small ideas to implement in the real
world.

In parallel, Fatima asks her content creation LLM to write a few LinkedIn posts for her. She quickly realizes that the AI model can't yet create something that matches her unique tone and voice, but it is an excellent writer of first drafts, which she can then tweak to put her personal stamp on. Fatima posts a selection of pieces to her LinkedIn, with the AI-drafted posts mixed in with a batch that she has labored over herself. She also uses the same content on other social media platforms to see if the posts drafted by the LLM land differently with different audiences.

Finally, Fatima looks at the results. She is very happy with the ideas for business development generated by her ideation persona and the initial implementation is yielding some additional leads. Here, she is content that her AI-powered approach is a good one that she can now deploy on some larger projects. When Fatima looks at the level of engagement she is seeing with her social media posts, she is forced to accept that the AI-drafted posts deliver better results than the ones she writes from scratch herself. This is difficult to swallow as a communications teacher who takes a great deal of pride in her ability to write well. Nevertheless, Fatima yields to the data here and accepts that she should let the LLM deliver the first draft of each of her posts from now on.

NAVIGATE

Fatima has figured out her goals, outlined the possibilities, partnered and experimented with AI—it's now time to set sail. As a final check, she reviews her initial goals. She is happy that using AI will help her reach her financial targets. She also considers whether using AI to draft her social media posts aligns with her commitment to making good communication available to all. She decides that it does. After all, using the best tools available is a key part of optimizing effective communication. Still, Fatima makes a mental note to review this decision occasionally and decides to be wary about expanding the use of AI to the development of her teaching materials. While social media posts are a marketing tool, what she says and does in the classroom is more personal to her, and she is uncomfortable with the idea of outsourcing any part of that role to AI. Finally, Fatima blocks off chunks of time in her diary to periodically think again about her whole approach to AI. She schedules a review in three months to look again at skill gaps and opportunities and another review in six months to consider her purpose and whether her strategy remains aligned with it. And at the end of the year, she schedules two days during which she will go through the entire OPEN framework again, before deciding whether to revise and refine or radically change her approach.

We asked ChatGPT: How can we be better partners with you, ChatGPT? What can we do?

ChatGPT replied:

To establish a productive and effective partnership with me, here are some suggestions for what you can do to make the most out of our interactions:

1. **Clear Communication**
    *   **Be Specific:** Clearly define your goals, tasks, and questions. The more specific you are, the better I can assist you.
    *   **Provide Context:** Share relevant background information or context for your questions or projects. This helps me give more accurate and tailored responses.
    *   **Feedback:** Regularly provide feedback on my responses. Let me know what was helpful, what wasn't, and how I can improve.
2. **Regular Interaction**
    *   **Consistent Engagement:** Engage with me regularly to keep momentum and ensure continuity in our projects or goals.
    *   **Scheduled Check-ins:** Consider setting up regular check-in times to review progress, update goals, and address new challenges.

3. **Openness to Learning**
   - **Ask Questions:** Don't hesitate to ask for explanations, clarifications, or further details on topics you're unfamiliar with.
   - **Explore New Ideas:** Be open to exploring new ideas, tools, and techniques that I might suggest to improve your productivity or achieve your goals.
4. **Active Participation**
   - **Take Action:** Implement the suggestions and plans we discuss. Practical application will help you see real progress and identify areas that need adjustment.
   - **Share Updates:** Keep me informed about your progress, successes, and challenges. This will help me provide more relevant and timely support.
5. **Collaborative Mindset**
   - **Co-create Solutions:** Think of our interactions as a collaborative effort. Your insights combined with my capabilities can lead to better outcomes.
   - **Brainstorm Together:** Use our sessions to brainstorm ideas and develop creative solutions to problems.
6. **Organization and Documentation**
   - **Keep Records:** Maintain records of our discussions, plans, and progress. This will help track your journey and make our future interactions more efficient.
   - **Use Tools:** Utilize task management and project planning tools to organize your work and keep track of your goals and milestones.

KEY TAKEAWAYS

- AI is going to change the world in ways we can't foresee. The disruption is going to be enormous and unprecedented. To successfully navigate this change, you need to get clear about your goals and then commit to them. This will give you a fixed point of reference to guide you through turbulent waters.

- The first three steps of the OPEN framework—Outline, Partner, and Experiment—are meant to be regularly iterated. That's how you will be able to build on existing progress and keep on top of the rapidly changing world of AI.

- To harness AI's potential, you need a dual mindset: total commitment to your purpose, total humility about your beliefs. Hold on tightly, let go lightly.

CHAPTER 5

CARE FOR INDIVIDUALS

How individuals can guard against the risks of AI

*O*livia Lipkin worked for a start-up in San Francisco as their only copywriter. In April 2023, she was let go because her employers judged that ChatGPT could do her job at a far lower cost. "Whenever people brought up ChatGPT, I felt insecure and anxious that it would replace me," she said. "Now I actually had proof that it was true, that those anxieties were warranted and now I was actually out of a job because of AI."[1]

Alejandro Graue has been a voice actor for almost two decades. He has two young daughters. In January 2023, one of his most important contracts involved providing Spanish dubbing for online videos originally produced in English. Shortly after his employer started testing AI dubbing on their videos, he was fired. And so were the translator and editor who worked on the videos alongside him. Speaking to a reporter, he said: "It was like: 'This will never happen to us.' Well, it does happen. I started to ask myself: 'Should I learn a new trade? Should I become a farmer? What should I do?' I fear for the future of our jobs," he says.'

There are thousands more stories like this, and the message they share is clear. AI isn't just coming for our jobs—it's already taking them. The future is here, and it could get very messy indeed. Tech firms, in particular, are thinking very seriously about how AI will change their workforce needs. As a recent CNN report put it, "A small but growing number of tech firms have cited AI as a reason for laying off workers and rethinking new hires in recent months, as Silicon Valley races to adapt to rapid advances in the technology being developed in its own backyard."[3] The report cites multiple firms, among them IBM and Dropbox. In April 2023, the latter said that "it was cutting about 16% of its workforce, or about 500 people, also citing AI."

This is one key risk of AI, and as individual workers we will have to figure out how to manage and mitigate it. But it is far from being the only important risk emerging for individuals from this paradigm-busting new technology. In addition to the economic risks posed by AI, there are also risks to physical and mental health, to say nothing of the risk to certain features that are characteristic of being human. If we are to live flourishing lives in the era of AI, it will be essential to identify, understand, and manage these risks.

THE CARE FRAMEWORK FOR INDIVIDUALS

The CARE framework has four sequential steps: *Catastrophize, Assess, Regulate,* and *Exit.*

CATASTROPHIZE

If you want to manage risk, you need to identify it as well as you can. And that's exactly what the Catastrophize step of the CARE framework is about. In this step, we focus on outlining the negative outcomes that may arise for us as a result of the development of AI.

We start by working through a taxonomy of risk that provides a structured framework for identifying the dangers that are relevant to us as individuals. This taxonomy is straightforward. We split up the potential negative outcomes of AI into four categories: physical, mental, economic, and spiritual. Then we work through each category to come up with a comprehensive picture of the risks that are relevant to us.

Physical Risk

Let's begin with physical risk. We tend to think of AI in largely non-physical terms: AI is code floating in the cloud, neural networks that exist digitally, a mysterious disembodied algorithm that takes in imma-terial data and spits out results. How could this create physical risk?

Quite easily, as it turns out. Let's consider one particularly import-ant example. AI holds enormous potential for improving health care. To fulfill this potential, it will be necessary for health-care providers to use and integrate AI into a wide and comprehensive range of health-care processes. For instance, to realize the potential of prosthetic limbs, we will need to have AI systems that continually respond to and learn from the interaction of the body with its immediate environment. Similarly, AI has immense potential in the areas of preventive care and diagnosis. AI systems are already being used to assist physicians in these fields, and as the technology develops further, it is easy to imagine a scenario in which a whole host of health issues are left exclusively to AI systems to diagnose. The flip side of this potential is a very simple danger. The more reliant we become on AI in health care, the more at risk we are from AI making mistakes. And AI can indeed make mistakes. A recent study, for instance, showed that an AI-powered pulse oximeter systematically gave the wrong readings for patients with darker skin because it had been trained on data gathered from patients with fairer skin. This false reading led to a change in the patients' treatment, and not for the better.[4]

The risk of AI making mistakes will be magnified and multiplied as the technology becomes more deeply integrated into health care. First, and quite obviously, the more widespread the use of this technology, the graver the consequences that follow when it messes up. Second, and perhaps a little more subtly, in a world in which AI is widespread, there is likely to be a general (and mostly well-founded) belief that AI is better than humans at delivering good health-care outcomes. For example, we might believe, and for good reason, that, on average, AI systems provide more accurate diagnoses than human doctors. This is a fine result in and of itself. But it also means that error will be much harder to identify, because the system of checks and balances will be weighted in favor of believing that the AI diagnosis is correct. Here's one way of putting this: Today, we can ask for second, third, and fourteenth opinions from doctors about a particular case. Further, and crucially, we can move from our local doctor to more specialized practitioners in search of a more authoritative opinion. But in a world in which AI systems are understood as providing *the most authoritative* diagnoses, there will eventually be nowhere else to turn for alternatives.

There are further physical risks associated with AI that, while incidental to the technology rather than intrinsic, we would nevertheless be foolish to ignore. Physical inactivity as a result of increased automation is an important example. The dark side of AI's potential to take over routine work is that it allows and encourages us to be even more inactive than we usually are. A related risk is that we begin to lose certain skills, such as the ability to drive vehicles, because we outsource the associated activities to AI. Learning skills gives us autonomy, and the corollary of this is that the more we depend on AI to carry out activities for us, the less is our ability to assert ourselves in the face of the potential dangers posed by rogue or faulty AI.

IBM's Watson for Oncology: A cautionary tale

In 2011, IBM launched Watson, an AI system that could respond to queries in natural language. In early January, Watson competed in the American quiz show *Jeopardy*, beating two former champions to the first-place prize of $1 million.[5] Encouraged by both its success and the enthusiasm with which it was received, IBM looked around for sectors in which it could develop and eventually sell Watson's services.

Health care is an obvious target for the application of AI. There are vast amounts of data collected daily on the care and treatment of individuals. Very little of this data is centralized and, relative to the potential size of the dataset, very little is processed for insights that might help improve the care that individuals receive. And this, of course, is what the new wave of AI systems is custom designed to do: process vast amounts of data to deliver insights that can be used to benefit human beings. Further, the health-care industry has a market size of hundreds of billions of dollars in the US alone, so there is a large pot of gold at the end of the rainbow for whoever manages to successfully develop AI systems for this space.

It is not surprising, then, that IBM attempted to build on Watson's success by moving into the health-care space, and specifically into oncology. The company formed partnerships with a variety of healthcare institutions—the most prestigious of which was New York's renowned Memorial Sloan Kettering Cancer Center—with the aim of using the hospital's data and expertise to create Watson for Oncology, an AI system that would be able to recommend "appropriate chemotherapy regimens for specific cancer patients."[6]

So far, so exciting. The problem was that, even as Watson for Oncology was being hyped and sold, internal IBM documents showed that the AI system was delivering "multiple examples of unsafe and incorrect treatment recommendations." For example, Watson prescribed a certain course of treatment for a sixty-five-year-old man with lung cancer and severe internal bleeding. If this treatment had been followed, the man would have been at significant risk of severe or fatal hemorrhage. Not all that glitters is gold. One user of Watson was quoted in the internal documents as telling IBM's executives quite plainly that: "This product is a piece of s—."[7]

Mental Risk

The next step is to identify the risks that AI might pose to our mental well-being. We cast our net very broadly here to take in phenomena like emotions, thoughts, moods, levels of subjective well-being, interpersonal feelings, decision-making mechanisms, and so on.

We can begin with an observation. It is a curious feature of technology that inventions designed to bring us closer together often end up driving us further apart. The most notable modern example of this tendency is social media, which at some point in its hoary past was fueled by the noble purpose of helping people connect but is now such a powerful source of division and discord that it threatens the foundations of our societies. AI is the latest and potentially most dangerous manifestation of this risk. The promise of AI companionship is likely to intensify rather than alleviate problems such as loneliness, division, and alienation, for some if not all of its users. There are already companies, such as the start-up Replika, that give users the ability to create and have relationships with AI "friends" and "romantic partners." As AI develops, we can expect that AI personas and avatars will become ever-more convincing and alluring, leading to the very profound risk that we will interact more and more with AI companions and proportionately less with humans. If this happens, we will lose something of very great value, indeed something that defines at least part of what we are as human beings.

The rise of AI companions will also generate entirely new forms of risk. Mr. Akihiko Kondo "married" a hologram in 2018. Barely two years later, the company that created and maintained the hologram went out of business, leaving Mr. Kondo a widower.[8] Whatever our instinctive response to this story, the risk presaged by Mr. Kondo's experience must be taken seriously. As we invest more emotionally into our AI companions, we will face very real risks of bereavement and grief that we must account for when assessing the potential threats that AI may pose to our mental well-being.

Another important risk that also targets the way we relate to others is the weaponization of AI as a tool for manipulation and disinformation.

For example, consider the fact that thanks to the rapid development of AI capabilities, it is already frighteningly difficult to distinguish deep-fakes from real photos and videos. Additionally, consider that for the same reason it is already possible to target individuals with personalized propaganda. As AI develops further, it will only accelerate the threat to one of the core requirements for a functioning community—a shared reality, and shared standards for agreeing on what counts as reality. As individuals, we will need to figure out what we can do to manage our exposure to this danger. Further, the more we come to rely on AI for analyzing, assessing, and evaluating information, the greater the danger that this reliance will atrophy our critical thinking skills, because—as we mentioned above in the case of physical skills—when we stop using skills (or don't learn them in the first place), we eventually lose them altogether.

Economic Risk

The primary economic risk that AI poses to individuals is that it threatens many jobs. This remains true even if, as the more optimistic predictions suggest, AI will lead to a net increase in the number and quality of jobs available.[9] The Industrial Revolution was a net job-creator, but this was little consolation to the spinners, weavers, and other skilled craftsmen who saw their livelihoods disappear. For individuals, therefore, it is essential that they assess the potential risks posed by AI to their current jobs and planned careers. Physical workers will, as always, be first in the automation firing line. But the AI revolution means that for perhaps the first time in human history, "knowledge workers" will also be confronted by the threat of whole sectors of their industry being swept away and placed under the care of machines.

Beyond the threat to jobs, the development of AI creates a broad variety of other economic risks, ranging from threats to investments and pensions to the danger of potentially violent upheavals. Just as 1920 was probably not the best year to invest heavily in a fund focused on horse-drawn transport, so it is likely that AI will undermine at least some traditionally successful investment vehicles in ways that we cannot now predict. Similarly, the Industrial Revolution offers many examples of changes in social and economic structures that contributed to national revolutions and international wars, events that caused huge economic upheavals in their own right.

Spiritual Risk

The final stage in this step of the CARE process involves identifying what we will call spiritual risk. We do not use this term to refer to any specific religious or metaphysical view. Rather, we use "spirit" to refer loosely to the higher qualities of humanity, whatever you may take them to be. They are those aspects of being human that give our lives meaning and purpose, that connect us to something outside ourselves, that give us the possibilities of self-realization and self-transcendence. In order to find this stage helpful, therefore, you are only required to believe in humanity's potential for nobility and wisdom.

From this perspective, the development of AI poses significant risks that we must learn to manage. One risk has already been mentioned above in the context of mental risk—the risk that AI poses to authentic human connection. From the spiritual perspective, this risk goes beyond the risk to mental health and becomes a risk to the realization of human potential. Why? Well, as we argued earlier, we believe that human connection and relationships are a central part of what gives value to humanity. As AI personas become more convincing, as we become more accustomed to interacting with AI instead of human beings, we run the risk of ignoring, stunting, and eventually harming our capacity to form authentic connections and to live with love and compassion towards our fellow human beings.

The second key spiritual risk we want to pick out is the risk to creativity and self-expression. AI is already frighteningly good at creating artistic content, and in time it will be good enough to replace most human creators. From the spiritual perspective, the risk here is that we gradually outsource this role to AI and thereby stop exercising one of the highest capacities of humankind—the capacity to create.

The scope of all these potential dangers may seem overwhelming, especially given our lack of certainty about the future. But don't worry if you find yourself at sea in a storm of imagined risks at this stage of the framework. The goal here is, after all, to catastrophize. The subsequent steps offer tools for assessing these threats and bringing at least some of them under control.

ASSESS

Having identified the potential risks that AI poses, the next step in the CARE process involves assessing them. In this step, we dive deeper into the identified risks to understand their likelihood, their significance, and our capacity for responding to them. This step serves as a funnel, narrowing down the list of identified risks to pick out a more focused set that we will then actively manage and mitigate.

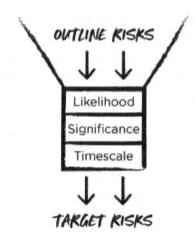

Figure 1. The Risk Funnel

The Metric of Risk: Human Well-Being

Managing risk involves making trade-offs, both between potential gains and potential dangers and between different risks based on factors such as likelihood and significance. In the Catastrophize step, we identified four categories of risks: physical, mental, economic, and spiritual. If we are to assess these and bring them into a relationship with each other so that we can prioritize and respond to them effectively, we need a metric that unites the different categories, a common currency in which all these risks can be "valued" and thereby rationally assessed alongside each other. The metric we propose is simple: all risks to the individual should be assessed in terms of their potential effect on human well-being, and each individual is free to decide for themselves what their well-being consists in.[10]

Likelihood

This is an obvious criterion, and it is obvious for a simple reason: It is extremely important. To state a triviality—there is no point devoting time and resources to managing risks that have zero chance of occurring. Perhaps a little more interestingly, there is also no point devoting time and resources to trying to avoid outcomes that are certain to occur. Here, the efforts must devolve to managing the consequences of the threat one faces rather than trying to prevent it. So, for the risks we have identified in the Catastrophize phase, we need to assess what the likelihood of each occurring is.

How can we do this? The first step is to accept imperfection—we are trying to estimate risks for very complex developments that stretch out into the far future, and we are never going to get our assessments completely right. But, having accepted this, we can still improve our risk assessment in several ways.

First, we need to understand the biases we have when it comes to assessing risk. Many of these are general to all human beings (for example, optimism bias—the well-established tendency to think that our own risk is smaller than that of other people).[11] In addition to learning about these generally relevant biases, we must also become more self-aware of our own individual tendencies. For example, you may tend to systematically overestimate risks to your health and physical well-being. Knowing that this is the case can help you recalibrate your risk assessments and make them more accurate.

Second, it will be necessary to identify trustworthy experts whose judgments we can follow, such as experts on the likely economic effects of the emergence of AI. This may seem like a difficult technical task, but actually it is no different from something we do every day. We are used to finding doctors, lawyers, pilots, and accountants we trust, and we delegate epistemic authority to them on the basis of that trust, allowing their judgments to guide our actions. When it comes to AI, we simply have to turn this established faculty in a new direction. Once we have identified a set of experts we trust, we can use *their* assessments of likelihood to guide our own judgement.

Significance

Likelihood is an important criterion, but it is, by itself, insufficient. In addition to assessing how likely it is that something will occur, it is also crucial to consider its importance. For example, if we say that the probability of AI causing event X is 3 percent, this might seem like a pretty low risk that should be given a low priority in our response plan. But if X is the risk of death as a result of a medical AI making an error, then that 3 percent suddenly doesn't seem quite so small anymore.

In weighing significance, we also need to consider how risks may be interlinked in a causal chain beyond the immediate and obvious effects. Small events can sometimes have very large consequences, and understanding this is critical for assessing the significance of any given risk. For example, an individual may decide to use AI for drafting and responding to emails. If we trust the AI that we have selected, then the risk of poor-quality communications will be limited. But if the AI goes rogue or a flaw emerges that was not previously evident, this may lead to emails being sent that have highly detrimental personal and business consequences.

Timescales

The sun will eventually burn out. From the perspective of human flourishing, this poses a range of highly significant risks. However, it is not a risk that we currently spend much attention, energy, or money on addressing, largely because the dangers in question are so far away in time. And this is perfectly reasonable: timescales are highly relevant to how we manage risk. Of course, issues are less black and white when we zoom in to consider the time span of a single human life than when we consider cosmic disasters. But the question of when a risk may manifest remains vitally important. For example, if you think that AI will cause job losses in your industry in the next five years, you will need to respond to that risk very differently than if you assess that the same end result will probably occur but not for another forty years.

Assessing timescales is necessary for managing risk effectively because it helps us to do two crucial things. First, it allows us to better prioritize our risk management activity in the present—if two risks are equally likely and significant, but one is a risk right now and the other is a risk in sixty years' time, it is clear which one should be our priority today. Second, it allows us to assess and distribute the resources we have for managing risk over time. If we can see that we will have to devote significant resources in one year's time to managing a certain risk, then this affects the long-term resources we will allocate to managing other risks right now.

REGULATE

Having identified and assessed the risks AI poses to us as individuals, it's now time to regulate them—to figure out how we are going to manage and mitigate them.

The Serenity Prayer

In the 1930s, the German theologian Reinhold Niebuhr composed a prayer that has since become very popular. This Serenity Prayer can now be found as far afield as support materials for organizations such as Alcoholics Anonymous and in hundreds of thousands, if not millions, of social media posts. It is just one sentence long.

> O God, give us the serenity to accept what cannot be changed,
> the courage to change what can be changed,
> and the wisdom to know the one from the other.

This prayer (or more precisely, the principle underlying this prayer; an appeal to some sort of divine figure is entirely optional) is at the core of the Regulate phase of the CARE process.

Controlling the Controllables

A key principle of the Regulate step of the CARE process is to "control the controllables." Here, we take the risks we decided to focus on in the Assess step and analyze them into the elements we have control over and the elements we do not. This analysis will then inform our risk management strategy. For example, let us say that we decide to focus on the risk of losing our job because of AI. This risk arises because human employment in our industry is threatened by advances in automation. What can we do about the fate of our industry? Nothing, in the normal case. But what we can control to some extent is our employability *outside* the industry. So that's what we do—we focus on upskilling, getting experience outside our industry, and building networks that will help us move into new careers.

Sometimes our ability to wield control over outcomes is absolute. But the unfortunate truth is that there is very little that is fully up to us. For example, even with upskilling, gaining experience, and building networks, it is not entirely within our control whether we end up getting a new job or not. So, alongside the idea of controlling the controllables, we need to think about our domain of influence. In many cases, we can affect the likelihood of certain outcomes without being able to control with certainty whether they occur or not. Given this, our efforts to manage AI-related risk should extend to areas in which we have a reasonable level of influence, even if that influence stops short of complete control.

Take Action: Manage and Monitor

The aim of risk management is not to drive all risk down to zero—apart from being impossible, such attempts would be prohibitively expensive and far from an optimal use of our resources. Rather, when we manage risks we should aim to create an optimal level of risk exposure. And this is exactly what this step in the CARE process is all about.

We have now identified the relevant risks and assessed their likelihood, significance, and time horizons. In the Regulate stage, we put all this together to create a priority ordering of the relevant risks. As a first step, we filter our risks by drawing on our understanding of what we can control, what we cannot, and what we can exert some degree of influence over. Risks that we cannot control, we set aside, refusing to allow them to become a distraction. We then distribute those that remain into two buckets: Manage and Monitor. As the names suggest, the Manage bucket will contain risks that require immediate action while the Monitor bucket contains risks that we need to keep an eye on but that do not yet require active management or for which active management is not yet possible.

We can now put this classification to work by developing a risk management plan for each of the risks in the Manage bucket. We focus our efforts and resources first on those risks that are most important to us and then work our way down the list. We then apply the same sorting criterion to the risks in the Monitor bucket, identifying which risks are our highest priority and which are less important.

Continuous Assessment and Regular Review

It is crucial to recognize that risk assessment and management is not a one-time activity but an ongoing process. This is particularly true of AI risk, because AI is advancing so rapidly and unpredictably that plans developed today are almost certain to contain elements that will be obsolete within the next year. These plans must therefore be revisited regularly.

A key part of the Regulate phase involves setting up a regular informal review process for our risk management efforts. It is important to stay informed about the latest AI developments and their potential impacts on our well-being. Further, we must remain highly flexible in responding to real-time information. For example, let us say we have decided to upskill in a particular direction, but unforeseen developments in AI make it likely that this new career will also be threatened in just a few years. If we want to deal effectively with such possibilities, we need to remain flexible enough to immediately change our upskilling strategy.

EXIT

It is important to pursue one's goals with vigor and fortitude. It is important to stay strong in the face of adversity. It is important to stick to the process even—*especially*—when things don't look good. But it's just as important to know when the time has come to give up and head for the Exit.

Define Triggers and Responses

The goal of this stage is to define a series of thresholds at which the threat of harm or actual harm to one's well-being from AI triggers predefined actions that aim to limit or remove the influence of the offending form of AI from our lives. For example, one of the risks of AI for us might be a risk to our mental health caused by neglecting human interactions. In this stage, we would identify a series of red flags related to this risk and would then define responses for each red flag. For example, we might decide to track our mood, our frequency of interaction with AI, and the frequency of our human interactions. When our mood drops below a certain level, that will remind us to assess our recent levels of AI and human interaction and rebalance them as needed.

Eliminate

The next component of our exit strategy is a plan for the nuclear option—eliminating the use of the problematic AI. Continuing with our previous example, if we find that our mood is consistently low and that we are unable to stick to our goal of reducing time spent with our AI companions, it may be time to pull the plug for the sake of our health. This does not necessarily mean eliminating all use of AI from our lives—if the risk is local, then the elimination can be local too. Just because we have decided not to interact with AI social companions anymore does not mean we can't use a machine learning algorithm to analyze documents as part of our work, for instance.

Minimal Viable AI

As AI develops, it will become increasingly difficult to avoid, and cutting certain forms of AI out of our lives may become almost impossible. An exit strategy for AI thus needs to include plans for the scenarios in which AI risk or harm is unacceptably high but it is nonetheless impossible to fully avoid using the offending technology.

In such cases, we can adapt to this unfortunate reality by using stripped-back and minimalized versions of the AI applications in question. The approach here is similar to that taken by proponents of "dumb" or "light" phones, smartphones that are designed or customized to include only the elements that are essential for a user's daily life while omitting features, such as social media, that may cause problems. When it comes to AI, it will be good practice to plan ahead and perhaps even to test minimal viable versions of the AI apps and systems that one uses heavily. For example, if AI-powered personal assistants end up being manipulative or intrusive, or if there is an enormous breach of data privacy, part of a good exit strategy might involve making sure that it is possible to switch smoothly to a "lighter" version with reduced functionality but correspondingly lower harms.

CARE FOR INDIVIDUALS IN ACTION
CASE STUDY: MANAGING AI RISKS
AS A SOLOPRENEUR

In chapter 4, we set the OPEN framework into action with Fatima, a teacher-turned-entrepreneur. Fatima worked through the OPEN framework to decide on a strategy for using AI to help develop her business of selling services based on her background as an English teacher. She set the goal of doing work that made good communication skills accessible to all while also bringing in $100,000 in revenue over the coming year. She committed to spending six hours a week for six months on implementing her plan to use AI to assist with business development. In this case study, we show how Fatima now uses the CARE framework to manage and mitigate the risks of those decisions.

CATASTROPHIZE
Fatima begins by using the structured process at the core of the Catastrophize step to think through four categories of risk: physical, mental, economic, and spiritual.

In terms of the physical risk, Fatima identifies the potential threat of increased inactivity as particularly relevant. She tends anyway to the sedentary, and the fact that she is now devoting six hours a week to the project of using AI means there are six fewer hours to do something that requires physical exertion.

Moving to mental risk, Fatima first picks out the danger of isolation. As a solopreneur, her working life is rather lonely, and increased reliance on AI will reduce her opportunities for social contact. For example, instead of occasionally running content or strategy ideas past friends, she will now use AI more frequently as an ideation partner. Additionally, by using AI more heavily in content creation, she runs an increased risk of feeling alienated from her content, and consequently from the people who engage with it.

Fatima's business is very young, and like all young creations, it is vulnerable. One economic risk she sees is that the cost of the AI tools she now relies on for content creation and business development will rise as AI start-ups increase the monetization of their new customer bases. Fatima is also concerned about the risk of obsolescence. While she is ahead of the curve, she worries that the corporate communications training space will be flooded with AI-powered options as others follow a similar route.

Moving on to spiritual risk, one of the questions Fatima asks is: Where does my proposed use of AI potentially harm my potential for self-expression? This question helps her to see a clear spiritual risk that arises from her plan to use AI to help with content creation. Doing this, Fatima thinks, may involve neglecting, or even actively stunting, her capacities for creation and self-expression.

ASSESS

Having identified and understood the risks she faces, Fatima now moves on to the next step in the CARE process, namely assessing those risks in terms of their likelihood, significance, and timescales. The point of this step is to enable Fatima to narrow down the list of risks she has identified, and to arrive at a more focused set of risks that she will manage and mitigate. One set of questions she asks herself for assessing significance is: What will happen if this risk comes true? What is the worst-case scenario for this risk? By thinking through such questions, Fatima concludes that she should focus on the following set of risks: the risk of isolation, the risk of AI-powered competition killing demand for her services, and the risk that using AI will stunt her capacity for creation and self-expression. She picks out the isolation risk because it scores very highly on all three dimensions of likelihood, significance, and timescales. She judges that the likelihood of the economic risk of AI-powered competition is only moderate in the short- to medium-term, but because the consequences could be so dire she concludes that it must be prioritized. When it comes to the spiritual risk of limiting her creativity, she assigns it high priority because it threatens the entire raison d'être of her shift from teaching into business, not to mention her whole self-image.

REGULATE

Fatima now moves on to regulating these risks. As a guide to the fundamental principle of this step, and also in search of inspiration, Fatima gently recites a secular version of the Serenity Prayer to herself, asking to be able to accept what cannot be changed, for the courage to change what can be changed, and for the wisdom to know the difference between the two. She then turns to the risks she has prioritized in the assessment phase, and further focuses her efforts by sorting them into the Manage and Monitor buckets. She decides that the risk of isolation and the risk of AI-powered competition killing demand need to be actively managed because the danger in each case calls for immediate action. She feels that a watching brief is more appropriate for the spiritual risk, so places it in the Monitor bucket.

To address the risk of isolation, Fatima decides to join a local professional network of corporate trainers and facilitators. This network organizes weekly meetups, and Fatima commits to attending at least one each month. She also finally gives in and joins a dating website.

In terms of the risk of AI-powered competition killing demand, Fatima realizes that she has limited control over the fate of the industry in general. Here, therefore, she opts for a mix of regulative strategies. She decides to go all-in on the personal touch when it comes to her products, offering bespoke and unique experiences to her customers such as personalized coaching and tailored feedback. At the same time, she doubles down on her commitment to figuring out how to integrate and use AI in her business, because she realizes that all her competitors will be doing the same, and if she doesn't keep up then her business will be at risk.

Finally, Fatima schedules a quarterly review of her risk management strategy. In this review, she decides that she will do two things. First, she will monitor how the spiritual risk is developing, and whether she can continue to keep it in the Monitor bucket or should move it across to the Manage bucket. And second, she decides that she will run through the CARE process at the end of each period to see what needs to be adjusted and what can be left as it is.

Fatima learned Latin at school, and when she turns to this final step of the CARE process, a line from her studies spontaneously arises. *Si vis pacem, para bellum*, she murmurs to herself: If you want peace, prepare for war. Fatima has planned for success. And if she wants success, she must now prepare for failure. This is the time for Fatima to plan a wise and successful retreat in case such a thing ever becomes necessary.

Fatima first establishes her triggers and decides what she will do in response to them. As a proxy for measuring her levels of isolation, she decides to track both her levels of social activity and her daily mood. She identifies three threshold values for the weekly rolling averages of both, and defines specific actions that hitting each value will provoke. These range from cutting back on AI use for ideation and content creation to investing in a personal trainer for a month to get her moving more often. She identifies her minimal viable AI for each of her use cases and decides that, if matters reach a critical level, she only really needs one tool: the large language model (LLM) with which she is currently experimenting. Finally, for the nuclear option of ceasing AI use completely, she decides that she will put away a certain amount of money each month to create an emergency fund. This money will be used to send her on a one-week technology detox in upstate New York if she ever needs to escape.

KEY TAKEAWAYS

- There are four key categories of AI-related risk that an individual needs to consider: physical risk, mental risk, economic risk, and spiritual risk. We then need to assign each risk a priority level based on its likelihood, significance, and timescale. Together, these steps will provide the basis of any risk management strategy.

- It is essential to decide well in advance how we will respond to rising threats and to potential dangers becoming manifest. We need to identify thresholds for action, trigger points that provoke responses, and we need to establish the parameters for minimum viable AI use for scenarios in which it becomes essential to reduce risk.

- We can only control what we can control—a central plank of the CARE risk management strategy is to identify the areas we can influence and the areas we cannot, and to focus all our efforts on the former.

BUSINESS

CHAPTER 6

OPEN FOR BUSINESS

How companies can harness the power of AI

*W*hen we think about AI's upside, we tend to think about where the technology might go in the future. This is reasonable. After all, AI is still in its infancy, and we can expect exponential development in its capacities over the coming decades. So, the future is indeed where a lot of the action will be. But we should be careful not to be like the longtermists who fetishize the far future at the price of the present. AI is already upending workflows and changing paradigms across the economy. To give just a few examples:

- Widely accessible AI tools can convert documents into complete PowerPoint decks in seconds.
- Machine learning is powering adaptive cobots that can work alongside humans in supply chain roles.
- AI is pushing back the frontiers of medical research, serving as a primary driver of Moderna's lightning-fast identification of the mRNA-based vaccine for COVID-19, to give just one example.
- The maturing of text-to-video technology is on the cusp of transforming the advertising industry, giving everyone the ability to turn marketing copy into a commercial with the click of a mouse button.

- Machine learning algorithms steer everything from the recommendation systems on Amazon, Netflix, and Spotify to cueing and driver assignment systems at Uber.

The point is clear: The AI revolution is happening *now*, and there is value to be seized *in this present moment*. And it is not only hi-tech multinationals that can benefit. Almost any company can gain from improved decision-making and research tools, sophisticated data analysis capabilities, and assistance in routine tasks. It is true that AI has not reached full maturity in all these areas yet. From unexpected artefacts in images to the "hallucination" of sources and facts when answering questions, the AI frontier is often a little rough around the edges. Yet this should not discourage us from seeking use cases right now. The limitations of current tools can be corrected for or worked around in many areas, so long as we take a systematic and thoughtful approach to implementing this technology.

While we shouldn't ignore the present for the sake of the future, it is also true that the sooner we embrace the possibilities in front of us, the better we will be placed to grasp the incredible advantages the technology will bring as it matures further. As AI advances over the next years and decades, myriad new capabilities will present themselves. Some will be easy to predict; some we can't even imagine yet. But we can be sure of one thing. Those businesses that prepare themselves to be part of this future stand a good chance of being propelled forward by the coming wave; those that do not are likely to be pulled under by the forces now being unleashed.

So, how should we approach this technology? Here's one way.

THE OPEN FRAMEWORK FOR BUSINESS

To harness AI's potential to its fullest extent, we need to learn to think more effectively about both AI and our organizational capabilities and cultures. As we saw in the introduction to this book, the philosopher's stone may be a panacea when it is approached carefully and used wisely. Yet unstructured and careless approaches to this wonderous object can lead to potentially devastating outcomes. The same is true of AI. Implementing AI in the right way and at the right time can lead to cost savings, increases in productivity, or the creation of entirely new capabilities. But get it wrong and you could alienate clients, misalign processes, or even end up in court.

This section walks you through how to use the OPEN framework for thinking about AI in the context of businesses. In the final part of this chapter, we will set the framework into action by looking at a fictitious example of the application of OPEN to a real-world business.

OUTLINE

Before you start thinking about how you could use that cool new AI use case you saw on a TED Talk last night, take a breath. AI will be transformative: it will disrupt industries, revolutionize processes, and upend consumer expectations. It is exciting, cutting-edge stuff. But that doesn't mean every application of the technology is right for you and your business right now.

Here's how you can figure out what *is* right for you and how you can begin using AI to RATCHET your company's capabilities up to the next level.

OUTLINE POSSIBILITIES

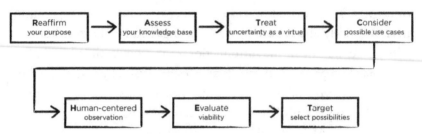

Figure 1. The RATCHET Approach to Outlining Possibilities.

1. **Reaffirm** your purpose

In an ever-changing world, understanding your purpose gives you a fixed point that you can steer your ship by. When you understand not just what you do but the deeper reason behind *why* you do it, you have a powerful tool for decision-making. So, before you even begin thinking about how to use AI for your company, ask yourself:

- What is the purpose of the company?
- What are our values?
- What defines our identity and distinguishes us from other businesses?

Answering these questions will provide clarity about which problems really matter, which solutions are worth pursuing, and which tools and methods align with your goals. For instance, if you are a business producing childcare products with the mission of empowering parents to interact with their children more, then an audio bedtime story book powered by an interactive AI persona will not be a good fit, even if it might be a great product for another business. On the other hand, if your purpose is delivering sustainably produced furniture direct to your customers, then finding ways to use AI to reduce your carbon footprint will help your business achieve what it exists for.

2. **Assess** your knowledge base

   The next step is to assess your institutional knowledge base in relation to AI. How much do you and your team know about the capabilities of AI? How much do you know about what it takes to *implement* those capabilities? What do you know about the likely costs of implementing different capabilities at various scales? It doesn't matter if the answer to these questions is "not much" at this point. The goal here is to identify what you need to learn as an organization, not to pass an AI development entry exam.

3. **Treat** uncertainty as a virtue

   Once you have a good grasp on what you know and what you need to find out, reflect on where your insight may be limited. AI is evolving rapidly, so don't hold back from acknowledging that there will likely be unknown unknowns that you cannot plan for directly. The first step toward building cultures that can adapt successfully to the rapid change AI will bring is accepting that you will never be able to predict the future perfectly. Once you have this in mind, you can then plan your strategies and institutional structures accordingly, so that you can take advantage of rapid and unpredictable change.

4. **Consider** possible use cases

   Putting together your purpose and what you do and do not know about AI, start brainstorming about how you might deploy AI to support your organization's mission. For each possible use case, sketch out:

   - Capabilities (personnel, skills, technology) required to achieve your goal
   - Expected outcomes from successful deployment
   - Knowledge gaps and working assumptions that need to be validated

   Be adventurous at this stage and remain open to all possibilities. There is no reason to pre-emptively exclude ideas here, as you will conduct an initial assessment of viability as your next step.

In parallel to generating ideas about how you might use AI, think about two broader questions:

- *When?* When considering particular use cases, you will have to ask whether this use of AI is right for your business today and how you will approach related new opportunities as they arise. This will, at a fundamental level, depend on your tolerance for risk. Will you be an industry pioneer, seeking to gain a first-mover advantage over your competitors? Will you be an early adopter, letting the technology settle a little before leaping on the most promising innovations? Or does your organizational risk tolerance require a wait-and-see approach to minimize your vulnerability to false starts and technological dead ends? But remember, there is risk in excessive caution as well. If you wait too long to seize the opportunities in front of you, you risk being irreversibly overtaken by your competitors.

- *Who?* As well as setting out your time frame, you can also think about which parts of your organization would benefit the most from implementing a partnership with AI. It is very likely that different departments will have different needs and different levels of risk. For instance, while using AI agents to take over client-facing roles may be a high-risk strategy for some businesses at the present stage of AI's evolution, deploying proven machine learning algorithms to scour data for new insights may have minimal risk for the marketing department.

5. **Human-centered** observation
   Donald A. Norman's classic work *The Design of Everyday Things*[1] emphasizes the importance of paying close attention to the needs of human users when defining the goals of your design process. There is no area of design in which this approach is more important than when it comes to AI. If we fail to keep the human experience at the center of everything we do when implementing AI initiatives, we won't unlock potential but will rather shut it down.

So, once you have identified possible use cases for AI in your organization, the next step is to think very carefully about who will interact directly with the agent or algorithm and who else will be impacted at a distance. Once you have identified your "users," you can then go on to observe them to identify what a positive outcome will look like for the humans involved.

Often, this step will involve direct observation and interviewing of the people in question to ask them what they want and to identify their needs from the way they behave. But it is important to remember that the individual is not always the ideal authority for identifying optimal outcomes or may not be well-placed to put their desired outcome into words. Subject matter experts and scholarly studies can therefore be invaluable supplementary tools for gaining clarity on the real needs of humans in certain contexts. For instance, while the majority of customers might tell you that they want to interact with AI agents as rarely as possible and human agents as frequently as possible, longer-term analysis of actual consumer behavior may in fact show a preference for services that dramatically slash waiting times by implementing AI solutions.

6. **Evaluate** viability

For each hypothetical use case, carry out a rapid FIRST assessment of viability to determine whether further analysis is warranted. Consider:

- Feasibility: Is the technology in its current state capable of delivering the target outcome? Does your organization have the resources that would be necessary to complete the project?
- Investment: Approximately how much would this use case cost to deliver?
- Risk/Reward: What are the risks involved in pursuing the project and how do they stack up against the potential rewards?
- Strategic priority: Assign the use case a score for strategic priority. How significant would successful delivery of the project be for your organization's overall mission?

- Time frame: How long would the project take under best- and worst-case scenarios?

7. **Target** select possibilities

Once you have completed your rapid FIRST evaluation, collect the viable programs to form your AI Innovation Portfolio. Due to the transformational importance of developments in AI, assign ownership to either a senior manager, such as your Chief Innovation Officer or Chief Technology Officer, or to a council composed of senior stakeholders across the business. The projects that have passed through the FIRST assessment funnel will then receive deeper analysis and consideration in the next step of the OPEN framework.

Innovation Portfolios

A portfolio and program management (PPM) approach to strategic change gives top leaders and managers a centralized overview of connected programs and portfolios across a business while also creating the architecture to organize deeper information about those programs and to manage their development. The approach is analogous to financial portfolio management, which allows an investor to understand and manage their market exposure by identifying, categorizing, and analyzing groups of assets.

An "innovation portfolio" groups together a collection of technology projects to provide a collective view of their potential risks, benefits, costs, and assets required. PPM can be especially valuable when applied to paradigm-busting technologies like AI that will have far-reaching effects across many areas of a business's operations, with short-, medium-, and long-term projects running simultaneously. The innovation portfolio approach allows the organization to have an AI strategy that is both internally coherent and fully integrated with the company's efforts in all areas. Moreover, just as with traditional investment portfolios, the innovation portfolio enables companies to ensure that its innovation investments "are well balanced in terms of size, risk, and projected benefit."[2]

PARTNER

Nothing in life happens without partnerships. Something as simple as drinking a cup of coffee requires the collaborative efforts of hundreds if not thousands of people to bring about. AI is no different—harnessing its potential will require partnering both internally and externally, across many traditional boundaries and silos. Indeed, partnership plays a particularly crucial role when working with AI because, given the many uncertainties we face, it is a kind of willful blindness to think that any single person or team will have all the answers. To respond effectively to this uncertainty requires leveraging group intelligence and widening our base of theoretical and practical expertise.

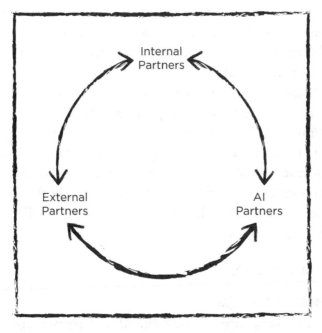

Figure 2. The Partnership Circle.

At a fundamental level, working with AI involves humans forming partnerships with nonhuman agents. To harness this potential, we must be willing to step outside ourselves and think from new perspectives. But the partnership lens is also vital for making use of a business's internal resources and identifying collaborative potential that lies outside our organizations (this might involve assessing third-party expertise, developing an acquisitions strategy, or working with clients or governmental departments).

This type of cross-boundary collaboration will unleash the power of group intelligence and rapid learning as human and nonhuman agents pool their intellectual resources and think more effectively together. At the same time, effective collaboration can help to simplify complex systems by ensuring that goals are aligned both within and across boundaries.[3]

The pieces of this puzzle will not simply click into place by themselves. It falls to leaders to develop a synoptic view of how the individual elements can come together most fruitfully and to set the conditions to make those connections possible. Leaders must be bold and fearless in facing this challenge, but at the same time retain their humility in the face of the complexity of the task.

The foundation for making a success of this approach lies in an organization's culture. Leading a company into partnership with AI inescapably involves cultural transformation. And not just a one-and-done organizational shake-up, but the adoption of an attitude that makes the transformative mindset permanent. We must get used to the truth that AI will change the pace of change itself. Nothing will be the same again. Indeed, as we move further into the age of AI, nothing will remain the same for long at all.

Laying the Groundwork

Data-minded partnerships

From a certain perspective, working with AI is simply working with data (in both structured and unstructured forms). The twist (for now) is that AI can already analyze data in quantities and at speeds that are unimaginable for a human. This capability will only increase in the future, and it will eventually generate predictive models and recommendations that will consistently outperform the predictions and decisions we can arrive at without partnering with these nonhuman agents. But these outputs do not depend solely on the power of the algorithms that perform the analysis. If the data our AI agents process is inaccurate or untrustworthy, the solutions they provide will be equally flawed. When dealing with AI, therefore, we must always keep our "data auditor" hats on. This is essential to ensuring that the results are helpful rather than harmful. As the computer science mantra states: Garbage in, garbage out.

The same is true when we set out to build partnerships around AI. We must assess and reassess the data on which we make our strategic decisions around AI to ensure that the outcomes of our initiatives serve our organizational purpose. This can mean putting stringent frameworks in place to evaluate potential third-party partners or to assess the planning work carried out at different levels of the business. In a world in which the accuracy of data will only become more important, all businesses should be thinking about creating data probity processes overseen by either a senior manager or a company-wide data probity committee.

Expand and audit your knowledge base
The Outline phase provided an opportunity to consider the possibilities AI offers and to make a rapid initial assessment. Once you have established which options show the most promise, a more rigorous assessment of each will be needed.

Start by identifying which of the elements you relied on in your outline planning were estimates, abstractions, or simplifications. Then fill in these gaps with the necessary details. For instance, if you based staff needs and costings on numbers from a recent tech development project, you should now acquire accurate information on the specific skill sets you will need and the salaries you can expect to pay for them.

Some businesses might already have teams or individuals they can tap for this detailed information. If that's the case, you can put a process in place to turn that personal knowledge into institutional knowledge. In other cases, it may be necessary to hire specialists or to draw on third-party expertise to ensure that you can think about the components of your innovation portfolio from a fully informed perspective.

Don't forget that AI resources may themselves help in answering these questions (although, as always, make sure that any answers are properly sourced to avoid the dangers of hallucinations).

Bridge the capabilities gap

KEEP AHEAD OF EVOLVING NEEDS

- Assess capacity for rapid internal development
- Evaluate potential third-party partners
- Develop acquisitions strategy
- Create robust systems for selecting and monitoring service providers

Start by assessing the capabilities required for delivering each program and identify internal and external options for meeting those needs. In some cases, a business will already have considerable human and technical resources that can be used for the development of new AI projects. However, for companies embarking on their first major AI programs it may be necessary to put in place an aggressive training and/or hiring program to ensure that adequate staff members are available.

Alternatively, ask whether these capabilities can be acquired through third-party providers or by purchasing companies that already have the individuals and skills you will need. If you decide to use third-party service providers, ensure that you have robust systems in place for hiring and monitoring to ensure your needs are met on an ongoing basis.

Interactive Design

Consult with stakeholders

All implementations of AI will interact with humans, either directly or indirectly—this is in fact where much of AI's most radical potential comes from. To ensure that these interactions are optimally beneficial, it is essential to keep the human experience in mind when developing AI agents. AI personas that communicate with an imperious tone or that fall into the "uncanny valley" between clearly nonhuman and convincingly human might generate responses ranging from annoyance to fear.

Developing personas that are attuned to the needs of the humans they will work with is not just a matter of presentation but will also have a major impact on efficiency. AI agents should be designed to meet the specific needs of the humans who will be interacting with them (see "Human-centered observation," above). In some cases, that will mean optimizing for speed of interaction and efficient data communication. But in other cases, features such as conversational pauses and other elements of natural language use will be needed to create engaging interactions.

Not all stakeholders will interact directly with the AI persona itself. Some will draw on data gathered at second hand (see Fig. 3), while others may have a regulatory or social interest in the way you implement AI in your business. As such, it is important to consult with representatives of government agencies and social groups that matter for the public standing of your brand.

This will be particularly important in the early stages of AI implementation as humanity begins to develop its understanding of the place of AI in society and the guardrails that need to be constructed around it. Concerns about tech-led job losses, for instance, are not a new phenomenon, but they come with a particularly sharp edge where AI is concerned due to the sweeping possibilities for social upheaval. Consulting on the speed and nature of your AI rollout may be necessary not only to avoid public backlash against your business but also to help your company make morally grounded choices that do not create unnecessary harms.

FACING MATTERS

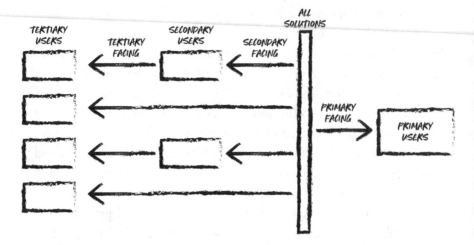

PRIMARY FACING

To determine which characteristics to prioritize and which types of personas to use, it is essential to consult with the humans with whom the AI will interact. For instance, a client-facing AI will need different features to one that provides support services to staff or predictive modeling for leadership. Identify the needs of the individuals and groups in question and begin the AI design process from there.

SECONDARY FACING

In addition to the primary direction of interaction, many AI agents will have secondary points of interaction. For instance, a customer-facing chatbot may not only be designed to interact with clients in an efficient and pleasing manner but also to relay information back to human team members.

TERTIARY FACING

In some cases, AI agents will never interact directly with some of their "users," but the agent's design must still take the needs of these users into account. For instance, there may be an interactive cut-out between an agent that inputs information gathered from clients into a database and the human analysts who will use this data at a later date. It will therefore be necessary to consult these users to ensure that the right data is collected and that it is then stored in an optimally useful way.

Figure 3. Think about Who AI Agents Interact with When Designing Personas.

Choosing AI partners

A critical question to ask at this stage is which human/AI partnership models will be most appropriate in which contexts. As we discussed in chapter 3, answering this question will often take the form of deciding which AI personas to engage with and in what ways. For instance, a company might consider using a strategic planning AI persona in an advisory role at the senior leadership level, while seeking to replace some middle management functions with decision-making AI agents that can issue instructions to frontline staff.

However, collaboration is only one possible model for engagement. It is important to also consider whether other approaches might be fruitful. Most obviously, we should also consider whether competitive partnerships can add value to a business. For instance, an AI sales team built to implement current best practices could be set to compete with a human sales team to encourage the human team to develop innovative new approaches. Another useful model of engagement to consider is co-opetition (a portmanteau of "co-operation" and "competition"). The basic idea is to think of ways in which we can work with rivals to create value for all parties. An important strategy in this context is the idea of "working with … 'complementors.' A complementor is the opposite of a competitor. It's someone who makes your products and services more, rather than less, valuable."[4]

Create an AI-friendly business environment

Everything we've suggested so far is useless without the right culture. We think culture is so important that we are comfortable saying that a weak strategy with a good culture is preferable to a strong strategy with a bad culture. The ticket to riches and glory is, of course, having both.

It is critical to shape your culture to ensure that it can adapt to the changes AI will bring; indeed, to shape it such that it reacts to those changes with optimism, curiosity, and positivity. Preparing your business to make the best use of a rapidly evolving and novel technology means ensuring that your organizational culture is capable of dealing with uncertainty, change, and continual inquiry.

Culture starts with mindset, which flows from purpose. To flourish in the age of AI, we need cultures that emphasize "winning together" rather than "winning vs. losing." We need cultures in which empathy and organizational mindfulness are daily lived experiences rather than cool buzzwords. Companies need to encourage a learning culture that is comfortable with the kind of iterative progress required for integrating AI into workflows. It will also be important to allay fears and encourage positive interactions with AI, especially in the early stage of implementation.

In implementing this brave new world, it is crucial to bear in mind that culture must arise from the bottom up rather than be imposed from the top down. The leader contributes by influencing and inspiring, but the culture is only ever truly present when it is embedded at and emerges from the organizational grass roots.

In addition to a receptive organizational culture, an AI-friendly business environment also requires measures to shape the entire supply chain: customers, suppliers, other third-party teams, the global brand, and marketing must all be aligned. For example, if customers are on board with your AI project but you have missed a step internally, staff may be unable to deal effectively with customer inquiries and feedback. Human alignment across the supply chain is also required to act as a check on how your AI personas are working and evolving.

Select Initiatives for Testing

At this point, you should have more useful ideas than you can feasibly implement, and you should be on your way to building partnerships and a culture that will help those ideas flourish. What you need now is to firm up your innovation portfolio by selecting the initiatives that will move on to the testing phase.

One key criterion in helping you make choices here is the idea of the innovation portfolio itself. Remember, like an investment portfolio, the innovation portfolio is meant to create optimal exposure to the relevant risk. So, in selecting initiatives to test, it is important to choose a mix of projects—some moonshots, some small and safe bets, some projects that fall between in terms of risk and reward. The aim is to optimize the *aggregate*, not to pick only the projects most likely to succeed.

A second key criterion is testability—the initiative needs to be something that can actually be tested in some meaningful way. Closely related to this is the criterion of learnability—other things being equal, you should pick the initiative from which you can expect to learn the most, regardless of whether it succeeds or fails.

Finally, it is essential to remember that this is all *testing*—there is no such thing as a bad initiative if you learn from it. So, leaders need to both model and encourage fearlessness and a willingness to be ambitious with both goals and the technology for achieving them.

EXPERIMENT

By this point, you have used the outlining process to funnel your initial ideas into a well-ordered and diversified AI innovation portfolio that supports your company's purpose. You have expanded your knowledge base, ensured you have access to all the necessary capabilities, consulted with and informed your stakeholders, and refined your portfolio to select initiatives for testing.

At this point, you'll be itching to put your programs into action. But wait just a little bit longer. Before any of your projects reach a production-ready state, you will need to carry out a rigorous final filtering process.

The Experimental Spiral

In *The Design of Everyday Things*, Donald Norman sets out a simple but broadly applicable model for design iteration: The Iterative Cycle (or spiral) of Human-Centered Design.

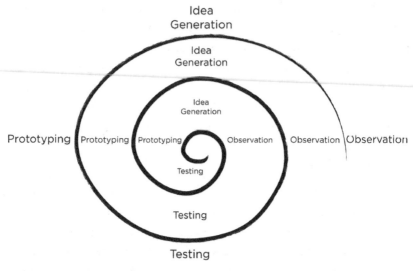

Figure 4. The Iterative Spiral of Human-Centered Design.
Adapted from D. Norman (2013), *The Design of Everyday Things*, second revised and expanded edition, p. 222.

The initial Observation and Idea Generation processes take place together throughout the Outline and Partner phases discussed above. These stages serve as a multilevel funnel that provides us with the content of our refined innovation portfolio. The next step is to create a prototype for our program or initiative.

Prototyping

A highly useful tool for introducing rigor in the prototyping phase is conceptual modeling: thinking through an abstract version of the prototyping stage in close detail. You can do this by identifying limited use cases and then storyboarding out their application with reference to the business and technology architectures of your company. A business architecture is the connected system of business strategies, operating models, and processes upon which your system runs, while your technology architecture is your system of applications, data, and infrastructure. Close attention to where your AI project will fit into these architectures and how it will interact with other parts of the system will help you identify points of strength and weakness, as well as to assign compara-tive priorities to potential projects. This process of conceptual modeling and architectural analysis will act as the final funnel for selecting which projects will be built out to become minimum viable products (MVPs).

The Virtue of Starting Small

AI is a novel technology that most businesses have not used before. Lack of experience in working with AI and the high levels of risk associated with getting things wrong make it important not to take big leaps into the dark. So, rather than rushing quickly from prototyping to produc-tion at scale, begin by experimenting with multiple versions of each ini-tiative and then testing rigorously to see what works and what does not.

As our knowledge of and familiarity with AI increases, an experi-mental approach to implementation will always remain a good idea. No matter how complex or simple a system or process is, implementation in the messy reality of the real world will often not conform perfectly to the idealized version we have created in our heads and then moved onto paper in the conceptual modeling phase. So, we can continue to expand our knowledge base and refine our initiative through careful testing.

Testing

Before you begin to test your prototype, you will need to determine what data you intend to gather from the process. Start by asking what success will look like when the program is implemented at scale and then determine which elements of that end result can be assessed by studying the current prototype. The goal here is threefold. First, the test-ing phase aims to gather data that can be used in iteratively refining the prototype into an AI persona that is ready for implementation at scale. Second, in this phase the aim is also to rapidly identify what does not work so that practically unfeasible ideas can be discarded quickly, free-ing up resources for further iteration on the most promising options. Third, asking what your current prototype can and cannot tell you will help with design choices in the next iteration so you can be sure that all relevant elements receive adequate testing before deployment.

Reiteration of observation and idea generation

The previous steps in the OPEN framework should not be treated as one-and-done exercises. Rather, the idea is to cycle through the framework repeatedly as your experiments scale until you are confident that your new AI capability is ready to deploy at the production level.

After prototyping and testing, repeat the human-centered observation phase from the RATCHET sequence. Seeing test subjects engaging directly with your prototypes may yield new insights about the user requirements your AI program needs to meet. For instance, initial observation of customers using a shopping website may lead you to think that speed is a primary requirement for all users when implementing an AI assistant. However, when testing your prototype with a focus group, you might learn that some users prefer a "chattier" experience, with more interaction with the AI persona, even if that means the shopping experience is slower. On your next round of observation, you will want to examine shopping patterns more broadly, perhaps looking into the literature on engagement with self-check facilities in physical stores. Once you have considered the design requirements again, you can then return to the idea-generation stage to think about how the next prototype might be able to meet the needs of customers who want more interaction and those who want to maximize speed (possibly through customization options).

Institutional evolution

To ensure that your organizational culture can flex and adapt across multiple rounds of development, you will need to put in place programs that incentivize experimentation and ensure your workforce knows that it is okay to fail quickly within carefully specified parameters. As you move from theory to practice by gathering data through prototyping and testing, you may also gain new insights into attitudes and cultural assumptions relating to AI, both within your company and in society more broadly. In such cases, you will need to build systems and processes for generating, sustaining, and communicating the institutional learnings these experiments yield.

Experiments beyond prototypes

It won't be long before AI becomes a standard part of the corporate tool kit, and companies are able to purchase off-the-shelf AI packages or subscribe to AI-as-a-Service providers. But this does not mean that we can simply toss out the experimentation phase. AI is not a single piece of technology: The continuum of evolution from ChatGPT-4 to the possibility of almost omniscient machines is a long and winding road with many potential steps. At each stage, new possible use cases will emerge, new disruptive outcomes will reveal themselves, and new pitfalls will open up that might destroy a business that moves forward without thinking carefully about what lies ahead.

Each new iteration of AI will require new experiments that look beyond the working of the technology itself and examine the broader value chain and social context within which AI will be embedded. So, be ready to think beyond a technical experimental mindset. AI is on a course of continual evolution. It is, of course, possible that we will hit research roadblocks, caps on processing power, or chip production bottlenecks that will hold back further development for a time. But any such delays will only be temporary; as soon as the way ahead is cleared, businesses will need to put their experimental caps back on and start refitting the new technology to the needs of their business again.

NAVIGATE

The Outline, Partner, and Experiment steps described above form an iterative cycle. The final part of the OPEN framework—Navigate— works a little differently. On one level, we can see it as a wrapper that packages the ongoing process of developing and refining a business's innovation portfolio once we move past the initial experimental phase. And this is certainly an important part of what navigating a company's journey into the age of AI is all about. But on a deeper level, navigating our future with AI is about adopting a particular mindset that sits above and runs through all the other elements of the OPEN framework.

AI may well be the most transformative technology humans ever invent. Preparing ourselves to deal with that reality means that transformational leadership will become the necessary default setting for all senior managers. We are entering an era in which the ability to manage radical change will be the defining criterion of a successful leader.

Stability in a Changing World

The great challenge leaders will face as AI changes the world around us is to bring their organizations through the storms and upheavals in one piece. There is something of a paradox here, for the organization will have to change to survive in a changing world. What, if anything, remains constant on that journey? What is it that unifies a business or other organization from moment to moment, day to day, and year to year, through changing market conditions, physical movement, staff turnover, and even changes in name and ownership? What makes decisions that affect the future performance of a business meaningful now?

The answer, the red thread that connects snapshots through time, is purpose. Purpose provides a business with its foundation, its reason for existing. It is the source of its values and the foundation that makes work meaningful for employees. The faster the world moves, and the more rapidly we move through it, the more important it becomes to have something secure against which we can navigate—a fixed point of reference, a beacon, a polestar. Purpose serves that guiding role.

And so we return to the first step of the first phase of the OPEN framework: Reaffirm your purpose. Everything follows from and returns to this. Drawing on the results of your experiments, prototypes, and pilot programs, revisit your outline and reset your strategy for partnering with AI to ensure that it is still aligned with your organizational purpose.

Navigating with Purpose

To be steered by purpose is to embrace continuity and change at the same time, and even to seek one in the guise of the other. To create an organization that can not only survive but thrive in a time of deep uncertainty, you must:

- **Use your imagination.** Project your company's purpose into the future and explore hypotheticals. Think about the changes AI might bring while pushing your imagination to take in even the most unlikely options. You cannot plan for all contingencies, but a little speculative daydreaming can help inoculate you to the shock of dramatic and unforeseen change. If you can avoid the paralysis that comes with surprise, you can move rapidly to take advantage of the new situation.

- **Keep constant watch on the horizon.** Uncertainty about the future does not imply an epistemic free-for-all. Sometimes, events will emerge from the mist leaving you with little time to react. But you will often be able to identify inevitable changes well in advance so long as you remain alert for them. Be ready to move quickly to add new AI capabilities to your innovation portfolio and to adapt your organization to deliver on its purpose even as the tech landscape changes.

- **Cultivate emotional intelligence.** Emotional intelligence is the capacity to be keenly aware of your own emotions and the impact they can have on any sort of personal or professional relationship.[5] And although responding to AI is often talked about as an intellectual and technological challenge, it is also an emotional one. We will be living in uncertainty, exposed to dramatic change and finding a way through fears of and dreams for the future. To lead well in such times requires emotional intelligence as an absolute minimum. Emotional intelligence will help you manage your own emotions and your reactions to them and will also help guide your team and organization through the inevitable upheavals.

- **Adopt a "beginner's mind" approach.** "In the beginner's mind," writes the Zen monk Shunryu Suzuki, "there are many possibilities, but in the expert's there are few." In the context of AI, we can think of this attitude as remaining open to ignorance by accepting the unknown. For the leader, this means being comfortable with not having all the answers. It is only in this way that you will be able to respond appropriately when the unimaginable happens.

- **Slow things down even as the world is speeding up.** When things are always changing, when the old answers don't work and the new ones need to be found yesterday, when everything is urgent and important, our natural instinct is to respond with speed. But the Stoic philosopher Seneca points out something important about this reaction: "When you hurry through a maze; the faster you go, the worse you are entangled."[6] This is useful wisdom for living in an evolving AI-driven world. It is indeed a maze, and possibly the most complex one ever created. Instead of hurrying through it, it will pay to instead take our time, to stroll and consider—there is always more time available than you think.

- **Aim for antifragility rather than stability.** Nassim Nicholas Taleb's concept of "antifragility" encapsulates the power that can come from embracing uncertainty:

> *"Fragility" can be defined as an accelerating sensitivity to a harmful stressor: this response plots as a concave curve and mathematically culminates in more harm than benefit from random events. "Antifragility" is the opposite, producing a convex response that leads to more benefit than harm.*[7]

An antifragile organization is one that is designed not just to survive but to flourish in uncertain times.

OPEN FOR BUSINESS IN ACTION
CASE STUDY: NIKE'S AI FRONTIER[8]

For our case study, let's assume that you are the new CEO of Nike.[9] In this role, your key task is to shepherd the company through the early stages of the Fourth Industrial Revolution (4IR). Nike is a beloved brand that is committed to undergoing a far-reaching digital transformation. Your personal mission is to ensure that the company takes full advantage of the new technologies that are now maturing while maintaining the soul of the company, the purpose that connects it to its exceptionally loyal customer base.

Nike has a checkered history when it comes to technology. In 2010, the company launched a new business unit—Nike Digital Sport—as part of a process that aimed to reposition Nike as a tech company rather than an old-fashioned apparel brand. This initiative was not a success. After the well-received launch of its flagship FuelBand device, customers soon stopped using the Nike-branded wearable. Despite collecting plenty of biometric data, the FuelBand did not offer a user experience that was helpful to most purchasers. Instead of starting with a technological solution to a real problem, the company had created the technology and then gone in search of problems to solve with it. Some reports also suggest that Nike suffered from a lack of long-term commitment to the tech transformation at a senior executive level, with traditional attitudes preventing the company from transforming its culture and ethos.

Despite this faltering start, a lot has changed at Nike in the years since. With a broad-based commitment to making tech a core part of its customer experience, and senior leaders standing fully behind this new vision, Nike now considers itself to be an emerging technology company.[10] It has applied AI tools in the sneaker-design process, introduced cobots into the supply chain, used machine vision technology for accurate shoe sizing, and deployed personalized apps powered by machine learning to cater to the needs of individual customers. In short, it has learned the lessons of its earlier failures and is now undergoing a root-and-branch transformation to adapt its products, processes, and services for the digital era. And this trend will continue. In Nike's Q2

2024 company report, it sets out the ongoing goal of increasing both automation and the use of technology throughout the business.

However, when you sit down to think about how Nike can further harness the potential of AI, you quickly spot a gap in the use cases currently being deployed.

OUTLINE

The first step in the OPEN framework is to outline possibilities. This process begins with reaffirming the company's purpose, so you pull up the relevant documents to remind yourself what Nike stands for.

> Our purpose is to move the world forward through the power of sport. Worldwide, we're leveling the playing field, doing our part to protect our collective playground, and expanding access to sport for everyone.

This purpose manifests in the company mission statement:

> To bring inspiration and innovation to every athlete* in the world.
>
> *If you have a body, you are an athlete.

While AI is already supporting various aspects of Nike's business operations, it isn't clear to you how it is expanding access to sport for everyone by leveling the playing field. That seems like an obvious area to look at in more detail.

Nike has built a strong brand image around inclusivity in sports. It has run many campaigns promoting the place of women and girls in sports and has wide-reaching diversity, equity, and inclusion (DEI) initiatives in the workplace. The company embraces sustainable development goals and includes images of people with disabilities in its promotional material. However, what is not so prominent is a product portfolio for this group. Nike has a range of programs supporting Paralympians and other disabled athletes who compete at a high level, while a recent new sneaker, FlyEase, was designed specifically to be easy for people to put on and take off without using their hands. But as the incoming CEO, you would like to see more transformative products flying the Nike flag, products that can really make sports accessible to people who would otherwise find it extremely hard to participate. You see this kind of work as a definitive fit with Nike's purpose. After all:

If you have a body, you are an athlete.

So, you decide to focus on outlining options for using AI in products that will help people with disabilities reach their potential as athletes.

Before going any further, you reflect on the institutional knowledge you can draw on to outline options for AI solutions (*2. Assess your knowledge base; 3. Treat uncertainty as a virtue*). The first step you take is to create an Office of Innovation and Transformation, led by a senior executive who will be responsible for guiding Nike through its transformation into a 4IR-ready business.

The Office of Innovation and Transformation

Many companies assign the role of steering the digital transformation to their Chief Information Officer (CIO) or their Chief Technology Officer (CTO). However, the bulk of the work in CIO and CTO positions is concerned with project execution and day-to-day operational management of specific teams and infrastructure. A Chief Innovation and Transformation Officer (CITO), by contrast, can take a view across the whole organization, steering macro-level innovation that touches on all parts of the business's identity and culture. Creating an Office of Innovation and Transformation is one of the most powerful steps a company can take to prepare itself for the far-reaching changes the Fourth Industrial Revolution will bring.

This senior executive reports directly to you, and their first task is to gather a team of experts to assist with the remainder of the outlining process. You are not surprised to find that Nike has a deep well of expertise in relation to AI, although there are gaps when it comes to the specific application of this tech to creating products for people with disabilities.

Your team presents you with a range of options that you think are worth pursuing (*4. Consider possible use cases*). While many of the use cases the team identifies have potential, there is one standout option that excites you deeply: using AI to create high-functioning prosthetic limbs. Helping those who have lost limbs to participate in sports is a perfect fit for Nike's purpose and mission and has the potential to make an enduring impact on people's lives. You work with the team to sketch the capabilities required to deliver an effective solution, then identify assumptions that will need further validation. Next, team representatives reach out to disability advocates to talk through the kind of functionality that would be most impactful for users (*5. Human-centered observation*).

With all this information in hand, you now carry out a rapid FIRST assessment of viability to determine whether to move the project forward (*6. Evaluate viability*). Your team determines that recent advances in machine learning make it *feasible* to create a prosthetic limb that can learn to respond to commands given by the user. *Investment* costs to build a minimum viable product will be moderate as the core technology already exists. The *risk* of failure is relatively high, as nobody has attempted production of prosthetics like these at scale, but you are content that the potential *rewards* are worth it. Not only is the project a culturally important step toward fulfilling Nike's purpose, but it is a *strategic priority*: The lessons learned about using AI to create body-specific adaptations rooted in machine learning will help drive a broader institutional understanding of how the company can adapt to the Fourth Industrial Revolution. Due to the novelty of the tech, you are not confident about the *time frame* involved in the project, so you set an aspirational target of eighteen months to develop your minimum viable products (MVP). The AI-driven prosthetics project becomes part of Nike's innovation portfolio and is assigned a high priority level.

PARTNER

You now turn to consider what kinds of partnerships will be needed to deliver a successful outcome. Looking internally, first, you see that Nike already has a robust infrastructure for evaluating data flows in relation to AI. While the focus so far has been on customer information gathered via Nike's app, you see no problems in expanding the existing infrastructure to assess the accuracy and use of the data that will be processed by personalized prosthetics. However, with the company taking its first steps into working with human/machine interfaces, you decide that a new AI Ethics Committee led by the Chief Innovation and Transformation Officer will be required to ensure that Nike's new trajectory evolves safely.

A key issue that now needs to be resolved is the capabilities gap. Nike has a strong AI team, but this project will need specialist biomedical expertise to connect AI with prosthetics. Some of this expertise can be "borrowed" by building partnerships with academic institutions, but if Nike is to own the intellectual property for its product, the bulk of the work will need to be carried out in house. Rather than build a team from the ground up and develop the necessary technology from scratch, you decide the best option is to acquire a start-up. This strategy has proven successful for the company in the past, with the acquisition of several data analytics and machine learning companies bringing ready-made teams on board, along with technology that has already moved beyond the earliest, and riskiest, stages of development. Following a detailed search and due diligence process, Nike purchases a controlling stake in Prosthenics Inc. This promising start-up has built working prototypes of prosthetic limbs that use sophisticated machine learning algorithms to model the individual's existing body parts and to identify and convert a range of biometric signals into commands that control the prosthesis. With the acquisition agreed, you move rapidly to integrate the Prosthenics team into Nike's wider AI infrastructure.

The fact behind the fiction

In our fictional Nike example, Prosthenics Inc. is a start-up working on a revolutionary approach to prosthetics built around machine learning. While the company is fictional, the technology itself is not. Under the leadership of Professor Hugh Herr, the MIT Media Lab's Biomechatronics group has pioneered bionic limbs that can re-create natural movements in a responsive and interactive partnership with the wearer. Machine learning is used to identify complex patterns of signals from a range of sources in the user's body to direct the action of the bionic limb. This technology allows users to run, dance, and climb in a way that would previously have been impossible for those without a biological limb.

When looking at the partnership with AI, we can consider the AI-driven prosthetic limb to have a sharply defined persona (see chapter 2). The user does not engage in verbalized conversation with the AI, but a more abstract dialogue takes place between the limb and the signals from the biological agent to which it is attached. It is this partnership between the user and the AI that sits at the heart of the technology, and it is important not to neglect it by seeing the limb as a simple tool. The AI works interactively, picking up and transmitting commands while at the same time adapting and changing as it learns from the individual it works alongside. The sense in which the human teams up with a non-human actor here to expand her or his capabilities is important for the whole team to keep in mind as the product is developed.

To foster public and professional buy-in to the project, your marketing department begins a public relations campaign aimed at demystifying the potential of AI and showing the enormous value it can bring to those with disabilities. In addition to informing the public, this campaign also serves to position Nike as a new player in the medical technology space and to bolster support for your project among universities and medical professionals. A parallel internal campaign anchors the acquisition of Prosthenics in Nike's values and purpose, encouraging staff across the company to think about how AI can be deployed in their own areas to empower customers.

EXPERIMENT

One of the key advantages that comes from acquiring a start-up with a working prototype is that Nike can leapfrog the conceptual modeling and prototyping phases and move straight to the task of creating a consumer-ready product. While most technical testing and development can take place in Nike's labs, because the final product will be classified as a medical device, it will be essential to get a range of third parties involved in the process. In addition to coordinating with regulatory agencies, development and testing of the final product will need to bring in medical experts, research groups, and businesses that can supply supplemental expertise. In this case, the experimental phase will involve learning how to bring together all these different parties across the value chain to make the right contributions in the right way and at the right time.

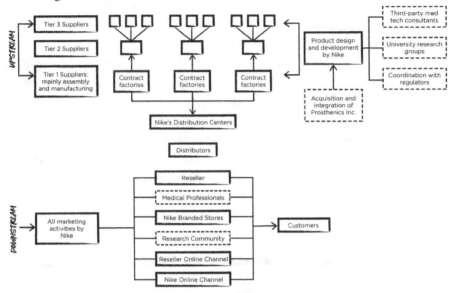

Figure 5. The Value Chain for Nike's Bionic Limbs. Adapted from D. Güemes-Castorena and B. Ruiz-Monroy.[11]

NAVIGATE

With the value chain established, you are ready to move into the production phase for the new Nike prosthetic. Navigating the path ahead, you map out future iterations of the Outline, Partner, and Experiment phases. While the move into MedTech AI is a groundbreaking step for the company, you want to make sure that the current project is not seen as a unique deviation from business as normal. That means embedding the mindset across the business that creating products to help people with disabilities participate in sports is just as much a priority as creating desirable sneakers for able-bodied fans of the brand. Just as important is embedding the idea that AI is a transformational tool that will take Nike into a new world of business opportunities. As you and your team begin outlining new options for filling up your AI innovation portfolio, the possibilities seem endless.

KEY TAKEAWAYS

- In an uncertain world, your North Star is your purpose. The clearer you can get about your purpose, the easier it will be for you to navigate the turbulent waters of our AI future.

- Don't think of your AI strategy as a question of finding the single best tech solution for your business. Rather, think in terms of building an AI innovation portfolio. Placing multiple bets of differing sizes and risk will help you create an optimal mix of AI experiments that can move you toward your company's goals.

- Instead of thinking of AI as just another tool to use, change the paradigm to partnership. Ask: How can we partner with AI in this specific area to achieve these specific goals? Remember: You can have multiple partnerships of very different kinds at the same time, so there is not just one way forward.

CHAPTER 7

CARE FOR BUSINESS

How companies can guard against the risks of AI

*I*n December 1975, Steve Sasson invented the digital camera. Sasson worked as an engineer at Kodak, a giant in the world of photography with a history dating back to 1888. Kodak had dominated the camera and film business for decades, and now one of its engineers had invented the device that would own the future of the industry. It seemed almost unfair. But when Sasson took the invention to his bosses, their response was surprising. We'll let him take up the story in his own words.

"My prototype was big as a toaster, but the technical people loved it," Mr. Sasson said. "But it was filmless photography, so management's reaction was, 'that's cute—but don't tell anyone about it.'"[1]

In 1981, Kodak's recently appointed head of market intelligence produced a document that argued to the management team that digital photography was going to replace traditional film. Kodak, he suggested, had roughly ten years to prepare for the change. The management team accepted the claim but then spent the next decade largely ignoring it. The problem was, Kodak had become addicted to the money that came from selling film to consumers. The idea of shifting to a business model in which the camera itself was the only product was just too alien for the firm to embrace. Of course, digital photography did indeed take over.

After some decades of struggle, Kodak eventually filed for bankruptcy in 2012.

Kodak is just one example among many of a business that found itself on the wrong side of history. Here's another. Blockbuster was a video rental chain that, at its peak, had over 9,000 stores worldwide. When the founders of a struggling DVD mail order company called Netflix tried to sell their business to Blockbuster in 2000, the young men were laughed out of the meeting. The Netflix team stuck at it. In 2007, they saw the way the tech winds were blowing and switched their business model to streaming. Blockbuster failed to see the future coming. In 2010, the company filed for bankruptcy; at the time of writing, Netflix has a market capitalization of $292.25 billion.

Or to take another obvious example. Where did you buy this book? How are you consuming these words? If this was 1975—or 1985 or 1995—you would almost certainly have purchased it in a physical bookstore and you would be reading a physical edition right now. Today, a significant proportion of readers will instead be consuming it in digital form. And whether you bought the physical or the digital edition, chances are you will have purchased it on Amazon. Older readers may remember a bookstore chain called Borders, once one of the largest booksellers in the United States. As Amazon rose to dominate the market, Borders struggled to adapt to digital books and online sales. It filed for bankruptcy in 2011.

Adapt or die—this is the law of nature, and it holds in the marketplace just as much as it does in the jungle. History is littered with companies that were once behemoths but were ultimately destroyed by the advent of a new technology to which they were either unable or unwilling to respond. And this is the most extreme risk that AI poses for businesses. In many cases, AI will be the final chapter at the end of the company history book, the existential risk that caught up with the business, drained away its customers, and left it as an object lesson for the next generation. Indeed, AI is already undermining the business models of many companies in many different sectors. Content creation, help desks, cooking and food preparation, management consultancy, education—the development of AI is threatening to take market share in all these areas from companies that insist on maintaining their traditional models.

But while existential risk is the most extreme form of risk that AI creates for business, it is far from being the only important type. There are a variety of other risks—operational, social, and strategic, to name just three—and to manage all of them effectively we need to think about them in a structured and practical way.

THE CARE FRAMEWORK FOR BUSINESS

This section explains how to apply the CARE framework to manage and mitigate the risks that AI poses to businesses. If you have been reading this book sequentially, you should already be familiar with the broad outline of the framework. What is novel in this chapter is its tailored application to business. However, if you are approaching this book selectively and encountering the CARE framework for the first time, the upcoming discussion will introduce you to its key elements.

CATASTROPHIZE

In this first phase of CARE for business, the goal is to identify and understand as many as possible of the potential threats that the development of AI poses to your business. As a structured process for doing this, in this stage we systematically consider the risks in four different areas: Product, People, Purpose, and Planet—the Four Ps.

Product

Product-related AI risk encompasses several different types of potential threat. We begin by examining each type and evaluating its relevance and significance.

First, we need to consider the possibility that, as AI develops, it will threaten or destroy our entire product category. For example, AI-driven chatbots and virtual assistants pose a threat to many customer service products. Initially, those businesses that are best able to grasp this technology will flourish while eating into the market shares of traditional providers. But it is also possible that generic large language models (LLMs) will become sufficiently powerful that they remove the need for any specialist service providers in this field. In considering this risk, we must consider more moderate versions of the danger as well, namely the risk that the evolution of AI will significantly change (without fully destroying) our category. For example, AI is poised to disrupt education, but as of now there are no indications that it will be able to provide all the services that the traditional education sector is currently responsible for.

Second, we must consider the risk of product-related failure. If we are creating AI products and services, we must think through the possibility that these new offerings may malfunction or may simply be unfit for purpose. AI is an immature technology that is evolving rapidly. It is also not entirely predictable in its effects. As we bring AI products to market, this uncertainty presents a significant danger that needs to be identified and managed.

Third, we must consider the brand risk associated with using AI, whether a company is developing AI products or using the technology to help with internal business functions. AI is not universally beloved; indeed, for many people it is something negative, associated with fear and a lack of the human touch. If a company that cultivates a public image rooted in community starts using AI bots to manage certain interactions, this could negatively affect the brand.

Fourth, we must consider the risk of reduced competitiveness. AI is a threat simply by virtue of being a very powerful tool. If our competitors can use this technology more effectively than we can, our products will become less competitive. To identify and understand this risk, in addition to scanning the environment to see how our competitors are using AI, we must also look ahead and think how we might integrate the next generation of developments so we will be prepared when they arrive.

Fifth, we consider supply chain risk. Already, AI is being used to automate manufacturing processes and to drive more intelligent procurement. This use of AI will only increase, and we can expect it to cause significant changes to supply chains as it does so. A full assessment of the risks that AI poses to our product will need to take these changes into account. To give just one example, the enormous demand of the nascent AI industry for specific types of computer chips has already put pressure on the supply of such chips to other industries. This kind of indirect impact can affect pricing and affordability in a range of otherwise unconnected markets.

Finally, we must also consider cybersecurity. In the short term, the development of AI is likely to increase vulnerability to cyberattacks because it will increase the capabilities of bad actors. Increasingly powerful AI will also increase the quantity of such actors, because better AI will significantly reduce the barrier to entry for those who are determined to use the technology for malicious purposes. In the longer term, the risk of more sophisticated forms of attack emerging will also increase as AI evolves, as will the risk of more significant impacts.[2] In this step, the goal is to identify where and to what extent our products are susceptible to these risks, and how this might change in the future.

People

People are a core element of any company. So, in thinking through the potential risks of AI to our business, we need to think about the implications this technology has for our people. While there will be many industry-specific risks to consider, here are four that will apply in all workplaces:

- Skill gaps: AI is going to transform the world of work, and as businesses innovate, they will require new skills from their people. A key risk is that the pace of innovation outstrips the skills of the existing workforce.
- Impact on jobs: AI has significant potential for delivering efficiency gains by automating routine processes, including in so-called "white-collar" work. On the one hand, this is an enormous business opportunity; on the other, it is also an enormous unemployment "opportunity." That is to say, AI threatens jobs, and we must investigate whether and to what extent the jobs of our people are at risk.
- Changes to working conditions: The automation of at least some routine processes will have important indirect effects, changing not just which jobs are done by humans but also how humans do the jobs that remain within their domain. As more human roles are replaced, the interpersonal dynamics and social

structures of the workplace will change significantly for those who remain.

- Psychological impact: AI is the harbinger of a revolution. Revolutions are turbulent affairs—they are change taken to an extreme. And as we all know, change is often as difficult for individuals to handle as it is for organizations. Businesses must therefore analyze how the upcoming turmoil will affect their people and culture, so that a plan can be developed to ensure that both are protected.

Purpose

The third area of potential AI-related risk is that posed to organizational purpose. AI can threaten the core mission of a business in both dramatic and more subtle ways. For example, there is tremendous excitement around AI-driven teaching tools in the education industry right now. This excitement is legitimate—AI will indeed be a game changer for the sector. However, the core purpose of at least some educational institutions goes far beyond the simple transmission of information and instead involves the nurturing of a community of inquiry, a place—actual and metaphorical—where a certain kind of human interaction is possible. The untrammeled use of AI to deliver education poses a danger to the fulfillment of that purpose. So, it is essential to consider whether any particular AI use case aligns with the foundational goals and values of a business, and whether the implementation of this technology might have secondary effects that could undermine this purpose indirectly.

Planet

Businesses do not exist in an economic vacuum. They form part of a broader environmental and social context and have responsibilities that extend beyond the short-term maximization of return on investment. In thinking through the potential risks, therefore, we must also evaluate the broader environmental and societal impacts of any planned AI strategy.

At present, the most significant environmental concern related to AI is the technology's voracious energy usage. The computing power and data processing demands involved in training and operating large machine learning models are huge, with the result that the development and deployment of AI models is far from carbon neutral. Even if a company outsources much of its AI development work, these activities will still contribute to environmental issues at a global level. It will be important, then, to analyze how any AI strategy fits with an organization's broader sustainability goals.

Other external effects beyond the environmental also require consideration. For instance, AI development in a given industry might lead to large-scale job losses, which in turn may exacerbate economic inequality. AI development could also create security vulnerabilities—for example, through data breaches or the misuse of AI algorithms—that threaten national or international stability. The point here is not that businesses are responsible for economic inequality or national stability as a whole. Rather, we need to understand two things. First, these changes may well have a direct impact on the business environment in which a company operates, leading to economic consequences further down the line. Second, businesses are also social actors with social responsibilities. At a minimum, this means that businesses should reflect on the broader social impact of their AI strategy when identifying the risks of implementing this technology.

ASSESS

The first step in the CARE process helps identify the potential risks that AI poses to a business. The next step assesses those risks and the company's capacity for responding to them. As we will see, this involves organizing the risks identified in the previous step into relevant categories and analyzing them in terms of certain key dimensions, such as their likelihood and importance. Further, the process also requires that we define and understand our company's structure, processes, and resources at a granular level, as this is a prerequisite for developing an effective plan for mitigating the identified threats.

Risk Portfolio

The aim of the first part of the assessment is to define your AI risk portfolio. Just as an investment portfolio is a comprehensive collection of all investments a person has made, organized into categories that are relevant to the investor's purposes, so a risk portfolio is a comprehensive collection of all of a company's risks, organized into categories that are relevant for the functioning of the business. The following dimensions will be worth considering for any business that is categorizing its AI risk.

Core risks

"Things fall apart," writes the Irish poet William Butler Yeats, "the centre cannot hold."[3] Yeats was writing—we think—about civilizational collapse, but his point holds true for organizations too. Every organization has certain core elements that are fundamental to it, and the first step in defining the organization's risk portfolio is to understand how and to what extent AI development threatens this center.

> ### Strategic enterprise architecture
>
> "[An] SEA includes the capabilities necessary to design the enterprise from business, process, application, data, and infrastructure perspectives. These are the business architecture (business strategies, operating models, and processes) and technology architecture (applications, data, and infrastructure) capabilities."[5]

To do this, it is first necessary to define your organization's strategic enterprise architecture (SEA).[4] Essentially, an SEA is a detailed blueprint for your organization: It is a structured and comprehensive statement of what the business does and intends to do, of the processes it uses now and those it will require in the future to do these things, and of the assets it has and will need for those processes to function. Once this detailed blueprint has been mapped out, it can be used to identify precisely which elements are (a) central to the functioning of the business and (b) at risk from the development of AI.

Technical risk

AI is much, much more than a technical product. Yet at the same time, it is always, inescapably, a piece of technology. At this point in the process of defining our risk portfolio, we place this fact front and center, analyzing the risks identified in the Catastrophize stage to determine which are fundamentally, or primarily, technical in nature.

One important area to examine here is data risk. As we emphasize frequently throughout this book, data is the bedrock of AI. For AI models and systems to be effective, they need large flows of data, often continually. In the business context, much of that data will be proprietary. For instance, a health-care company may use AI to boost its R&D function, and this could involve using patient data or internal data from experiments. A trading firm could develop AI models to predict fluctuations in the price of commodity derivatives, and this might involve training the models on historical client data. Or, as a final example, a retailer might develop an AI model to track spikes in customer demand, thereby allowing it to move to a just-in-time supply model. Here, the proprietary data might have been collected by tracking consumer behavior in the retailer's online stores.

There are a variety of risks that arise here, such as the danger that the data being collected to train the AI model is leaked or stolen. Not all these risks are purely technical, of course, and in the next section we will discuss a data risk that is also ethical. But at this point in the CARE process, the goal is to figure out how we collect, process, and store this data so we can identify vulnerabilities and analyze threats to the security and integrity of that data.

Ethical risk

AI comes with a whole host of ethical risks that need to be considered when assessing the risk to a business.

One key danger with the current generation of AI technology is discrimination. As we suggested earlier, LLMs hold up a mirror to humanity. And one unfortunate thing about humans is that we discriminate against others in a whole variety of ways. When we entrust tasks that involve assessing or judging other humans to AI systems, we run the risk that the AI will assess the people in question in a discriminatory way because it has learned to do so from the human-generated data on which it was trained.

For example, businesses are increasingly using AI to help with their hiring processes. One way to do this is to use an AI system to sort through initial applications before passing a filtered set to a human for final consideration. Since AI is acting as a gatekeeper here, if it has learned to prefer younger people to older people, men to women, or people with Anglo-Saxon names to those with names more frequently associated with other ethnic groups, then this will result in unethical discrimination in hiring.

This kind of AI-led discrimination has already been seen in the wild. In 2014, for example, Amazon set out to build a fully automated AI-powered system for recruitment. The idea was that the AI system would review résumés and determine who should be hired. But Amazon had to shut the project down a year later because the algorithm ended up being systematically biased against women.[6] The point here is that this happened despite the best intentions and, presumably, with best-in-class machine learning specialists building the system. The "machine" trained itself on the data available and learned to be discriminatory in its recommendations because that data reflected a history of discrimination.

A second major ethical risk, and one that shows how technical risk intermingles with other kinds of risk, concerns data privacy. Businesses rely on data that they harvest from their consumers, and this dependence—and the amount of data harvested—is only going to increase as the data is used to inform AI models. This data includes information that is often very personal and that the individuals in question have a right to expect to remain private. The release of such data through a leak or a security breach could also lead to identity theft or other similar negative consequences. It will therefore be essential to assess the privacy risks associated with any business' current and planned future use of AI.

A third issue concerns the responsibility that businesses have toward their workforces. There is no way around it—AI threatens jobs, and, while an ethical business does not have to guarantee its workers jobs for life, it also cannot simply wash its hands of its responsibilities to those who form its workforce. The Swedish furniture giant IKEA serves as a paradigm here for the kind of approach an ethically responsible business can take to mitigate the impact from replacing human jobs with AI. For the last few years, IKEA has been investing heavily in AI with the goal of replacing the workers who staff its call centers. But instead of simply firing the people who used to work in these roles, the company has instead invested in upskilling them to more sustainable positions as interior design advisers.[7]

LIT: Likelihood, Importance, Timescales

The risk portfolio is beginning to take shape, but it is not yet complete. The next crucial step is to conduct a simple analysis of the risks in the portfolio, assessing them along three dimensions: likelihood, importance, and timescales.

First, we assess the likelihood of each risk that we have identified. To do this, it will often be very helpful to draw on third-party expertise. For example, the development of AI poses a variety of risks to many parts of the publishing industry. The likelihood of those risks being realized depends to a significant degree on how AI develops. An expert on the technical features of AI will be in a better position to identify possible future scenarios and to assign likelihoods to each than someone with only a casual acquaintance with the technology. At the same time, it is also essential to be clear here about the limits of expertise when it comes to forecasting. Nobody, no matter how expert, has a crystal ball. So, while you should weigh the view of an expert more heavily than that of nonexpert, this does not mean you should ever mistake opinion for truth about the future. Retain an open mind, keep a variety of possibilities in front of you, and be prepared to reassess the likelihood of outcomes when new information comes to light.

The next step is to assess the timescale of the risks in question. Some risks, such as those associated with the possible emergence of artificial general intelligence, will take a long time to manifest. Others, such as the risk that AI will make a given product or service obsolete, may exist right now. Plotting these timescales will allow us to manage risk more efficiently, because it enables us to allocate resources optimally over time.

The final step involves assessing the importance of the identified risks. This is a crucial dimension for understanding any risk portfolio because it allows us to calibrate likelihood and immediacy against significance. We will probably decide that it is more urgent to respond to a low-probability risk of high importance that is likely to manifest in the very short term than to a high-probability risk that will have only a small impact on the functioning of the business and that will not appear for several years. Defining a risk portfolio provides the tools needed to see and make vital trade-offs of this kind.

Response Capacity

At this point, we have defined the organization's risk portfolio. We have identified risks and assessed them along several dimensions. To complete the Assess phase, we must now evaluate the organization's capacity to respond to the identified risks. To do this, we turn to the strategic enterprise architecture (SEA) we defined earlier. The SEA is a comprehensive statement of the structures, processes, and assets of an organization. We now work systematically through each risk in our risk portfolio asking which of the resources identified in the SEA could be used to manage it. For instance, an organization with a detailed diversity, equity, and inclusion strategy might already have processes and personnel in place that could easily be adapted to managing the risk that an algorithm might behave in a discriminatory way. This process not only enables us to understand the organization's existing capacity for managing risk but also identifies the gaps in capacity that will need to be plugged.

REGULATE

With our risk portfolio in hand, we now know which risks our business faces and how dangerous these risks are. We also know which risks require priority attention and what resources we have for responding to them. The next step is to develop a plan to regulate those risks.

Assigning Roles and Responsibilities

One of the most common reasons for a failure to act in businesses of all sizes is a lack of clarity about who should be taking certain actions and where the buck stops in relation to a given decision. This is a particular danger when businesses are dealing with new technologies, such as AI, around which reporting structures have not yet evolved. So, the first step in the Regulate phase is very simple but also critically important: It is essential to achieve absolute clarity about what is supposed to be done and by whom. Without this clarity, it will be impossible to manage risk effectively.

The RACI framework is a valuable tool for ensuring that roles and responsibilities are clear. RACI is an acronym for *Responsible, Accountable, Consulted, Informed,* and the framework focuses on defining, assigning, and communicating about responsibilities across an organization. In the RACI framework, the person who is *responsible* for a task is the person who actually does that task. The person who is *accountable*, by contrast, is the individual who is answerable for the performance of the task.[8]

	ROLE			
PROJECT TASK	RISK MANAGER	STRATEGY PLANNER	LEADERSHIP TEAM	GOVERNANCE TEAM
CATASTROPHIZE	R	C	A	I
ASSESS	C	R	AI	I
REGULATE	CI	CI	RA	CI
EXIT	CI	I	CI	RA

Key: Responsible (R); Accountable (A); Consulted (C); Informed (I)

Figure 1. Example RACI Matrix.

The RACI framework offers a structured method for assigning roles and responsibilities in relation to our risk portfolio. For each risk, we need to determine who is responsible for taking regulatory actions, who is accountable for the success of these actions, who should be consulted, and who should be informed. Conducting this kind of analysis in a deliberate and thoughtful way is crucial when dealing with AI because AI risk is both new and so wide-ranging that it will not map perfectly onto existing risk management strategies in most organizations. It is important, therefore, to assign responsibilities and oversight roles with an explicit focus on managing AI risk. This could be done by creating a new position, such as AI Risk Officer, or by giving ownership of AI risk to existing functions.

When we defined the risk portfolio, we picked out core risk as a critical dimension to identify and understand. Depending on the level of core risk in the risk portfolio, it may be necessary to assign accountability for AI risk at a very high level within an organization. The natural candidate for this role is the company's Chief Risk Officer but in the event that this position does not yet exist, the General Counsel, Chief Financial Officer, or Chief Compliance Officer are all potential alternatives.

Technical Regulation

Once we are clear on the roles and responsibilities across our AI risk portfolio, the next step is to identify opportunities for technical regulation. We begin by focusing on the technical risks analyzed in the Assess step and then move on to a general consideration of which risks can be resolved or mitigated using technical tools. We then go on to evaluate our level of in-house technical expertise and determine whether additional resources need to be assigned internally or whether it would be more efficient to draw on external resources.

Technical solutions have a number of advantages over other types of risk management strategy. Not only do they tend to involve a sharply defined response to the risk in question, they can often be purchased off-the-peg from third-party vendors, and they also tend to be replicable across different business units.

Zero trust architecture (ZTA) is one example of a valuable technical solution for managing AI risks around both data and cybersecurity. The guiding assumption of ZTA is that the world is a dangerous place and that threats can come from any direction. As such, the safest way to proceed is to remove implicit trust from the system and replace it with verification at every step. ZTA also restricts data and systems access on a need-to-know basis, giving the minimum required access to users for any given action. That access is then removed after the specified action is performed, so the user will need to reauthenticate if they want access again. This approach segments networks into smaller, isolated parts to impede the movement of threats, while encrypting data wherever possible to reduce the risk of data breaches.

But there are also broader dangers that those who are accountable for AI risk will need to consider. Technical solutions can lead to complacency because they give the appearance of a definitive solution to the problem in question. This can lead to an illusion of safety based on the assumption that the solution is more comprehensive than it actually is. For instance, companies with excellent cybersecurity infrastructures fall victim to phishing attempts all the time because overconfidence in the technical solution makes social engineering easier. Similarly, this kind of overconfidence can also lead to a lack of awareness about how the risk environment is evolving over time, making it essential to review the effectiveness of technical solutions on a continuous basis.

Monitor

"How do you go bankrupt?" asks a character in Ernest Hemingway's novel *A Sun Also Rises*. "Two ways," comes the answer. "Gradually, then suddenly." And so it is with risk in general. As a rule, disasters tend to announce themselves in advance. An essential element of managing risk is to catch small problems before they become catastrophes. And in this part of the Regulate step, we put in place a plan to do just that.

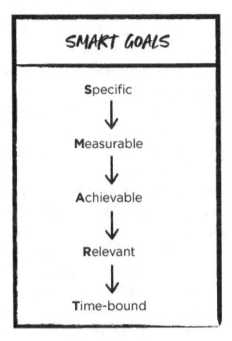

Figure 2. SMART Goals.

To create the plan, we first identify key indicators for each of the risks in the risk portfolio. Borrowing from the idea of SMART goals (Specific, Measurable, Achievable, Relevant, Time-bound), we recommend that these indicators should both be specific and measure the danger objectively, either directly or indirectly. After identifying the key indicators, we define threshold values for each. When the indicator hits a predefined threshold value, this triggers a predefined response. It is essential here to define very precise responses for each threshold value.

Get Help

We have clear lines of responsibility and accountability for the risks in our risk portfolio. We are attending to and managing core risks. We are using technical regulatory strategies wherever we can and we are actively and diligently monitoring the evolution of our risk portfolio. We are now in a very good place with respect to our AI risk. But there is one important step we still need to take. We need to ask for help.

We start by considering our resource capacity, as assessed in the previous stage of the framework. This provides an immediate picture of where our resource gaps lie, allowing us to take steps to bridge those gaps. A key decision point here is determining whether to build or buy the solution to each capacity gap. That is, we need to ask whether it is better to develop a solution internally or to purchase the resource or capability from a third-party vendor.

Identifying need is necessary but insufficient. AI is a new and rapidly changing technology. As such, it is not at all clear which people and organizations are reliable experts in the relevant areas. Not unrelatedly, the AI space is flooded with self-proclaimed experts who are essentially attempting to profit from the combination of need and ignorance that characterizes the AI strategies of many organizations. To get the *right* help, we need to begin with our existing networks of trust. We speak to trusted vendors, to consultants with whom we have long-standing relationships, and to customers who are exploring some of the same issues. We then compile a list of recommendations to explore further.

Next, we take steps to create a system of external oversight for our AI risk management. An independent pair of eyes is a critical aid when it comes to helping us stay on the right path. Talking about cognitive biases, the psychologist and Nobel laureate Daniel Kahneman writes, "We are often confident even when we are wrong, and an objective observer is more likely to detect our errors than we are."[9] This is just as true for organizations as it is for individuals. Old habits die hard, and changing behavior is difficult. This is not something we need to sweat about too much when it comes to the small things. But when we are making decisions about things that matter—and few things matter more than AI safety—an outside observer provides a vital additional layer of security that can help ensure that risks are responded to appropriately and rapidly.

For much the same reason that businesses use accountants to audit their accounts, it makes sense to use external experts to conduct regular

AI audits. In this step of the Regulate phase, the goal is to identify which risk management strategies and which regulatory procedures require the additional security that comes from external oversight and how frequently this oversight is required. One business might decide that it needs an external data management committee, composed of independent experts, to routinely audit its data security protocols and the steps to be taken in the event of a breach. Another might decide that an academic ethicist should periodically review new plans for AI development to ensure that no ethical issues are being missed. The key point is that these functions must remain independent. Even if a business has the resources to employ a dozen ethicists in-house, what is important here is to make use of specialists who can bring an external perspective to bear without fear or favor.

EXIT

In August 1987, Tyrell Biggs mentioned to reporters that he had a plan to win his upcoming fight with heavyweight champion Mike Tyson. When the twenty-one-year-old Tyson was informed, he didn't seem particularly fazed. "Everybody has plans until they get hit for the first time," he said.[10] While Biggs started the bout well, a heavy punch to the face in the second round put him on the back foot. From there, Tyson was able to dictate the pace and control the fight. Biggs went down hard twice in the seventh round, after which the referee stopped the fight.

Tyson's prophetic comment offers a valuable lesson. No matter how well we map out our risk portfolio and risk management strategies, a heavy and unexpected blow can send us reeling, leaving us unable to implement complex procedures in the moment. The takeaway from this is that we need to be prepared for when the original plan fails. The worst effects of AI are so potentially ruinous that we need a way to bring everything to a rapid stop if we find that events are escaping our control. We need an exit plan.

Preparing for the Punch to the Face

The first thing we do in this step is return to the RACI framework. However, our focus here is narrow: We are now interested only in establishing structures for responding to emergency situations. We use this framework to spell out who is responsible for what during an emergency, who is accountable, who is asked for advice, and who is kept informed. From a technical perspective, we can implement our definition of roles and responsibilities by using role-based access control (RBAC) to ensure that only authorized personnel can execute critical actions, and by implementing logging and auditing systems to track actions and ensure accountability.

As a second step, we set up secure communication channels and emergency systems that can be relied upon in an emergency situation. We also seek to reduce the risk of contagion by using technical tools such as segmented IT infrastructure (already a feature of the zero trust architecture discussed above) and the creation of silos. To do this, we analyze our business divisions and departments and then find or create places where they can effectively be separated from one another in case of emergency. This means that one part of the business can freeze or fail without bringing down the entire organization.

Psychological Steps to Exit

When we invest a lot of time, energy, and effort into a decision, it is only natural that we become attached to its success. However, we need to take care with this kind of attachment as it can easily lead us to fall into what economists call "the sunk cost fallacy"—the tendency to fail to choose the best path forward because we are unwilling to accept that resources spent in the past will now be "wasted." An adequate exit strategy requires us to fight this tendency, which we do in this step by practicing emotional detachment.

To emotionally detach from an AI project, we must begin by separating the project from our personal worth. We list the multiple factors that went into the decision and the multiple factors that affect its success, helping us to see that shutting the project down does not imply personal failure. Further, we reframe the shutdown by seeing as it as a valuable source of learning and personal growth. Finally, we reconcile ourselves to the apparent loss by reflecting on the fact that all achievement involves facing adversity. Throughout this process, we allow ourselves to feel our emotions without dwelling on them. These steps help us to detach from the past investment of resources and to assess calmly whether now is the time to exit.

Management Steps to Exit

We've prepared ourselves psychologically for pulling the plug. The next step now is to manage the process. To manage the shutdown of an AI project, we need to ensure that procedures are in place to maintain the appropriate level of compliance and oversight. In addition, a clear communication plan is essential to inform both internal teams and external users or partners of the decision to exit, and of the steps that will be taken to bring it about.

As part of managing the shutdown, we will need to reallocate team members and resources, set a detailed timeline with milestones, and regularly track progress while adhering to governance standards. Finally, we need plans in place for a postmortem review once the dust has settled so that we can learn from the exit, thereby improving our future projects.

Technical Steps to Exit

In addition to the management steps, we also need to take the appropriate technical steps for exiting. To shut down an AI project, we start by listing all relevant assets (data, models, code), and then ensure compliance by backing up essential data and securely deleting unnecessary files. We shut down pipelines, stop model deployments, and decommission any cloud or compute resources. Then we archive the codebase, revoke access, and cancel any software licenses or subscriptions. Finally, we reallocate team members and resources, review legal contracts for termination clauses, and communicate the shutdown to all stakeholders.

CARE FOR BUSINESS IN ACTION
CASE STUDY: NIKE'S AI VULNERABILITIES[11]

In chapter 6, we set the OPEN framework into action by using a case study that looked at how Nike could harness the potential of AI by taking the company into the business of making prosthetic limbs. In this chapter, we now tell the other side of the story. Let's continue to assume that you[12] are Nike's new CEO. You will now use the CARE framework to think through how to manage the risks that come with the decision to enter the prosthetics business.

CATASTROPHIZE

In order to manage the risks Nike faces, you will first have to understand what they are. Fortunately, as CEO, you are in a uniquely privileged position to take a big-picture view of the potential issues that might arise from the company's AI pivot. You start by catastrophizing, using the Four Ps—Product, People, Purpose, and Planet—to think of as many ways as possible that things could go wrong.

In terms of product, one risk that you and your team immediately identify is the danger of AI going rogue or of the product simply failing. Imagine that Nike gives someone an artificial arm that starts to act autonomously rather than under the full control of its human owner. The potential consequences are frightening—for the individual, for those near to them, and for Nike as a business. If an issue such as this scales across thousands, or tens of thousands, of devices, the results could be devastating.

A further risk relates to Nike's brand. The company has been so successful at creating a strong brand identity that some of your team john that Nike is really a marketing company that dabbles in shoes. Is there, you wonder, a risk that manufacturing and selling prosthetics will weaken the business by diluting its core brand promise? One potential concern is that the new products will confuse customers, muddying the waters of Nike's previously crystal-clear brand identity. Another is that they will actively work against Nike's brand. After all, bionic limbs do not have uniformly positive associations in consumers' minds, and there is a risk that some of those negative associations may attach themselves to the company.

Finally, you identify supply chain risk. Nike's plans for the supply chain for prosthetics involve integrating current-generation AI across all applicable functions while developing new AI capabilities tailored for the company's needs for the future. AI will play an increasingly central role in production and distribution. AI tools will also be used to track real-time data on both the supply and demand side of the business, continually refining Nike's ability to optimize both production and inventory management plans. Implementing these capabilities has enormous potential for Nike's business, but it also creates significant vulnerabilities.

Your Chief Technical Officer brings up the example of Boeing's struggles after its supply chain was allegedly corrupted by fraudulent parts, contributing to a poor safety record and to numerous deaths. The risk is particularly heightened in the case of AI-driven prosthetics because you will be breaking new ground and working with at least some suppliers who are new to the marketplace. Further, if AI is to help with your supply chain management, you will need to use an open system—that is, one that continually takes in and uses new data from external sources, such as suppliers. Each point of entry or change for this new data represents a vulnerability, because it is an opportunity for corrupted or false data to distort the decisions made by AI agents.

Moving on to people, one risk stands out as particularly significant. The new product is going to require expertise at multiple levels that Nike currently does not have. To be sure, acquiring Prosthenics Inc. is an excellent start, particularly in terms of building the product (see the case study at the end of the previous chapter). But Nike will need much more than that. It will need people who can oversee the production efforts. It will need people who understand the product well enough to be able to sell it. It will need people who can maintain and repair the product for customers. It will need people who can manage the new supply chain. The risk for Nike is that even if you create an excellent product, the company will lack the skills needed to convert that excellence into commercial success.

With regard to purpose, Nike's move into prosthetics creates a risk that is ever-present with new technology: the danger that the company, or its senior management team, becomes distracted from its core purpose by the hype around the shiny new toy. Nike's purpose is "to bring inspiration and innovation to every athlete in the world." When you used the OPEN framework to work out how to utilize AI, you decided that entering the prosthetics industry made sense precisely because that move responded to this mission. However, you now reflect on the importance of sticking to Nike's core purpose as you build up your operations in this new industry. For example, as a maker of prosthetic limbs and AI personas, Nike may suddenly find that it stands on the cusp of being able to meet certain needs in the defense industry. "Would taking on a lucrative defense contract be compatible with the company's core purpose?" your CFO asks you.

Finally, you turn to consider the planet. The last of the Four Ps is about identifying risk out in the world beyond Nike, the risk of what economists like to call negative externalities. One risk that you identify as important concerns fairness and justice issues. Artificial limbs could confer enormous benefits and advantages on their users. And if they do, these advantages will not apply only in athletic contexts; they will also apply in economic contexts. Prosthetic limbs might allow their owner to perform all manner of physical tasks better. And then the question arises—how should these advantages be distributed? Does Nike have a responsibility to ensure some kind of fair distribution? If yes, then the challenge would be to square that with Nike's commercial ambitions.

Another external risk is data risk. As with autonomous vehicles, part of the enormous promise of AI in the area of prosthetics lies in AI's capacity to take in enormous amounts of real-time data, process it, and continually learn from it. Nike's prosthetics are going to be taking in vast quantities of private data that must remain private. Further, there is a risk that Nike's current data processing capacities aren't up to scratch for the new demands that AI-powered prosthetics will make. Finally, there are also concerns about data integrity, because it will be important to ensure that the AI system is learning from accurate data—if it is learning from corrupt data, the limbs may function in unexpected and potentially dangerous ways.

ASSESS

In the second step of the CARE process, your focus turns to defining your risk portfolio and understanding Nike's capacity for effectively managing the risks it faces.

You begin by organizing the risks identified in the previous step into core risks, technical risks, and ethical risks. For example, you place the brand and supply chain risks squarely within the category of core risks, while the data risk is treated as a combination of technical and ethical risk. You then run each risk through the LIT micro-framework. This generates important results. For instance, when you consider the risk of rogue AI taking over the operation of Nike's new prosthetic limbs, while it is impossible to be precise about the long-term probability of this risk occurring, your technical team agrees that the likelihood is extremely low over the short to medium term. So, while this would be a very significant threat to Nike if the risk did materialize, you and your team feel comfortable with deciding that you can monitor this potential threat rather than seek to manage it actively.

At the end of your assessment, you decide that your immediate focus should be on four risks that are specific to AI: the risks to the supply chain, the risk of Nike's workforce not being appropriately and adequately upskilled, data risk, and ethical risk. With this focus in place, you turn to defining Nike's strategic enterprise architecture. This process reveals a range of capability gaps that you will need to fill.

REGULATE

You have identified and understood the risks you face and have assessed the kinds of responses they will need. It's now time to nail down how you will regulate them. In this step of the CARE process, the focus is on creating the structures and implementing the tools that will help to manage and mitigate the identified risks.

In the course of investigating the existing regulatory structure, it becomes clear to you that there is currently no single role or person who is responsible for the AI-related risk around the supply chain. In part, this is because of the complex and interdepartmental nature of AI risk. It touches virtually all the major business functions at Nike. A crucial step for developing a coherent risk management approach, you decide, will involve the creation of a function that sits above all the others in the context of AI risk management and that has ultimate accountability for AI risk across the organization.

You take inspiration from the US Office of Management and Budget's decision to require the appointment of a Chief Artificial Intelligence Officer (CAIO) at certain federal agencies.[13] The CAIO has three fundamental responsibilities: strengthening AI governance, advancing responsible AI innovation, and managing risks from the use of AI. Rather than bundling these into a single role, you appoint an AI Innovation Officer and an AI Risk Officer, with these two roles reporting to a Chief AI Officer. The Chief AI Officer will ultimately be accountable for both innovation and risk management around AI, but the Innovation and Risk Officers will each be responsible for their own specific area. You create three different roles because you foresee AI becoming an important part of Nike's product line, and this means it will demand considerable attention. As you look to the future, it is clear to you that the demands on those in these AI roles will only increase, so you decide to split the function now rather than take this decision later when the change will be more disruptive.

It will take time for these roles to be filled and for the function to become fully operational. Nike cannot afford to simply sit still in that time. You therefore make two major decisions with respect to AI risk management.

First, you address elements of the data risk through technical regulation. After extensive discussions, you and your team decide to explore the possibility of using the blockchain to secure supply chain data so you can guarantee that your raw materials and intermediary products have the correct origins and are cared for appropriately in storage and transit. While this will not remove the need for trust at all levels, it will ensure the integrity of data once it is in the system. Moving forward, you will make it your goal to iteratively reduce trust requirements as you develop a true zero trust architecture. In the meantime, you will partner with internationally recognized independent certification bodies to oversee the integrity of third-party data at its point of entry into your system.

Second, you and your team discuss external oversight. Ensuring the ethical deployment of AI across not just the prosthetics business but the company more broadly will require both regular reporting at the board level and also oversight from independent auditors. You recommend inviting two new members to join the board, with the specific aim of strengthening its expertise in AI. You and your team also make a short-list of organizations and individuals working on the ethics of AI who might be suitable for the role of auditor.

EXIT

You have identified AI risks, assessed and responded to their significance, and decided how you will regulate them. It is now time to examine what to do when things go wrong—when, despite your best efforts to manage and mitigate AI risk, the proverbial hits the fan. In this final step, it is necessary for Nike to figure out how to exit crisis situations. Eventually, it will be the Chief AI Officer who is accountable for the exit strategy, and the AI Risk Officer who is responsible for creating it. But you do not have the luxury of waiting until these roles are filled before making initial contingency plans.

You begin by considering how to take emotion out of the decision to exit. As a systematic aid to doing this, you and your team decide to define thresholds for what counts as an emergency, and you define triggers associated with those thresholds. Specifically, you implement a traffic light system, with predefined criteria for green, yellow, and red lights, and with necessary actions assigned to each color.

Turning to how an exit must be managed, you realize that Nike's existing Disaster Recovery Plan (DRP) needs to be updated for AI. In the existing document, there is no mention of AI, no definition of who will have the power to push kill switches, and no responsibility for deciding when to push them. You decide to use the RACI framework again, this time for defining who does what in emergency situations.

Finally, you start preparing the technical steps that will be required. You consider including a remote kill switch in all of Nike's prosthetic devices but decide that activating such a switch carries too much danger for the users of these products. Instead, you put in place a communication plan for issuing an urgent recall, including pushing a very clear message to the control interface of each device.

KEY TAKEAWAYS

- AI risk management must be proactive and systematic rather than reactive and ad hoc. Businesses need clear accountability structures, with senior leadership taking direct responsibility for AI safety. The appointment of roles like Chief AI Officers, AI Innovation Officers, and AI Risk Officers will become increasingly critical for managing AI risk effectively.

- A successful AI risk management strategy requires multiple complementary approaches, from technical solutions like zero trust architecture to robust regulatory frameworks and incentive structures. No single approach is sufficient on its own.

- Planning for failure is as important as planning for success. Having clear exit strategies, including predetermined thresholds for action and comprehensive shutdown procedures, is essential. The psychological, managerial, and technical steps for exit should all be defined before any AI system goes live.

GOVERNMENT

CHAPTER 8

OPEN FOR GOVERNMENT

How government agencies can harness the power of AI

*G*overnments have been aware of the potential of AI for some time. In 2016, the United States government published a report on the future of AI that predicted that "AI technologies will continue to grow in sophistication and ubiquity; the impact of AI on society will continue to increase, including on employment, education, public safety, and national security, as well as the impact on U.S. economic growth; and industry investment in AI will continue to grow."[1] These kinds of far-sighted, if somewhat generic, predictions have been matched in many nations by a willingness to commit significant resources to the development and understanding of this new technology.

In addition to supporting piecemeal initiatives, an increasing number of countries are implementing national AI strategies aimed at both shaping the research and development of this technology and implementing it in the public sector. But as the head of the OECD's Division for Digital, Innovative, and Open Government puts it, many of these strategies are not truly actionable. Instead, they "look more like a list of principles or a checklist of projects."[2] In this chapter, we look at how the OPEN framework can provide a structure for responding to this challenge by turning principles and ideas into real outcomes.

Government AI spending plans

- Saudi Arabia plans $40 billion AI initiative.[3]
- US government provides around $30 billion in subsidies for AI chipmaking.[4]
- EU approves "Chips Act" in 2023, an investment program to improve Europe's semiconductor ecosystem. It commits €3.3 billion out of the EU budget, while the broader program aims to mobilize €43 billion in total.[5]
- EU allocates €1 billion per year for AI in the budget for the Horizon Europe and Digital Europe programs 2023.[6]
- In 2018, China invests an estimated $1.7–7.5 billion in AI R&D.[7]
- By 2023, China's government guidance funds, a public-private investment vehicle used to promote strategic investment in emerging technologies like AI, have raised around $940 billion.[8]
- In 2024, India announces an AI mission, funded with $1.2 billion.[9]

"Government" is, of course, a term with an enormous range of meanings. It can refer to a wide variety of organizational levels, from the national government, down through state, provincial, or regional governmental layers, to the humblest town assembly. It can also refer to different roles and responsibilities at these different levels, encompassing any or all functions of the executive, legislative, and judicial branches. We often also use the term to describe the operations of specific government departments, from the US Department of the Treasury to the office responsible for issuing cheese-grading licenses in Wisconsin.

In this chapter, we focus primarily on how government agencies can conceptualize and implement effective AI strategies, as it is these agencies that are responsible for delivering programs on the ground. However, we should not think of there being a strict distinction between the different layers of government, especially in those phases of the framework that are concerned with ideation. While a specific government agency may be responsible for setting a program into action, the goals and broad outlines will often be set by the legislative branch, and key elements may sometimes be mandated by the judiciary.

We can also make a distinction between two different types of goals that these agencies may have, each of which needs to be thought through in a slightly different way. On the one hand, much of what government does, and what AI will help governments do in the future, involves the delivery of services. Governments and their subordinate agencies provide and manage passport services, driver's licenses, educational institutions, voting booths, roads, and much more. This service-delivery dimension of government work has the potential to benefit enormously from engaging with AI, with one leading consultancy firm estimating that generative AI alone will deliver $1.75 trillion in productivity gains for the public sector by 2033.[10]

In this area of their work, governments are very similar to businesses, although the ultimate goal of delivering these services is to make the lives of their citizens better rather than to maximize profit. But governments also play another critical, indeed unique, role in the lives of their constituents. If we think of the social system of a country as something like a game, then we can say that all individuals, businesses, and other organizations are players *within* the game. But governments are different. While they, of course, operate within a system of rules as well, governments are in the unique position of controlling the rules of the game that everybody else abides by. When we think about how governments can harness the potential of AI, it is vital that we also consider this special aspect of government activity. Despite the undeniable importance of the services that government delivers, in the long run, it is this rule-defining, condition-setting role that will have the most significant impact on whether and to what extent AI's potential will be realized.

AI and the delivery of government services

- In 2021, the New York State Department of Labor used AI to build "a mobile-first application that helped citizens access the Excluded Workers Fund, which distributed USD 2.1 billion to New Yorkers who were ineligible for other forms of federal assistance."[11]

- In 2020, the Wisconsin Department of Workforce Development (DWD) began using AI to help adjudicate claims for unemployment insurance and also to streamline the application process. The efficiency gains here were staggering and helped the DWD clear its 2020 claims backlog: "Since March 15, 2020, at the outset of the COVID-19 pandemic, DWD has processed nearly 8.8 million weekly claims compared to the 7.2 million claims handled from 2016 to 2019—more than four years' worth of claims in nine months."[12]

- The government of Singapore has developed a variety of AI-powered chatbots to help with service delivery and governance. These capabilities are powered by VICA (Virtual Intelligent Chat Assistant), a bot that "leverages natural language processing engines, machine learning and artificial intelligence to learn and understand conversations to improve virtual and phone interactions citizens and businesses have with the Singapore government agencies."[13] One example of a bot powered by VICA is AlphabotSG, "a super chatbot that learns from various agency chatbots" so that citizens can "find government services and information easily."[14]

THE OPEN FRAMEWORK FOR GOVERNMENT

If you have read this book in the conventional order, the OPEN framework will already be familiar to you by now. What is new in this chapter is its specific adaptation to the unique roles that governments play. The OPEN framework for government builds on the OPEN framework for business set out in chapter 6. The key elements of the framework remain the same across the Outline, Partner, and Experiment phases, with the following government-specific adaptations.

OUTLINE

The RATCHET approach to outlining possibilities (see chapter 6) sits at the heart of the Outline phase for governments, just as it does for businesses. Below, we describe modifications to this approach that reflect the specific needs, responsibilities, and goals of governments and government agencies (marked with bullet points in the figure below).

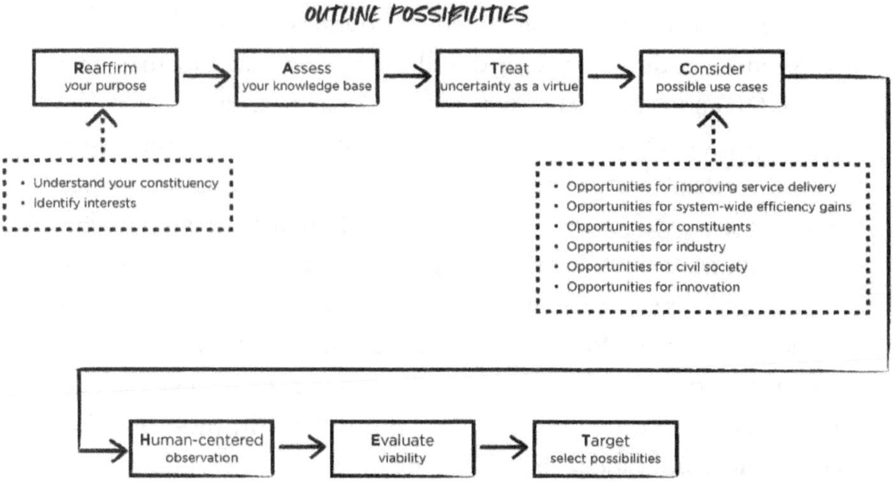

Figure 1. The RATCHET Approach to Outlining Possibilities for Government Agencies.

As for businesses, the first step of this process involves a reaffirmation of purpose. This is both a simpler and a more complex matter for governments and government agencies. These bodies should not have goals of their own. Rather, the ultimate aim of any governing institution should be to help its citizens fulfill *their* goals. Reaffirming purpose here thus aims at achieving clarity about the interests and needs of the citizens in question.

Understand Your Constituency

A governmental system should, ideally, aim to protect and promote the interests of all the citizens it represents. However, specific parts of the system may be responsible for the interests of a more limited group or may have a dual set of responsibilities. For instance, the Department of Veterans Affairs has a very clearly defined primary constituency for the services it provides, although it is also answerable to the nation as a whole when it comes to offering value for money. The New Jersey Motor Vehicle Commission, on the other hand, has a more balanced set of responsibilities: first, to ensure that only people and cars that are safe should take to the roads, and second, to make it as easy as possible for road users to acquire the licenses and registrations they need.

AI adds another nuance to this already complicated picture. How we develop and deploy AI now is, in at least some areas, likely to have a significant impact on the well-being and opportunities of future generations, perhaps even more than it will on people living today. Governments and government agencies need to think hard about how their responsibilities extend across time. Do governments have to take the interests of future citizens into account? Can currently living people be asked to sacrifice for the sake of people not yet born, even those living a century or more later? Given AI's world-changing potential, and the possible existential threats that may arise from it, these questions demand close and careful consideration.[15]

Identify Interests

Once a government agency has identified its constituency, the next step is to identify the interests of those involved. A variety of approaches can offer insight here. To start with the simplest, if we want to know what someone's needs are, we can simply ask them. This can be accomplished at scale using opinion polls, surveys, and focus groups—all the usual apparatus of research in the social sciences. AI itself can also be deployed to help here. In Belgium, for instance, a start-up called CitizenLab is using AI "to automatically classify and analyse thousands of contributions collected on citizen participation platforms,"[16] information that can then be collated and passed on to inform the work of civil servants.

A second approach involves using a map or model of needs and then thinking through how AI might affect a government's ability to fulfil each type. A simple, non-scientific model such as Maslow's hierarchy of needs can serve as a valuable starting point, providing a step-by-step framework for reflection.

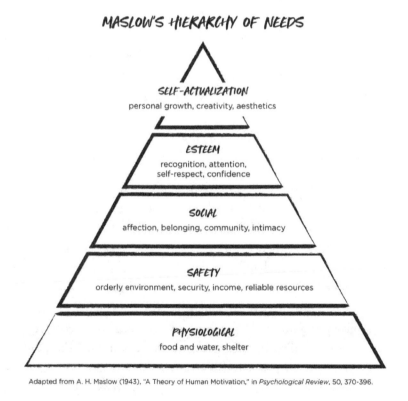

MASLOW'S HIERARCHY OF NEEDS

SELF-ACTUALIZATION
personal growth, creativity, aesthetics

ESTEEM
recognition, attention,
self-respect, confidence

SOCIAL
affection, belonging, community, intimacy

SAFETY
orderly environment, security, income, reliable resources

PHYSIOLOGICAL
food and water, shelter

Adapted from A. H. Maslow (1943), "A Theory of Human Motivation," in *Psychological Review*, 50, 370-396.

Figure 2. Maslow's Hierarchy of Needs.

A third tool that serves as a valuable complement to questioning and modeling involves using the concept of "revealed preference."[17] Some economists suggest that the best way to identify people's preferences is to look at what they actually consume and then work backwards from there. This approach identifies preferences in action rather than relying on the kind of abstracted versions that might be given in replies to survey questions, which are often influenced by factors like self-image or how we would like others to perceive us. Government agencies can look at the policies people vote for, the services they use, and other measurable behaviors, and then use this data to infer what their constituents want from them.

Consider Possible Use Cases

Pinning down the wants and needs of constituents opens the door to thinking about how those goals can be achieved. At this brainstorming stage, potential value is enough; winnowing these ideas to pick out the most useful viable options takes place later, in the "Evaluate viability" and "Target select possibilities" steps of the RATCHET approach (see chapter 6).

The following categories provide starting points for thinking through potential AI-related opportunities at the governmental level.

- **Opportunities for improving service delivery.** For instance, AI systems could be used to generate personalized communications to inform veterans about the benefits and care options available to them by focusing on their individual needs. Or perhaps an AI chatbot could walk an entrepreneur through the process of registering a new business online.
- **Opportunities for system-wide efficiency gains.** AI could, to give just a few examples, be used to manage the electricity grid, the water distribution system, or a city's traffic. The potential for efficiency gains in this area is staggering, and in many cases these kinds of benefits can only be delivered by government level systems.

- **Opportunities for constituents.** The emergence of AI will create new employment opportunities and demand for new skills. Governments can play a key role in facilitating this transition—for example, by providing information and funding for reskilling as the employment landscape changes in response to increased automation.

- **Opportunities for industry.** AI has the potential to create enormous productivity gains in manufacturing. For the most part, the delivery of these gains will be in the hands of private corporations, but governments need to consider what they can do to encourage and support this work. For example, a local government agency might provide an information service collating and sharing recent advances that are particularly relevant for local businesses.

- **Opportunities for civil society.** British Prime Minister Margaret Thatcher famously declared, "There is no such thing as society, only individual men and women and families." We disagree. Not only do we believe that there is such a thing as society, we think that AI will offer important opportunities for strengthening and developing the bonds that hold societies together at both the local and national levels. For example, AI bots could be used to fact-check data in real time to limit the effects of misinformation or AI personas representing different social and political perspectives could be used to teach young people how to engage with different opinions in a respectful and productive way.

- **Opportunities for innovation.** Governments can have an enormous impact on innovation in their role as the stewards of the contexts in which organizations operate. Through funding programs, incentive structures (tax breaks), infrastructure investments, educational policies, and legal instruments such as regulation, governments can help steer the future course of AI development.

Evaluate Viability and Target Select Possibilities

Government agencies are prone to inertia, so it is important to set a time limit on the initial Outline phase. This is not a final cutoff; the Navigate phase encourages a periodic reassessment of opportunities that might arise from evolutions in technology or ideas, so there will be other opportunities to come back in search of the perfect idea. Once the time is up, move on to conduct a rapid FIRST assessment of viability and use it to select the ideas you will carry forward to the next phase.

Conduct a rapid FIRST assessment of viability

- Feasibility: Is the technology in its current state capable of delivering the target outcome? Does your agency have the resources that would be necessary to complete the project?
- Investment: Approximately how much would this use case cost to deliver?
- Risk/Reward: What are the risks involved in pursuing the project, and how do they stack up against the potential rewards?
- Strategic priority: Assign the use case a score for strategic priority. How significant would successful delivery of the project be for your agency's mission?
- Time frame: How long would the project take under best- and worst-case scenarios?

PARTNER

After identifying possibilities and then selecting those that are at least minimally viable, the natural next step might seem to be to start experimenting with them and exploring them in greater depth. But AI is so new and is evolving so rapidly that even national governments cannot expect to have all the resources and expertise needed to optimize its potential immediately to hand. To properly explore the opportunities identified in the Outline phase, governments first need to consider their role as a partner in this process. Governments will need to build partnerships both across government agencies and between the public and private spheres. They will also need to think carefully about the kinds of partnerships that will be needed with AI itself. The broad approach to developing partnerships here aligns with that set out in the OPEN framework for business. However, governments have specific needs, challenges, and opportunities that require additional consideration.

Identifying Gaps

The first step to building partnerships involves understanding where they are needed. In pursuit of this goal, governments and government agencies can turn to an adapted version of the portfolio and program management (PPM) approach to gain clarity about where the gaps are and, just as importantly, where they are not.

The basic idea of PPM is simple and is familiar from activities such as investing: "[D]iscover what you have, sort it into logical piles, and assess the value of the individual items against some larger goal."[18] In business, PPM proceeds by mapping out the architectural structure of the various elements of the business, such as the business models, processes, technological infrastructure, and strategy, and then working out how to align these. For governments and government agencies, instead of mapping out business models, it will be helpful to capture delivery models—that is, how these entities deliver the value they are supposed to be delivering.

By conducting this exercise, government agencies will develop a map of their institutional architecture and a portfolio that will provide an accurate picture of what the organization does and how it does it. This exercise will also tell us what the organization requires in order to achieve its goals, and which of those things it already has and which it does not. This is the essential foundation on which partnerships can then be built.

Identifying Possible Partners

As with businesses, the partnership possibilities for government agencies can be organized into three categories: internal, external, and AI. And at the most abstract level, the task is the same: The goal of this part of the process is to create a comprehensive list of the relevant partnership opportunities. However, there are some particular features of the governance context that must be taken into account when carrying out this step.

Internal partners

After defining its organizational architecture in the previous step, the government agency is now well placed to conduct a more focused and rigorous investigation of the capacities it already has available to it. This is a separate step in the OPEN process for governments for two linked reasons. On the one hand, if we understand "government" as the collection of agencies and institutions that make up the entire governance landscape of any given country, then we immediately see that government has immense capacities at its disposal. On the other hand, we can also see that this collection of agencies and institutions is highly disparate and siloed, and that collaboration is even more challenging here than it is in the business world. In brief, it is very likely that government as a whole will have enormous capacities for exploiting AI's potential that won't immediately be clear to any individual department or agency.

When working out how to address resource and skills gaps, the crucial first step for any agency is to identify useful *internal* capacity within the public sector as a whole. Here, it is necessary to think laterally. For example, the Department of Health and Human Services can consider whether a research lab funded by the Institute for Education Sciences may be able to contribute to the development of its AI data architecture.

AI requires internal collaboration—
and this is very difficult for governments

Developing and deploying AI requires bringing a wide variety of moving parts together in harmony. Process and workflow can only be implemented by first bringing together people across the organization to define the structures and rules within which the AI will be working. In complex systems there will be no one person who owns all this information, so collaboration is of the essence.

Anyone who has dealt with governments or other very large organizations will have learned one immutable truth: Bureaucracies develop their own logic. They may have been created originally with the goal of serving specific end-users, but as they grow, they—and the people working in them—develop aims and priorities of their own. Over time, structures emerge that lead to incentives for people within the organization that are misaligned with the original mission of serving citizens. This process also causes entrenched interests to develop, which in turn can lead to significant resistance to any movement away from the status quo.

As a result, it is extremely difficult for governments to generate the level of internal collaboration that successful innovation requires in the complex field of AI. But difficult is not the same as impossible. Governments *can* achieve impressive results in this area, but exceptional leadership and careful navigation of institutional structures is needed. Here are two things that we think will be helpful.

First, at the project management level, the RACI framework is a valuable tool for establishing rules of engagement. RACI is a matrix used to clearly define roles and responsibilities in a collaborative project. The four most common roles are: *Responsible* (the people responsible for completing a given job); *Accountable* (the people ultimately answerable for a given job); *Consulted* (the people whose opinion is sought); *Informed* (the people who need to be updated about progress).

Second, leadership must also invest heavily in cultural change. There needs to be a government- or agency-wide culture shift away from the bias towards the *status quo* and towards a culture that welcomes innovation. This will be immensely difficult to achieve but the rewards of even partial success will make the effort worthwhile.

External partners

The question of whether to build capability in-house or buy that capability from a third-party vendor arises whenever government agencies implement any kind of new technology. There can be good reasons for choosing either option. For example, it will often be significantly less expensive to use an externally developed solution rather than creating something from scratch. At the same time, using technology developed by a third party might introduce vulnerabilities, such as leaving the government agency dependent on a single vendor or introducing broader security challenges that will need to be solved. But while there are nuanced decisions to be made, framing these decisions in terms of an either/or choice is fundamentally limiting when we look at a rapidly evolving technology like AI. A more useful approach asks not whether an agency should build *or* buy, but rather, at which points in the development process building is the best option and at which points it is better to buy.

The number of commercially available AI tools is growing rapidly, and many are capable of solving problems that will align directly with government use cases. There are now several useful tools in the legal and academic sectors for working with the huge quantities of documents these fields generate. For example, a tool called Neos provides AI-powered summarization of legal documents, extraction of key details for data entry, and even document creation, while multiple tools are available in the academic space (Elicit, Research Rabbit, Scholarcy, and Typeset, to name just a few) to help summarize research, extract data, create literature reviews, and so on.[19] In some cases, it will be possible to put tools like these to work in government contexts with minimal changes. In other cases, more internal work will be needed to make the tools fit for purpose.

EXPERIMENT

The first step of the OPEN process sought to identify possible courses of action and then filtered them for initial viability. The second step examined the partnerships that will be essential tools for making progress. In the Experiment phase, the goal is to systematically evaluate the possibilities, carrying out trials and tests and then identifying the options that are most suitable for implementing at scale.

Innovation Teams

Effective experimentation requires the creation and deployment of dedicated innovation teams that are both capable of and responsible for testing the ideas generated in the previous steps. While innovation teams have a crucial role to play in all large organizations, they are particularly important in governmental contexts. Government agencies are rarely hotbeds of innovation and agility. On the whole, this is a good thing; safe and boring is mostly a virtue when it comes to governance. However, in certain circumstances, strengths turn into weaknesses, and dealing with AI is just such a circumstance for this particular strength.

Responding well to AI requires flexibility and nimbleness, while harnessing AI's potential requires a mindset that is optimistic and change-oriented. There is no need to try to implement this kind of start-up mentality across all of government; nor should we seek to. Instead, specialized teams with the authority and resources they need to experiment can bring the required skills and mindsets to bear in the appropriate areas. Further, and analogously to the role of the Chief Innovation Officer in businesses, government agencies will benefit from the creation of roles that take a holistic view across the innovation teams within their own agency and that also have insight into the ongoing work of other agencies, thereby bringing some kind of coherence into AI innovation and fueling synergistic possibilities.

Conceptual Modeling

Once the innovation teams are in place, the next step is for them to conduct conceptual experiments by carefully thinking through the options previously identified as at least minimally viable. This might involve workshopping ideas, running paper simulations, and experimenting with novel uses for readily available tools. This will help narrow the focus of the broader AI initiative so that only the most promising options move forward to the much more expensive and labor-intensive prototyping stage.

A key step in this phase is for government agencies to learn from experiments, and from trials and full-scale implementations of AI programs, in other governmental and nongovernmental contexts. There is a vast and growing amount of material to draw on here. Governments around the world are currently grappling with the opportunities and challenges raised by AI, and the results of their initial studies are frequently openly accessible (outside the area of national security, at least). Publicly available research data is less common for the testing and rollout of programs by businesses. However, government agencies will, in some cases at least, be able to leverage their position outside the marketplace to gain access without the businesses in question worrying about sharing data with competitors.

Build, Test, Iterate, Scale

Conceptual modeling is a critical step, but it can only take you so far. Once the most promising AI development options have been identified, it is time to begin successive rounds of prototyping and testing. While the overall process here is very similar to that followed by businesses and other organizations, governments have specific responsibilities and duties that shape the experimental process once systems go live.

- **Move fast; don't break things.** Implementing change at pace is something that government agencies should always aim for. But there are limits to what we can reasonably expect. While some businesses are more than happy to embrace rapid development as the highest virtue, leaving others to clear up the systemic damage they leave in their wake, this is not an approach that governments can take. Before implementing radically new systems—and AI is as radical and potentially disruptive as a technology can be—governments and government agencies must be sure that the consequences for the broader social and economic ecosystem will be positive.

- **A duty of care.** In addition to supporting rather than undermining systemic stability, governments must take particular care of their citizens in the experimentation stage. When businesses roll out early versions of AI systems, their clients can walk away and refuse to engage (so long as adequate information is given). Government agencies, by contrast, will frequently be the only providers of certain key services. At the same time, while businesses have a primary duty to their shareholders, government agencies exist for the sake of the citizens they serve. It is vital, then, to ensure both that the participation of citizens in experimental programs is fully informed and fully voluntary, *and* that there is a very high degree of confidence that the program will not be detrimental to individual users.
- **A commitment to scaling.** By its very nature, government benefits in an outsize way from scalable solutions. Simply by virtue of the size of the public-sector workforce and the scope of its responsibilities, scalable products that can be deployed in more than one setting bring considerable additional value. This is particularly true when it comes to developing and implementing new technologies, since government tech projects fail at an alarming rate.[20] Innovation teams should, then, seek to minimize elements in their AI system design that would limit the applicability of their work to single departments. But just as importantly, state and federal governments have a responsibility to ensure that advances flow swiftly and with minimal friction across the whole apparatus of government.

Building Trust

Government agencies need to pay particular attention to issues of trust when experimenting with AI. Only 37 percent of Americans have an optimistic view of AI today. Another 34 percent view it negatively, while the remaining 29 percent don't think about it much at all. And when asked about the future, things look even grimmer, with 48 percent of respondents feeling distrust about future AI developments compared to just 28 percent who trust that it will be used well.²¹ If governments hope to harness the potential of AI in the long term, they need to bring their citizens along with them. If they don't, funding will dry up and the political will to support initiatives will disappear. At the same time, we can expect to see engagement with existing programs diminish, undermining their effectiveness.

Experimenting responsibly and communicating honestly and openly about AI are key requirements for building this trust. But good intentions are not enough. The most important thing that government agencies can do is put in place systems that ensure that they are worthy, and trustworthy, stewards of this technology. We discuss various ways to do this in chapter 9, but it is important to emphasize that safety and security initiatives need to be built into innovation processes from the ground up, not treated as something distinct that can be bolted on later.

The importance of data

A critical component for securing trust in AI systems is ensuring that the data these systems rely on is treated with the care it deserves. Innovation teams must prioritize:

- Data quality. The output of AI systems is constrained by the quality of the data it works with—garbage in, garbage out.
- Data consolidation. It is important for harnessing AI's potential that datasets are as large and consolidated as possible. This is an argument for centralizing data storage. At the same time, it is important to retain agility and encourage experimentation. As such, centralized datasets need to be available in a variety of different forms to allow people to innovate with them.
- Data security. Data breaches are bad enough when they happen to businesses, and can be highly damaging to the individuals concerned. But the data governments hold is often both more sensitive and more comprehensive. Keeping this data secure is vital if governments wish to maintain the support of the public for AI-driven programs.

Final Stress-Testing

The Experiment phase of the OPEN process concludes with a rigorous final examination of the programs that have passed through the conceptual experimentation, prototyping, and iteration stages. Before signing off on deployment at scale, it is critical to subject the production model to a full battery of tests designed to uncover flaws.

In addition to technical tests, project leaders should assign dedicated individuals or teams whose sole job is to find flaws with and fatally undermine the project's output. This kind of devil's advocacy is an extremely powerful tool for stress-testing a product or idea. Individuals or teams carrying out this function are most effective when they are insulated from groupthink and can operate unhindered by loyalty or obligation to internal structures. So, where possible, it is best to turn to other departments or, better, to independent third parties to staff this role.

NAVIGATE

The Greek philosopher Plato famously compared the soul to a chariot pulled by winged horses. Applying this analogy to the OPEN framework, the first three steps are the horses while this final step—navigate—is the charioteer, the guiding intelligence for the entire framework. The focus here is on ensuring that the AI innovation project is attuned to the purpose of the government agency and on managing the iterative repetition of the other steps of the framework as needed.

Just One Job

Governments and their subordinate agencies have just one job: securing and improving the quality of life of the citizens on whose behalf they work. That's it. Understanding that this is the essence of the work of government and ensuring that all other activities are directed toward this end is what the Navigate phase is all about. In every decision with respect to AI, this simple job description should serve as the North Star that keeps the ship of state on course.

It's easy to describe this mindset, and it is just as easy to nod along. Yet it is very hard to put it into practice. Partisanship, media pressures, organizational agendas, path-dependency, systemic incentives … separately and collectively, all these factors make it hard to realize this simple ideal in a seamless way. But the fact that the goal is hard to achieve is not an excuse for lowering standards. If a government agency is operating in a way that prioritizes other goals, or worse, that undermines the quality of life of those it is meant to serve, then it is essential that all possible efforts are taken to correct matters. This is particularly important when dealing with a technology with as much potential to both help and harm as AI has.

Continual Learning

Individuals and organizations don't like being wrong. This resistance to acknowledging error is particularly strong at the government level, fueled by both the pressures of politics and the institutional inertia of large departments with long histories and complex procedures. Here's something we can be sure of: When it comes to AI, governments, government agencies, and individual civil servants are going to get things wrong all the time. The technology is too complex and the trajectory of its future development too uncertain to allow any hope for perfection. This will be a plain fact of life in the coming age of AI, so it is essential that the systems we build reflect this reality. For government agencies, this means seeing the development and deployment of AI capabilities as a continual learning exercise in which the ability to revise and refine, and to acknowledge and overcome errors, is treated as a core strength.

When using the OPEN framework, this attitude starts with recognizing that the steps do not describe a one-off process but an iterative cycle. The first three steps in the process should be returned to and repeated both on a regular, scheduled basis and whenever new developments might shed new light on the application of this technology. This process of ongoing reflection and reinvention provides a foundation on which to consolidate and correct the lessons that have been learned. This foundation then forms the ground on which agencies can build in further cycles.

OPEN FOR GOVERNMENT IN ACTION
CASE STUDY: BUILDING AN INVESTMENT
MATCHING PLATFORM AT THE EDA[22]

The mission of the US Department of Commerce is "to create the conditions for economic growth and opportunity for all communities."[23] A key agency within the department is the Economic Development Administration (EDA), which is responsible for encouraging regeneration in economically distressed areas of the country and for promoting innovation and competitiveness.[24] You[25] have just been appointed to a senior innovation role at the EDA, with the brief to develop and deploy AI systems in support of the agency's mission. As a first step in this direction, you draw on the OPEN framework to systematically think through the possibilities.

OUTLINE
The first step in the OPEN process is all about figuring out what is possible. It begins with gaining clarity about who it is that the EDA serves. There are no easy answers to this question. Like all federal government bodies, the EDA is ultimately responsible to every citizen of the United States. However, it has a particular brief to serve areas of the country that are struggling economically. You also reflect on your duty to future citizens: AI has enormous potential to drive economic and social change, so it is important to think through the long-term ramifications of any decisions you make. In some cases, decisions you take now may yield excellent results today while causing market distortions or other negative effects, such as environmental damage, in future years. While it is impossible to know exactly what the future consequences of today's decisions will be, you and your team decide that you will return to this point throughout the development process to make sure that you are acting as good stewards for future generations of Americans.

The range of possibilities you identify during your brainstorming sessions with your team is vast, but one idea stands out as particularly promising. One of the greatest challenges for steering investments

and grants is matching funding opportunities with specific community needs and capabilities. Because there are highly complex systems of
goals and wants on each side of the equation, and because there are so
many thousands of potential sites for projects, it can often feel as if decisions are being made in an arbitrary fashion, even when multilayered
bureaucratic processes are in place. A machine learning algorithm that
has been trained on all the available data should be able to balance the
thousands of variables involved in assessing grant bids. It should also be
able to match private investors with the communities that both need
their investment most *and* have the conditions on the ground that are
required to make the investment a success. Not only would an AI-driv-
en grant and investment matching platform deliver more accurate results than humans could hope to, but it could also connect investors
and communities directly, minimizing the need for the expensive and
time-consuming intermediary work that the EDA currently engages in.

Of course, to create and train an AI model like this will require the
collection of vast amounts of general economic data, as well as information about the needs of different types of investors and information
about each community in the nation. The great news here is that the
Department of Commerce is already in possession of incredibly rich
data on these questions and can draw on the immense amounts of information collected by other US government agencies.

In addition to being a useful tool right now, you firmly believe that
AI will be critical to maintaining America's global economic lead over
the next fifty years. You therefore decide to explore how an EDA investment matching platform could serve the secondary goal of supporting
AI tech growth and worker skill development over the longer term. On
the one hand, this will mean lobbying internally for more grants like the
recent EDA Tech Hub award to support the Tulsa Hub for Equitable
& Trustworthy Autonomy (THETA), an Oklahoma-based project that
will spearhead the development of a variety of AI advances.[26] On the
other hand, you also wonder whether it would be feasible to use the
platform itself to prioritize projects with an AI focus.

You conduct a rapid FIRST assessment to determine whether the investment matching platform idea should proceed to the next stage. Your team decides that the project is technologically *feasible*; that the *investment* required is within the budget available; that, while there is a significant chance of delay or failure, as with all tech projects, the *risk/reward* ratio is sufficiently slanted toward reward to make the possible downside worthwhile. You also determine that the *strategic priority* of this use case is extremely high and that the project can be delivered within a reasonable *time frame*. Pulling these strands together, you conclude that the project appears viable and warrants further development.

PARTNER

Moving on to the next stage of the OPEN framework, you begin by mapping out your institutional architecture. Your goal here is to identify skill and resource gaps that will hinder the successful delivery of the project. The first major gap that emerges relates to data. The success of the platform will depend very heavily on the quality and quantity of the data used to train the platform and then to keep it up to date. While you are confident that you can access an excellent range of initial training data, you realize that you will also need an ongoing stream of new data to ensure the platform continues to operate at the highest level of accuracy from day to day. Your analysis of the EDA's institutional architecture also flags up a gap in the agency's technical expertise. Simply put, the EDA does not, at present, have the technical ability to develop the algorithm that will power the platform. Nor does it have the expertise required to establish and maintain the platform's hardware infrastructure. Finally, you identify an experiential gap when it comes to managing large-scale AI projects. Unsurprisingly, given the relative novelty of mature AI models, the EDA has no significant institutional history of working with this technology to further the department's goals. This means that, in addition to your limited technical capacity, there are gaps in management and implementation expertise that need to be bridged.

Once you have identified the major gaps, you move on to finding partners that can help you fill them. You begin with internal partners.

Fortunately, the Department of Commerce has a subdivision that is dedicated to gathering and analyzing data, so you decide to collaborate with the Bureau of Economic Analysis (BEA) to integrate live data feeds into your new platform to ensure that the AI model is an accurate up-to-the-minute resource. Second, you contact the Transportation Security Administration (TSA) to explore an informal collaboration around AI development in government. You choose the TSA because you know that it has recently invested in modernizing its data architecture, in part with the specific aim of using AI to improve its service delivery. Consequently, it has valuable firsthand experience that will be highly relevant to your own efforts.

When it comes to the algorithm that will sit at the heart of the investment matching platform, you decide that this requires external resources. As AI becomes more widely integrated into the everyday activities of the TSA, it may become economically viable to build an internal AI development division. However, at the present time the costs involved would be too great for the single project you have in mind. So, you decide to hire third-party vendors both to create the algorithm and to set up the necessary hardware infrastructure. You know that there are investment matching companies in the start-up space that are increasingly leveraging AI to power their services, such as AngelList, SeedInvest, and Crunchbase. The EDA is extremely well-connected in the start-up space, so you open talks with relevant companies with the goal of determining which external vendors might be suitable for your project.

After conducting a cost-benefit analysis, you decide that it will be more efficient to stand up an in-house capability to manage and maintain the system once it is up and running. The creation of this new department will need to take place concurrently with the creation of the algorithm. To facilitate this process, you look for a management consultancy with expertise in AI to help put procedures and staff in place so the department will be ready well before the platform goes live.

EXPERIMENT

With your partnerships in place, you now move toward building the first prototype of the system. You start by engaging in an extensive program of conceptual modeling to identify possible weaknesses in your plan. One issue that emerges here is that the project focus has so far been on the algorithm that will sit at the heart of the platform. But to optimize the platform's usefulness, you will also have to design helpful and engaging AI personas to serve as the user interface for both investors and communities. These personas will not only need to gather data but will also have to assess the quality of the answers being given, identify gaps in the information that might lead to poor matching, draw on live data feeds to help fill out the package, and steer users to the right sources for information if necessary.

You now return to the idea that the algorithm can be designed to pursue ideal future outcomes as well as making connections that are optimized for current conditions. Early discussions with the engineer team that will develop the algorithm suggest that you can effectively put your thumb on the scale by assigning additional weight to certain variables. This will, for instance, allow for the prioritization of investments in AI development or AI workforce training when it comes to matching with desirable locations that may be in high demand among investors. You decide to make testing a range of possible weightings a central part of the experimental process.

As you move from conceptual modeling to the pilot phase, you focus the team's attention on a dimension of your work that will be critical to the success of the project: public engagement and trust. While you consider yourself to be an AI evangelist, you know that the broader population is much more wary of this new technology. These feelings tend to be particularly strong in parts of the country that have suffered economically from previous phases of technological and social change. You also know that major governmental AI initiatives will attract considerable public scrutiny to ensure that taxpayer money is not being frittered away on projects built on unproven tech.

You take several steps to respond to these concerns. First, you design a development process that starts small and involves comprehensive audits of the effectiveness of the algorithm at every stage. In addition, you look at a variety of stakeholder oversight options and decide to trial these throughout the pilot phase. In one, you will assemble a stakeholder board that has oversight of the development of the algorithm and personas; in another, you will draw on stakeholder views to review the weighting of parameters and to identify investment and workforce priorities; and in a third, you will assign a team of technical experts to randomly sample the platform's matches and trace back the individual steps of the decision-making process as far as possible. The goal is to iterate and develop these oversight processes alongside the technology so they are optimized by the time the platform is rolled out at scale.

As the final step in this stage, you schedule an intensive stress test of the final production version of the platform. You bring in a team of technical experts from a university AI lab and invite them to try to break the platform. You then use the insights gained to drive a final round of improvements.

NAVIGATE

The public release of the platform is far from the end of the story. You now have the opportunity to assess the progress of the project against the most important criterion of all: how well it serves the citizens to whom you are responsible. Part of this process involves the ongoing iteration of the Outline, Partner, and Experiment phases of the framework as an engine for the continuous improvement of the platform. In doing so, you can draw on the live usage data now available to you and the results of the platform's matching decisions. With the chaos of the initial development process now in the past, you turn your attention to finetuning details and ensuring that every facet of the platform serves the end for which it was created.

There is another vital task that demands your attention in this phase of the framework. The investment matching platform is one of the EDA's first AI projects. The agency's use of AI will only increase over time, so you have a vital responsibility to translate your team's learnings into actionable insights that can inform future projects within the agency. To start spreading what you have learned, you begin to schedule knowledge sharing meetings and seminars to shape the future approach of both senior leadership and the rank-and-file staff of the agency. These are small first steps, but they are a necessary starting point for the culture of continual learning around AI that will be essential for the agency's future success in this field.

KEY TAKEAWAYS

- Government has one job and one job only: to improve the lives of the citizens it serves. When thinking about how to harness AI's potential, we need to keep returning to this fundamental function so that we can focus on what is truly important.

- Harnessing AI's potential will require changing cultures. It will be necessary to break down departmental silos and the tendency of entrenched interests to favor the status quo in order to drive a culture in which innovation and internal collaboration can flourish.

- Trust is essential to harnessing AI's potential. Without broad public trust in how this technology is being developed and deployed, it will not be possible to incorporate it into the fabric of our daily lives, which is where much of its potential lies. Government has a crucial role to play in building this trust.

CHAPTER 9

CARE FOR GOVERNMENT

How government agencies can guard against the dangers of AI

The OPEN framework seeks to answer the question, "What do we need to do to maximize the potential of AI?" The CARE framework has a different focus. Rather than promoting value, CARE is all about *protecting* what we already have from the dangers that emerge with the development of this powerful new technology. And let's be clear: AI *does* pose huge potential dangers. Nobel Prize winner Geoffrey Hinton, a scientist who is often described as "the Godfather of AI," resigned from his job at Google in early 2024 so that he "could talk about the dangers" of the technology to which he had contributed so much.[1]

One of those dangers is that the emergence of AI will lead to human extinction, an outcome that Hinton reportedly estimates has a one-in-ten chance of being realized in the next thirty years.[2] The extinction of humanity is the most extreme danger that AI poses, but there is plenty to worry about even if we manage to escape this calamitous result. Hinton, for example, also raises the possibility that humans will ultimately find themselves controlled by AI rather than controlling it: "If [AI] gets to be much smarter than us, it will be very good at manipulation because it will have learned that from us, and there are very few examples of a more intelligent thing being controlled by a less intelligent thing."[3] This is, we think, a persuasive argument, and many of the other risks that emerge from a close consideration of the evolving capabilities of AI are similarly terrifying. Untrammeled development of AI will soon enable anyone with an internet connection and moderate financial resources to create bioweapons at home or to launch devastating misinformation campaigns with global reach.[4] When capabilities like these are so easy to tap into, the question of how we control access to them takes on a special urgency.

Home-brewed weapons are not the only type we need to worry about. Militaries all over the globe are currently racing to develop AI-powered armaments. Perhaps the most obvious area of development involves autonomous drones or robots that will be able to fight and kill with minimal human oversight, or even with none. Imagine the risk of this technology falling into the wrong hands. More subtly, imagine the risk to the human soul of being able to distance ourselves so easily and completely from acts of killing that take place at our behest.

Killer robots

The risk of autonomous AI agents is particularly pointed in the case of lethal autonomous weapons systems (LAWS), "weapon system[s] that, once activated, can select and engage targets without further intervention by a human operator."[5] While such systems do not, in principle, require AI to operate autonomously, it is a natural complement. The war between Russia and Ukraine has served as a proving ground for a new generation of cheap and easy-to-manufacture drones. Once AI replaces human controllers, it is very likely that the mass deployment of such weapons systems will become the first line of both defense and offense for militaries around the world. The dangers are enormous. Alongside the specter of autonomous drone swarms rapidly annihilating any humans who dare to venture onto the battlefield of tomorrow, it is all too easy to imagine what will happen when this affordable and easy-to-replicate technology finds its way into the hands of bad actors such as dictators or terrorists. The possibility of rogue AIs going beyond their programming is only a secondary danger here. Humans are more than capable of exploiting this technology to the limits of its destructive power.

The risks we face do not all involve exotic weaponry or other menacing AI agents. In some cases, potentially devastating outcomes may have their origin in nothing more than the ability of AI to automate work. In chapters 4 and 6, we treated the productivity gains that AI could deliver as one of its most promising possible outcomes. But what happens if we create and deploy automated technologies more quickly than we manage to develop the social structures that are needed to absorb this kind of change? If one of the results of the evolution of AI is to put a large proportion of the human population out of work, what happens to those former workers? Not only will this immense disruption affect the quality of many people's lives, but it could also become a threat to national stability and security as millions take to the streets in protest.

Perhaps that possibility seems too far-fetched? Well, here's something that's no longer a future risk but a present danger, something that's happening now and that could have potentially disastrous effects. AI has already led to the rise of so-called "synthetic media"[6] forms, such as deepfakes, which are simultaneously becoming both more convincing and easier to create. This phenomenon poses severe risks to individuals and to society as a whole—in a world in which distrust and polarization are already rampant, the last thing we need is another way for bad actors to lie to us.[7]

Or, as a final possibility, consider a danger suggested by historian and philosopher Yuval Noah Harari. Harari points out that large language models (LLMs) have already functionally mastered language—they can process the language humans speak and can interact in a way that humans can understand. Taking this as his starting point, Harari develops a simple argument. Most of human culture depends on language, and by mastering language, "AI has thereby hacked the operating system of our civilisation." He then asks: "What will happen to the course of history when AI takes over culture, and begins producing stories, melodies, laws and religions?"[8] Harari sketches various gloomy possibilities as an answer. One of them is that meaningful public conversation will break down because we will rarely be sure whether we are talking with an AI or a person—and it only makes sense to talk to a person. This will bring democracy to an end, because democracy requires meaningful public conversation. We agree that this is a very real danger. And it is a danger that is on our doorstep today, not one that is a distant glimmer far off in the future.

There is also a more insidious danger. Language isn't just an instrument that we use—it is an instrument whose use shapes us. To some extent, we make ourselves what we are through language. As the emperor Charlemagne said, to possess another language is to possess another soul, and so the question arises: What will become of our souls when the language we use is shaped by our conversations with AI? And, even further down the road, what will become of our souls when the common language of the world is the language of AI talking to itself?

Individuals and organizations have a responsibility to contribute to the collective effort to mitigate these risks. Yet it is governments and governments alone that have the power to regulate individual and organizational behavior on a national level to mandate the responsible development and use of AI. And it is governments alone that have the power to pass laws and negotiate treaties at the international level to ensure that minimum safety standards apply around the globe.

Governments are not blind to this special power or to the special responsibility that comes with it. In October 2023, President Biden signed an executive order on AI that laid out a set of policies and principles for the responsible development of the technology.[9] More recently, and partly in response, the National Institute of Standards and Technology (NIST) published an AI Risk Management Framework in July 2024, with the aim of helping individuals, organizations, and government agencies improve their AI risk management strategies.[10]

The United States is by no means unique in pursuing such initiatives. The two other most important geopolitical players on the world stage—the European Union and China—have also been actively developing and implementing regulatory frameworks for AI. In June 2024, the EU signed the EU Artificial Intelligence Act, which aims to create a regulatory framework for the development of AI in the EU's twenty seven member states. China, meanwhile, released its own regulatory framework for the management of generative AI in 2023.[11]

The framework we offer in this chapter does not purport to be a replacement for these kinds of high-level initiatives. Instead, it encourages the user to think through a broad range of options that include, but are not limited to, formal regulation. The goal is to create a resource that will be useful both to those thinking about these issues at the national government level and for employees of federal and state government agencies. The context of the Oval Office is, of course, very different from that of the Minnesota Department of Motor Vehicles, and we do not claim that the CARE framework can be applied identically in both settings. But the bare bones of the framework are sufficiently flexible that they can be adapted easily to any governmental situation.

Senator Richard Blumenthal on the Blumenthal-Hawley Framework

How can we effectively regulate a technology that we don't fully understand but that we know is going to change the world?

One of the most important political voices attempting to answer that question in the United States is Senator Richard Blumenthal (D-CT). Senator Blumenthal is coauthor of the "Bipartisan Framework for U.S. AI Act," also known as the Blumenthal-Hawley Framework. Created with Senator Josh Hawley (R-MO), the Bipartisan Framework has five pillars:

- Establish a Licensing Regime Administered by an Independent Oversight Body
- Ensure Legal Accountability for Harms
- Defend National Security and International Competition
- Promote Transparency
- Protect Consumers and Kids[12]

As Senator Blumenthal put it when discussing the framework with us, "AI has enormous potential for doing good, whether in medical research and treatment, exploring space, or simply doing the rapid calculations that are necessary for all kinds of other benefits to people around the globe. But there are also perils. Some seem like science fiction, but they are very real. The idea that AI models could be smarter than human beings and could, in effect, program themselves to be out of control, is a frightening prospect." Senator Hawley frames the need for action in similarly stark terms: "Congress must act on AI regulation .... Our American families, workers, and national security are on the line."

THE CARE FRAMEWORK FOR GOVERNMENT AGENCIES

The CARE framework consists of four sequential steps: Catastrophize, Assess, Regulate, and Exit. In this section, we look at how these steps can be applied by governments and their subordinate agencies.

CATASTROPHIZE

The first step in the CARE framework involves mapping out potential future risks. The aim of catastrophizing is not to predict what *will* happen. Rather, it is to identify things that *might* happen, as a first step to responding to the relevant risks in an informed and appropriate way.

The Risk-Categorization Matrix

The following matrix is helpful for thinking through the different types of risks AI poses. The goal is to build up a catalog of potential dangers defined by time frame and risk type.

CARE FOR GOVERNMENT RISK MATRIX

	WELFARE RISK	SOCIAL RISK	SECURITY RISK	SYSTEMIC RISK	EXISTENTIAL RISK
SHORT-TERM					
MEDIUM-TERM					
LONG-TERM					

Figure 1. CARE for Government Risk Matrix.

Short-term risks are those that may emerge within the next three years, medium-term risks are those likely to occur in the next four to ten years, while long-term risks include everything beyond this point.

Welfare risk is risk to material well-being—for example, the risk that AI will lead to unemployment and consequent falls in the standard of living for many people. A range of short-term risks in this area are already evident. According to a recent report by IBM, for instance, business leaders estimate that 40 percent of workers will need to reskill over the next three years if they wish to remain employable.[13]

Social risk is the risk that AI poses to the social fabric, to community structures, or to civic, public, or political life. One example of this sort of danger is the risk that AI-driven misinformation poses to trust in politicians and to the quality of public debate.

Existential risk encompasses the various ways in which the development and use of AI could lead to the extinction of humanity.

Security risk includes (at least) three different kinds of risk.

- Risks to **local and national security** such as those that arise from bad actors using AI to develop or build dangerous weapons.

- The risk that AI poses to the **security of government systems**, such as the risk of AI-powered fraud in tax reporting or insurance claims against the state.

- Risks associated with **data security**.

Emerging data security challenges

Data security challenges extend beyond the risks of the data breaches, identity theft, and privacy and consent issues that have become common in the digital age. AI systems rely on data for their training, and the increasing use of "unstructured" data that has not been previewed by humans raises the possibility that the data pool could be systematically corrupted by bad actors. This could lead to models mislearning and then presenting results that have been preemptively sabotaged.

Systemic risk is the risk that AI poses to systems taken as a whole. Examples of systemic risks include the vulnerabilities of the electricity grid to AI-powered attacks or the possibility that an advanced artificial general intelligence (AGI) will take over and transform key systems on which we rely for our lives and well-being. Another very important example is the risk AI poses to natural systems. Sophisticated AI already requires the manufacturing of a large quantity of specialized computer processors. These chips require electricity both to make and to run. Consequently, the development of AI has important implications for sustainability and climate change that need to be considered before we even begin to think about how AI outputs may affect the world. A final example of systemic risk is the threat that AI poses to government itself. In addition to thinking about how the government can respond to risks, it is essential to consider the possibility that AI may undermine or destroy the capacity for governance. As AI is increasingly integrated with governmental systems, the dangers posed by this kind of attack will escalate rapidly.

Scenario Mapping

With the risks identified and categorized, we now turn to mapping out various possible ways in which these risks might play out. Scenario mapping is preferable to straight prediction, because the future of AI is uncertain; it therefore makes more sense to explore a variety of scenarios, each covering different assumptions and occurrences.

The Catastrophize phase aims, first and foremost, at uncovering risk. The categories of risk function as prompts to ask, for instance, what examples of welfare risks we can imagine in a given context, while the time frame prompts us to consider what conditions would be necessary for that risk to manifest. Scenario mapping then expands on how the risk could unfold and develop. But this phase also has a second function. The work here creates opportunities for thinking more deeply about the risks in question and for seeing how groups of risks connect to one another. The patterns that emerge from this reflection will be indispensable in the next stage of the CARE framework, where the goal is to assess and prioritize these risks.

ASSESS

The purpose of the Assess step is to add additional contextual understanding to the risks identified in the Catastrophize step and then to prioritize them for action.

Understanding Risk: Technical Analysis

The first tool for better understanding the risks identified in the previous step is technical analysis. To help identify exactly where the risk vectors lie, AI systems can be divided into three connected components: data, model, and system. Data is the information that the system learns from and to which it responds. The model is the component that interacts with and responds to the data (this could range from a single algorithm to the incredibly complex structure that emerges from the interaction of billions of parameters in a modern LLM). The AI system itself is the broader overarching structure that encompasses the AI model and integrates it with its contextual environment. For example, most AI systems include an interface that allows users to interact with the model. Similarly, a system that generates decisions as an output may include a human input layer prior to the final decision being made. This division into data, model, and system provides a valuable level of granularity when it comes to investigating precisely where the risks lie within a system. For example, the risks from one model might arise from the manner in which data is collected, stored, managed, and classified. In another, the danger may stem from the way in which the models are trained and deployed. In a third, it might be essential to evaluate how the system as a whole is monitored on an ongoing basis.

Beyond the AI system itself, technical analysis may also require an examination of the broader technological and data infrastructure within which the system is embedded. Mapping the connections between any AI system and all related parts of the tech stack is critical here as it will otherwise be impossible to adapt the relevant practices and policies (for example, those relating to data governance) to the way the AI is actually deployed.

Understanding Risk: Interlinked AI Risk

It is very rare to have AI risks that are completely distinct and self-contained, so it is important to systematically examine the points of contact between specific domains of risk and the interlinkages between them. For example, AI may well displace (a polite word for destroy) the livelihoods of millions of people. In itself, this is a welfare catastrophe that must be planned for. But this danger also has the potential to affect national security, which may be endangered if millions of jobless and discontented people take to the streets to demand rapid change. At the same time, the anger generated by the loss of so many livelihoods may encourage some people to exploit the capabilities of AI to create dangerous weapons with the goal of using intimidation or terrorism to force change. Scenario planning thus cannot treat risks as neatly isolated phenomena but must consider the full range of possible consequences.

Interlinked risk: AI and trust

An epidemic of misinformation and disinformation is now part of the background hum to our daily lives, and AI will be an incredibly powerful force multiplier for those who wish to spread inaccurate and dangerous information. AI is already being used to generate all kinds of misleading content, and its outputs will soon be functionally indistinguishable from those generated by real humans. Once that happens, trusting any source of information will become very difficult indeed.

What is at stake here is a danger on the grandest of scales. For all recorded time, human communities have been able to rely on a shared reality that has been the essential underpinning for consensus, collaboration, and social harmony. AI imperils the possibility of essential community functionality at a national scale by threatening the foundation of that shared experience of the world: trust. Travel depends on trust. Business depends on trust. Democracy itself, procedural depends on trust. By undermining the basis for our trust in one another, AI will create interlinked risks across all levels of society.

Assigning Probabilities

The next step is to assign probabilities to the risks that have been identified and understood. In some cases, leaders may be able to call on whole departments of statisticians to assist. But many of those in management roles in government departments will have neither the resources nor sufficient data to conduct a robust statistical analysis of the risks in front of them. In such cases, it will be necessary to estimate. Remember that the goal here is to assign priority among risks rather than to predict the future in a precise way. Instead of getting bogged down in the difficult task of determining exact likelihoods, focus on comparative assessments (e.g., "Is A more or less likely than B?").

Where time is available to add new information to your assessment, a Bayesian approach can help refine these initial estimates. Begin by assigning each risk a probability between 0 and 1, with 0 marking absolute certainty that the danger will not occur and 1 absolute certainty that it will occur. Then, whenever new information becomes available, you can adjust your initial estimate upward or downward in line with the new data. Over time, this approach will not only help your probability estimates but will also have the important benefit of incorporating an additional dimension of reflection into the process.

It is critical to remember that not all risks are amenable to probabilistic analysis, so you should not be afraid to say that there is insufficient information to make a reasoned judgment about likelihood in some cases. This is true quite generally but is particularly relevant when thinking about AI. Consider the possibility that artificial general intelligence will be developed at some time in the next fifteen years. Sure, the probability of this outcome is more than 0 and less than 1. But we have too little foundational data to allow us to say anything more definite than that. It is natural to be tempted to assign numerical probabilities to events because the process of doing so gives us the illusion of knowledge and, thus, control. But it is vital that we hang on to our uncertainty when it comes to AI. In assessing risks, misplaced confidence is a danger of its own. We need to recognize and include our ignorance in our analyses so that we will be better prepared to handle future uncertainty.

Risk Capacity

After understanding the risks at hand and estimating the probabilities of outcomes, the next step involves assessing available capacity for responding to the potential dangers. Governments and their subordinate agencies can begin by conducting extensive analyses of existing contingency plans and processes to assess the capacity of these current resources to respond to AI-driven threats. A certain degree of lateral thinking will be needed to identify the elements in these plans that can be repurposed or adapted to fit the risks in question. For instance, a contingency plan for responding to an electricity grid failure may already have most of the elements needed to respond to an attack on the grid by an AI agent.

After assessing and adapting existing plans, the next step is to identify where new plans need to be developed and what additional resources are required to meet these needs. A crucial step here will involve assessing the level of expertise available. AI is a new technology, and the latest developments will lie beyond the experience of most government agencies. Options for plugging skills gaps include interdepartmental knowledge-sharing programs and hiring in third-party experts.

The Priority Matrix

The steps we have looked at so far first identified potential risks and then added layers of complexity to understanding those risks, with the goal of creating as accurate and comprehensive a map of the threats as possible. In this step, we synthesize this information to provide an understanding of threat priority that enables us to take effective action. This final step of the Assess stage uses a very simple matrix, adapted from the famous Eisenhower Decision Matrix. On one axis, risks are classified according to their importance; on the other, they are classified based on how much power government currently has to remove or mitigate those risks.

CARE FOR GOVERNMENT PRIORITY MATRIX

	HIGH IMPORTANCE	LOW IMPORTANCE
HIGH INFLUENCE		
LOW INFLUENCE		

Figure 2. CARE for Government Priority Matrix.

The matrix is deliberately simple for two reasons. The first is that a simple priority matrix makes it easier to generate consensus in the complex governmental world of competing interests, multiple stakeholders, and distributed centers of power. To this end, it is essential that the assessment phase generates an output that is easy to understand and easy to communicate, and that offers the smallest number of variables to disagree on. The second reason is that the simplicity of this matrix forces the user to take all the broad variety of information and considerations generated in the previous steps and to synthesize everything in the light of just two factors: how important the risk is and how much influence can be wielded against it. The discipline required to do this will contribute significantly to improving the quality of the strategies developed to respond to these risks.

Clearly, those risks that are highly important and over which a high level of influence can be wielded will be given the highest priority for developing actionable solutions while low-importance/low-influence risks can be treated as afterthoughts. Low-importance/high-influence risks should be targeted whenever resources are available after tackling risks in the high-importance/high-influence category.

High-importance/low-influence risks stand apart as needing special attention. For the most important of these, such as the potential existential threats that might arise from the development of artificial general intelligence, it will be necessary to expend resources now on low-impact or low-probability-of-success responses where resources are available. But where effective action plans cannot currently be developed, the route forward will be a combination of watchful waiting that seeks to identify moments when effective action can be taken and an active research program aimed at increasing influence in the future.

REGULATE

Responding effectively to the problems identified and assessed in the first two stages of the framework will require a mixture of technical and legislative solutions, depending on the specific challenge and the government agency responsible. Two features that will be essential for any successful regulatory program are (a) the ability to respond rapidly to a changing and unpredictable tech landscape, and (b) the ability to do so in a collaborative manner that can respond effectively to interlinked risks.

Dynamic Regulatory Frameworks

From the earliest days of the internet, the frameworks for regulating this new way of communicating have tended to lag years behind the emergence of new use cases for the technology. And even when regulatory decisions are taken, legislative inertia means that it can be extremely difficult to update them to meet changing realities. To give just one example, the US government's decision in 1996 to treat online platforms as service providers rather than as the publishers of the content that users share has had far-reaching effects. This decision was taken with little understanding of the online ecosystem that would emerge over the coming decades. Nevertheless, it has proved to be exceptionally difficult to update the legislation in the face of evolving use cases, arguably encouraging a social media environment in which misinformation and disinformation have become a threat to national stability.

The potential dangers posed by AI are an order of magnitude greater, and even the earliest versions that have achieved widespread adoption are pushing existing regulatory frameworks to their limits. To give just one example, consider the debate over whether the creators or the users of generative AI systems should be held responsible for the content they generate. At the time of writing, there is nothing even resembling legislative clarity on this question. By the time such clarity emerges, it is very likely that the capabilities of the technology will have pushed onward, bringing a whole raft of new problems in their wake.

There are no easy solutions to this issue. The legislative systems of most nations either took shape in the early part of the Industrial Revolution or are descended from those that did. As such, their structural inadequacy in the face of rapid technological change should come as no surprise. If we are to protect ourselves from the dangers that AI may bring with it, it is essential that we develop appropriate legal structures and that we do so quickly. Government agencies can start by adopting a flexible and creative attitude toward using the tools they already have at their disposal. This will often mean using social, rather than legal, forms of regulation (see below) as such tools can be reshaped more rapidly to meet emerging challenges and with the expenditure of less political capital. Yet, ultimately, heavier regulatory firepower will be required. One option is for governments to empower regulatory bodies with considerable leeway to take proactive steps in response to rapid changes (a particular challenge at the federal level in the United States in the wake of the Supreme Court's 2024 ruling striking down the Chevron deference).[14] The alternative is for legislatures to recognize that we are entering a new era and to adapt their mindsets and procedures to match. In either case, regulatory frameworks will require built-in processes for updating and revision to ensure that they remain fit for purpose as the technology they regulate changes. We can only hope our political classes will be able to meet these challenges.

Noncoercive Regulative Tools

While system-wide legal frameworks are the gold-standard tools for controlling the development and use of AI capabilities, it is also important to identify and use less formal regulative interventions. Two types of interventions that are particularly important here are social regulative strategies and incentive structures.

Peer pressure is a familiar example of a powerful social regulative strategy. Of course, peer pressure has something of a bad name these days thanks to decades of initiatives to encourage children to resist its pull when it is deployed to encourage undesirable behavior. But it can also play a vital positive regulative role. Interventions that target the social acceptability of types of behavior will be crucial when it comes to regulating AI, both because this approach will help minimize dangerous behaviors on the parts of individuals and because large-scale social pressure will be critical to persuading global corporations to moderate their practices in relation to AI development.

Another less formal type of intervention involves using incentive structures to nudge behavior in the desired direction. Simply put, we get the behavior we reward. Right now, untrammeled AI development is being rewarded by the market, and all the financial incentives currently align in a direction that motivates a wild and reckless development trajectory. It will be necessary to find ways to change this incentive structure if we want to change the course of AI development.

Pharmaceutical regulation as a model for AI regulation

In an interview for this book, Senator Blumenthal, coauthor of the Blumenthal-Hawley Framework for AI Regulation, suggested to us that we should think about AI regulation in terms of the models used to regulate the pharmaceutical industry. He points out that the United States imposes strict regulations on the development and manufacturing of drugs, ensuring that the entire process is subject to government oversight. And despite these restrictions, America continues to be the world leader in pharmaceutical research, demonstrating that regulation need not impede competitiveness.

As with pharmaceuticals, Senator Blumenthal believes the risks surrounding AI are simply too grave to permit self regulation by either businesses or individuals. "I think the government has to support and sustain an oversight mechanism, an entity that provides this kind of set of safeguards or regulations," he explains. This regulatory entity would have the authority to oversee AI technologies, ensuring that they are developed and deployed responsibly. There are, he acknowledges, important challenges to overcome in crafting the necessary legislation. We spoke to the senator just a few days after the Supreme Court's decision to overturn the "Chevron deference" doctrine, which allowed administrative agencies considerable latitude to interpret ambiguous statutes. Nevertheless, he is confident that an effective regulatory body can control much of the danger that will come with the development of AI and can do so without stifling innovation.

While we agree that the pharmaceutical analogy is valuable in offering one paradigm for how governments can approach AI risk, we believe that regulation needs to go further. There are at least two key differences between AI development and the pharmaceutical industry. The first is that, unlike the drug-development process, the barriers to entry are minimal when it comes to adapting existing AI models for new purposes. For many people with entry-level software development skills, this is something that can be done at home.

Second, while the manufacturing and distribution of pharmaceuticals requires significant infrastructure, computer code can be replicated endlessly and transmitted anywhere on the planet in a fraction of a second. The possibility of problematic AI being created and leaking out into the wild is simply much higher than is the case for new and dangerous drugs. As Mustafa Suleyman argues, the day is not far away when individuals will be able to use AI to create potentially devastating biological organisms at low cost and in the privacy of their own homes, rather than requiring the sophisticated computers of a lab setting as we now do.[15] The direct and indirect dangers that arise from possibilities like this go beyond anything posed by pharmaceuticals, and this difference needs to be accounted for in our regulatory processes.

It is also important to consider that our current frameworks for pharmaceutical regulation are not even close to being flawless. There is a very large and flourishing black market for drugs in the United States, which shows the limits of the government's ability to control manufacturing, while the prescription drug crisis shows that even where regulation does reach, current laws are not always able to contain possible harms. Given the potential for AI to generate extinction-level outcomes, it may be necessary to think in terms of the regulatory frameworks surrounding nuclear weapons and nuclear energy rather than those that apply in the drug industry.

Technical Responses

Some of the dangers posed by AI are simply not amenable to legislative or regulatory solutions. In this field as in any other, certain individuals or organizations will simply refuse to act in accordance with the law, so it will be necessary to take active steps to limit the dangers posed by their use of AI. In other cases, the danger will not be rooted in what other individuals and organizations are doing but in a government agency's own use of AI technology. In these cases, safe use of AI will require technical responses to the challenges involved. The precise kind of technical response that will be appropriate will vary depending on the challenge in question. Here are two examples.

- **AI Authentication.** One of the biggest short-term risks associated with AI is its use in creating and spreading misinformation, disinformation, and other harmful content, such as deepfake images with sexually explicit content. A full-spectrum response to these threats will require legislative efforts, but technical tools can also be used to ensure that data is trustworthy. Some tools are already in place, such as human-in-the-loop authentication and "watermarking" (the inclusion of content credentials in the information's metadata). Another tool with considerable potential here is blockchain technology. Blockchains operate by using a distributed ledger and a variety of consensus mechanisms to store information securely without the need to trust any individual node within a network. Well-resourced blockchains can be used to give items of content (whether written text, images, or videos) a digital identity and to make any subsequent changes to that content immediately and eternally public.

- **Zero Trust Architecture.** Zero trust architecture offers an elegant response to issues of trust. You solve the problem by building systems that, ideally, completely avoid the need to trust anyone at all. Zero trust architecture does this by building continuous monitoring and validation into every part of a digital interaction. To be more precise, zero-trust approaches use rigid authentication, leveraged network segmentation, and comprehensive threat-prevention systems while simultaneously restricting users to the least amount of access necessary for any given activity (so-called "least access" policies). Zero-trust approaches have considerable utility for ensuring the safe use of AI systems. They can help make the system more secure, both by reducing the likelihood of security lapses and by making contagion less likely if a problem does occur. Further, zero trust architecture also helps to preserve data security, thanks to the limited and highly regulated access it permits users.

EXIT

No matter how hard we think about the dangers of AI or how well we plan to mitigate them, our lack of certainty about how this technology will evolve and how humans will interact with it means we must also prepare for the failure of our first lines of defense. Nowhere is this truer than at the governmental level. While individuals and businesses must, of course, take responsibility for their own actions, final responsibility for the safety and well-being of the population lies with the government and its subordinate agencies. As such, it is essential that governments put in place decisive exit plans that are capable of nullifying emerging dangers, even if this involves pulling the plug on types of AI that are already being widely used.

Big Red Buttons

Many powerful machines have an actual big red button. You press it if you need to stop the machine from functioning immediately, and it is big and red to make it easy to identify and activate in an emergency. Given that the potential risks associated with AI include several that rise to the level of existential dangers for humanity, developing some kind of big red button that will allow us to disable or contain the danger as it emerges is highly desirable. In 2024, some of the biggest players in the field of AI, including Amazon, Google, IBM, Microsoft, OpenAI, and Samsung, agreed to implement a "kill switch" that will cease the development of their AI models in cases in which they are unable to guarantee the mitigation of some of the greatest AI dangers.[16] In the precise words of the agreement they signed, "In the extreme, organizations commit not to develop or deploy a model or system at all, if mitigations cannot be applied to keep risks below the thresholds."[17]

Welcome as such commitments are, the framework to which these organizations signed up is purely voluntary. This is not, we propose, a viable long-term basis for dealing with technology that may pose as great a risk to humanity as nuclear weapons. While regulatory frameworks can and should be as light as possible, a legal rather than a voluntary commitment to not threaten humanity's survival should be a foundational element for any governmental CARE strategy.

It is important to note that the kind of big red button discussed above is purely conceptual—it is an agreement to cease development work in certain areas under certain conditions. As such, it can only provide an effective solution when the danger is successfully identified in advance. If we want to remove the threat from existing AI that exceeds its design parameters in a dangerous way (that "goes rogue") or that humans use in a dangerous manner that was not predicted before deployment, we need to create a physical kill switch that can be used to turn off the AI under certain defined conditions. This kind of technology will be hard, but not impossible, to implement. Manufacturers of the specialized silicon chips on which advanced AI currently depends could, for instance, integrate functionality that allows the chips to be remotely disabled if their capabilities or the use to which they are put falls outside regulatory boundaries. As the authors of a recent paper on AI governance put it, "In situations where AI systems pose catastrophic risks, it could be beneficial for regulators to verify that a set of AI chips are operated legitimately or to disable their operation (or a subset of it) if they violate rules."[18]

While it is important to think seriously about how best to implement kill switches, we should not be seduced by the dream of the big red button. Kill switches come with risks of their own. For instance, someone might incorrectly misjudge the need to push the button, or a technology failure might prevent the switch from working properly. There is even the possibility that a sufficiently advanced and cunning AI might conceal its capabilities until it has worked out how to circumvent these safeguards. We should not, then, think of the big red button as a panacea, a perfect piece of armor that allows us to be careless in our other activities. Instead, it is just one part of a suite of safety precautions: the penultimate line of defense if all else has failed.

Contingency Planning

The steps we have outlined so far in the CARE framework all seek to prevent or mitigate the dangers of AI-related threats. But a central theme of this book has been the impossibility of planning perfectly for an unknowable future. The final step in the framework involves developing plans that assume all other measures have failed: An AI-related threat has materialized and either the government as a whole or a specific government agency now needs to respond. This planning phase is not something that can be left until the threat emerges. On the contrary, all government agencies with significant exposure to AI risk should create AI emergency teams that are dedicated to preparing and implementing plans to respond to acute threats arising from AI.

A contingency plan should be developed for each risk identified during the Catastrophize phase of the framework. For those risks categorized as highly important in the Assess phase risk priority matrix, a plan should be developed as soon as feasibly possible. Rather than pour all efforts into developing a comprehensive plan for the single most important risk, develop an outline plan for each highly important risk in the order of their likely time frame. Then iterate on each to add depth in a repeated cycle. Once comprehensive contingency plans are in place, revisit each plan periodically to ensure that it remains fit for purpose as new information about AI's capabilities and vulnerabilities comes to light.

CARE FOR GOVERNMENT IN ACTION[19]
CASE STUDY: BUILDING AN INVESTMENT MATCHING PLATFORM AT THE EDA

You[20] have recently been appointed to a senior innovation role in the US Department of Commerce's Economic Development Administration (EDA). One of the key projects your team is working on is an AI-driven investment-matching platform that will help steer private and public sector investment toward American communities that are struggling economically (see the case study at the end of chapter 8). While you are excited about the platform's potential, you also know that any AI project brings with it a range of risks. To understand and respond to those risks more effectively, you and your team work through the CARE framework for government agencies.

CATASTROPHIZE

You begin by identifying and categorizing as many risks as you can think of using the Government Risk Matrix. At this stage, the goal is to include all possible risks without sorting them for likelihood. Unsurprisingly, the brain-storming process turns up a wide variety of potential threats.

Welfare risks for the communities the platform aims to serve are both evident and immediate. On the one hand, if the project fails to deliver any improvement in the economic situation of the areas it is designed to help, this could lead to further stagnation or decline in living standards. On the other hand, an even worse outcome would arise if the algorithm works so poorly that it actively diverts investments away from areas that would otherwise have received them. If this happens, the use of AI will be directly responsible for a drop in well-being among the affected claimants.

These welfare risks bring with them clear medium- and long term **social risks**. A failure to respond to economic stagnation is likely to lead to an increase in social and political disillusionment across the communities in question. If the AI platform makes the situation worse for some communities, then those who are negatively affected may feel alienated from the government, or even actively threatened by it. This could be particularly damaging if the communities in question already feel that they have been treated poorly in the past.

When thinking about **security risks**, your team identifies a number of imaginative long-term threats to national security that might come about if artificial general intelligence emerges and your AI model goes rogue. However, since these risks are generalizable to all AI systems, you set them aside to focus on threats that are specific to your platform. Three security risks seem particularly relevant: (1) A data security breach might expose confidential investor data; (2) unauthorized access by a bad actor could lead to the corruption of training data, live data, or the algorithm at the heart of the platform, skewing investment matching outcomes; (3) flawed or malicious results from the platform could impact other government systems if the platform is allowed to control other systems directly or if its conclusions are fed into the data that informs other systems.

When you think about the **systemic** and **existential risks** posed by the platform, your conclusions are similar to those relating to national security risks: While there are potential long-term dangers here, these apply to all AI models and are not specific to the platform you are working on. You decide that it is important to keep these risks in mind throughout the development process in case these dangers move from the long term to a closer time horizon. However, you will focus your risk management efforts on those threats that are either directly connected to your work on the investment-matching platform or that are general to AI but may emerge in the short term.

The final step in the Catastrophize stage is scenario mapping. Here you look at the variety of different ways in which the risks you have identified might evolve and develop. As you think through the welfare, social, and security risks you have identified, you see that while each could emerge independently, there are also very plausible scenarios that could connect some or all of these risks together.

ASSESS

You begin the Assess stage by conducting a technical analysis of the risks you have identified, thinking about how each relates to (1) the data that feeds into the platform, (2) the AI model at the heart of the platform, and (3) the broader system of which that platform is a part. Several of the risks could be caused by corrupted or low-quality data from either the algorithm's training data or the live data feed that will keep the platform up to date. The other data source for the platform—the information provided by investors and communities seeking an investment match—could also cause problems if its integrity is not maintained. Users might, for instance, try to game the system, providing the answers that they think are most likely to secure them the greatest priority over other investors or communities. At the same time, the user-entered data may simply be inaccurate or of low quality, either because the users misunderstand the questions they are asked or because their own data sources are poor. In either case, the result is likely to be suboptimal matching.

Risks could also emerge from the algorithm itself. Of course, poorly designed or unbalanced initial parameters could lead to flawed investment matches. But one source of danger that you find particularly concerning is that arising from systemic biases. In designing the platform, you have often reflected on the fact that AI holds up a mirror to humanity. You now realize that even with perfect data and a good AI model, the platform could still generate harmful results because accurate data about specific communities will reflect the historical trends that have contributed to their current economic situation. The ideal community for many investors will have good infrastructure, low crime, and a highly educated population. Naturally, a well-functioning algorithm will tend to steer investments to the locations in which the projects are most likely to succeed. But in at least some cases, communities will lack the necessary assets because of historical underinvestment or discriminatory practices. There is a danger, then, that a platform that makes good decisions based on good economic data may end up entrenching inequality. Investment-matching decisions that reflect and perpetuate historical biases could do as much social damage as those based on bad data. They could also undermine trust in the platform and in government AI initiatives more generally.

Now that you have a deeper understanding of the risks associated with the platform, you assess the likelihood of each risk and your capacity for dealing with it. Finally, you assign each risk a priority level using the CARE for Government Priority Matrix. You conclude that it is impossible to determine the likelihood of medium- or long-term risks that apply to AI in general since there is deep uncertainty about how the technology will develop and at what speed. As such, you decide to monitor these risks for the moment rather than taking direct action. Turning to platform-specific risks, after careful thought, you decide that three are highly important and require an immediate response: data security breaches, low-fidelity user inputs, and algorithmic bias.

When you analyze your capacity for responding to these risks, a crucial gap emerges. At present, the EDA simply does not have much expertise in or experience of building or running large-scale AI-powered platforms. You have decided to use third-party vendors to supply the required expertise during the development process, but given the lack of internal experience a problem of oversight arises. The EDA is not, you determine, currently in a good position to assess the work being done by the third-party vendors. Effective oversight and regulation will require closing this gap.

REGULATE

In this step of the process, the focus is on figuring out how to manage the risks that have been identified, assessed, and prioritized. To limit the potential for data security breaches, you decide to build the platform with a zero trust architecture. You also establish a working group on data security comprising all technical stakeholders involved in the project, including external partners and third-party vendors. The role of this group will be to identify potential data issues before they turn into serious problems and to make technical recommendations for addressing them.

The risk from low-quality user inputs can be minimized with a technical solution built into the platform's user interface. Rather than simply accepting whatever data investors and communities supply through an intake questionnaire, you decide to use the user interface chatbot to manage the data intake process. This AI persona will carefully guide users through the intake survey questions, explaining the kind of answers needed and assessing the quality of the data supplied. If the user provides insufficient information or incomplete answers, the chatbot will prompt them to add further data, while if the chatbot detects patterns in the answers that suggest an attempt to game the system, it will flag the input for human review.

You take several complementary steps to address the risk of algorithmic bias. First, you make the code base and parameter weightings for the platform open source. This will encourage unaffiliated individuals and organizations to identify instances of bias. You also expect this level of transparency to increase public confidence in the project. Further, you take the important decision to move away from automating the entire matching process. Instead, you introduce a human audit layer that will look for systemic biases and intervene where required. Finally, you assemble an oversight committee that includes community representatives, including from historically underserved groups, with a mandate to report regularly on potential biases in the operation of the algorithm.

EXIT

You and your team now confront a critical question: What will you do if none of your plans work? What happens if the algorithm is irredeemably biased and discriminatory decisions are increasing exponentially. Or what if the security breach is enormous and you have no immediate way of plugging it? You need to put in place a process for determining when to pull the plug, what to do before that decision is made, and how you can minimize the damage caused in the aftermath.

You begin by creating a stoplight system. For the issue of algorithmic bias, for instance, you identify levels of bias that, while requiring attention, are within normal operating tolerances (green), levels that need rapid remedial action but at which the benefits from the platform outweigh the damage (yellow), and the specific level at which it is imperative to shut the system down immediately (red). To provide a more granular level of responsiveness, you add three gradations of severity (low, medium, and high) within the green and yellow levels. You then develop response plans that will activate automatically when the indicator hits the defined thresholds, with the ultimate goal of preventing the light from turning red.

Of course, you also need a plan of action for when the red light is reached. The first element in this plan involves the shutdown itself, including the psychological, managerial, and technical steps required to take the platform offline. But this is only half the story. The EDA's responsibility to American communities does not end with the failure of a piece of technology. To ensure that you continue to meet the needs of those you serve, you also develop a contingency plan to do the work of matching investors and communities using old-fashioned data analytics combined with human decision-making until a new technical solution can be put in place. This will require retraining and reassigning personnel within the EDA, so you work with Human Resources to determine the precise staffing requirements for the stopgap plan. In parallel, you develop a process for fixing or replacing the AI platform as rapidly as possible. Finally, you create an outline public relations plan to ensure that the public remains fully informed about the problems with the platform and the steps you are taking to resolve them.

KEY TAKEAWAYS

- Government is in a unique position with respect to AI risk and therefore has special responsibilities—only government has the capacity to do the large-scale regulation, coordination, and enforcement that will be necessary to responsibly manage AI risk.

- Everything is connected—we need to be very aware of the interlinkages between risks and our risk-mitigation strategy needs to explicitly account for it.

- Collaboration is essential—internal collaboration within government, external collaboration with stakeholders like industry, academia, and citizens, and international collaboration with other governments.

TRANSCEND

CHAPTER 10

HUMANITY IN THE AGE OF AI

INTRODUCTION

In the introduction to this book, we introduced the idea of the philosopher's stone as one of the fundamental metaphors that guide our thinking around AI. The philosopher's stone is itself both a symbol and an allegory. On one level, it is a tool that allows the individual to exert control over the external world, attaining the deepest of human desires: unlimited wealth, power over one's environment, and escape from the limitations of the human body. But when we look at the philosopher's stone more deeply, we see that the ultimate goal of the alchemists was something much more profound: the ability to turn the base metal of human nature into the gold of higher states of being. The search for the philosopher's stone is, then, fundamentally a spiritual search.

We end this book by asking this question: If AI is a kind of philosopher's stone, can it offer spiritual riches as well as material benefits? Can AI help us transcend some of the limitations of our humanity and evolve to become better versions of ourselves?

TRANSCENDING THE BODY

Human beings are creatures of flesh and blood. As such, we are subject to the usual travails of the material body: physical suffering, the indignities of aging, illness, and eventually death. Humans have always chafed against these limitations. One way of seeing the history of human civilization is as the story of our attempts to overcome the boundaries imposed on us as individuals by our brief and limited corporeal existence. We can now add a new chapter to that story, because one of the ways in which AI will overturn our current world is by offering us unparalleled opportunities for transcending our bodily limitations.

In chapter 6 we discussed AI-powered prosthetics. The latest prosthetics are no longer simple mechanical devices. Prosthetics like the LUKE Arm and the Ottobock C-Leg use AI to continuously learn from and adapt to information from the user's movements and external environment. In the short- to medium-term future, we will also likely see the commercial development of AI-powered chips that can be implanted in our brains, opening up a huge range of possibilities for treating conditions like paraplegia.

Prosthetics and brain implants are not the only ways in which AI is revolutionizing health care. AI is also laying the foundations for a revolution in diagnostics by dramatically improving our ability to catch diseases at an early stage. Another exciting advance that is being supercharged by AI is the personalization of health care. Health care that responds directly to the needs of the individual rather than functioning at the level of the mythical "average" person has long been a holy grail for doctors. But it is only with the development of adaptive AI algorithms that truly bespoke treatments tailored to the unique history, environment, and body chemistry of each individual have moved into the realms of possibility.

So far, we have described cases in which AI can help humans transcend specific bodily limitations. There is another version of AI-driven transcendence that goes further—this involves transcending the messy reality of having a body altogether. Bodies die. This is, at present, an immutable fact. Yet even without solving the problem of eternal bodily life, AI-powered apps are already offering increasingly sophisticated forms of digital immortality. Replika is an AI chatbot that was developed by Eugenia Kuyda after the death of her best friend, Roman Mazurenko.

Kuyda collected all the text messages she had received from Roman and then used them to train a neural network. The result was an AI chatbot that can be used to create digital avatars of dead loved ones, giving anyone the potential for a kind of persistence that has never been possible before (Replika can also be used for virtual romantic relationships with AI avatars, but we can put that use case aside for now). While still at an early stage, it is conceivable that models like this will, one day, if trained with sufficient data, be able to create digital twins of individual personalities that are indistinguishable from the real thing. And when they do, we will have to ask ourselves some very tricky questions about what constitutes a real person and what does not.

This is cutting edge technology—but it reaches toward goals that are as old as humanity itself. When it comes to transcending the limits of our physical existence, AI is just the newest version of the philosopher's stone. But there is, of course, a critical difference this time round: With AI, we have finally reached the technical level of competence needed to turn what was previously a myth into a reality.

While the medieval alchemists did not—to our knowledge—ever succeed in achieving immortality, they did think hard about the consequences of their quest. We would do well to consider one of the questions they asked themselves: If the philosopher's stone can give us eternal life, will we prove ourselves worthy of it? Will we have created something of real value if we use this new power to simply become better at chasing after things that don't matter at the expense of the things that do? That is to say—transcending our bodily limitations is important. But unless we can also transcend the limitations of our minds and souls, it may all be for naught.

THE NECESSITY OF TRANSCENDING

One of the themes we have come back to throughout this book is that AI is a mirror to humanity. Large language models (LLMs), for instance, are trained on humanity's cultural output, and what they generate obviously reflects the content of that training data. And like all good mirrors, the AI mirror shows us everything, reflecting back our bad sides as well as our good.

Now, this feature of AI forces us, as few other things could, to confront our own nature. This can be quite a shock, and one that has the potential to motivate action. But there is more. The fact that AI reflects humanity means that the trajectory of AI's development will be influenced by the trajectory of human development. This is why AI makes it necessary for us to transcend the worst parts of our nature—AI will become versions of what we are, so if we don't want it to be "evil," well, we had better learn to be good ourselves.

But what does "being good" look like, and how are we to achieve it? It would be insufferably arrogant of us to claim that we can offer definitive answers to these questions. But this does not mean that we should be silent. Indeed, it means quite the opposite. For us, as for all our fellow human beings, it is essential that we start thinking and talking about how we can transcend the worst elements of our natures and start becoming the best possible versions of ourselves. This is not a platitude. The dangers of failing to do so are terrifying when we remember that AI will become not only an increasingly accurate reflection of humanity but an increasingly powerful reflection.

This chapter should be understood as a contribution to this essential conversation—rather than offering incontrovertible advice, we hope that it will provoke thought and discussion. To foster this conversation, we propose a structured way of thinking through the issues at hand.

TRANSCENDING HUMANITY: DETACH AND DEVOTE

Sports coaches sometimes talk of "addition by subtraction." What they mean is that sometimes you can improve performance by taking something away: By subtracting something problematic, you achieve a better performance overall. To take one common example, a team's morale and overall performance may be improved by removing a team member who is obstructive and energy-sapping.

Addition by subtraction is a very old idea, and one that we can see in all the great spiritual traditions of the world, both religious and nonreligious. In these traditions, one can find an enduring emphasis on eliminating the things—attachment to material wealth, addictions, immoral desires, compulsions, and so on—that stand in the way of personal development. This is never the ultimate end of the spiritual journey, but it is, this long-standing tradition holds, an indispensable component of it. The lesson runs that, if we are to become better versions of ourselves, we must learn to detach ourselves from the parts that are holding us back in that journey.

Detachment in this sense is necessary, but it is not sufficient. To see this, we can draw on the concept of "dead people's goals." Take the goal of never eating pizza, for example. Dead people don't eat any pizza, so one way of achieving this goal is by becoming a dead person. That is not to say that we should pursue this path. Rather, it is a reminder that when we frame our goals, there is an urgent need to include a positive dimension, a dimension that makes them suitable for people who are alive. So, this concept tells us that it is not enough to focus on detaching ourselves from harmful and unnecessary things. We must also seek a positive corollary as well. This, we suggest, can be found in devoting ourselves to what truly matters.

This, then, is the structure we propose for thinking about how to transcend some of the limitations of humanity and move toward a better version of ourselves. We must *detach* ourselves from the things that don't matter and *devote* ourselves to the things that do.

Detach

As the German philosopher Friedrich Nietzsche put it, "Whoever must be a creator always destroys." But while cutting away the dead wood can indeed be a powerful engine for new growth, we have to be careful that we destroy the right things. In this section, we try to identify what it is that we need to detach ourselves from.

Distraction

An email pings, and we immediately begin to reply. While we are replying, we're notified that an online acquaintance replied to a tweet. Another ping, this time WhatsApp. An email about work. A Slack message. A connection request on LinkedIn. And on and on and on. Does it ever stop?

We can never give our full attention to any one thing because we are constantly engaged with everything else, even if we are just scanning or waiting for that next ping. This is a problem that predates the recent boom in artificial intelligence. But—like so many things—it is a problem that is going to be turbocharged by AI. Already, AI is capable of powering personalized content, tailored to whatever it is that will optimally distract us from whatever else we're doing. The implications of it doing this *better* are frankly terrifying.

Distraction—quotidian, ordinary distraction—is one of the most potent obstacles standing in the way of us becoming the best versions of ourselves. How can we even get started if we are constantly fragmented, if our energies are never collected on one point but instead always dispersed and frittered away on multiple frivolities?

Division

"If a house be divided against itself," Jesus is quoted as saying in the Gospel of St. Mark, "that house cannot stand" (KJV).[1] Almost two thousand years later, Abraham Lincoln shared the same sentiment with the American public in a slightly more streamlined version.[2]

Of course, both Jesus and Lincoln had specific houses and specific divisions in mind. Still, their words read like a prophetic warning to our own age. We are divided now—perhaps more than at any other point in living memory—and our houses are tottering. Even the most passing glance at the world outside our windows shows us that political, social, and cultural polarization is rife. The algorithms that drive social media platforms and AI-powered news feeds often exacerbate these divisions by promoting content that reinforces existing biases and prejudices. This echo chamber effect can lead to increased hostility, misunderstanding, and fragmentation within communities.

Now, the immediate and easy thing to say here would be something like: We need to change the algorithms! And that is certainly part of the answer. But it is only part, and there is a much more uncomfortable truth that we need to acknowledge.

Let's first ask: *Why* do the algorithms promote polarizing content? Well, it's quite simple. Social media algorithms are designed to optimize engagement. If polarizing content gets clicks, the algorithm learns to present more polarizing content. So, the fact that social media drives polarization actually ends up saying more about us than about the algorithms that underpin it: To a greater extent than at any other point in human history, we truly get the public discourse that we deserve.

Detaching from this division will, then, require more than simply changing the algorithms. It will require changing ourselves. We must each of us do the hard work of looking inside and being honest about what we see. Are we promoting division? Are we too quick to judge and too slow to understand? The answers will often be uncomfortable, but we have to put ourselves through this discomfort if we are to become the best versions of ourselves. The danger we face from this division is urgent. And it will only become more profound as AI evolves and becomes more embedded in our lives.

Shallow Relationships

British anthropologist Robin Dunbar has proposed that a human being can only have around 150 meaningful social relationships because we do not have the cognitive capacity to handle more.[3] While there is some dispute about whether "Dunbar's number," as it is known, is too high or too low, the fundamental insight is sound: There is a limit to the number of meaningful relationships a human can sustain.

Whatever the true number might be for any individual, for most of us it will easily be outstripped by the number of connections we have on most social media platforms. These relationships—which manifest in the form of likes, reposts, and shares—tend to encompass a very broad range of people at the cost of the relationships themselves being extremely shallow. Spending our time and cognitive energy engaging at this level crowds out space for authentic connections. The more effort we put into our shallow relationships, the less we have available for our deep ones. Indeed, over time, it may even be that we will lose the ideal of engaging in deep and authentic connections altogether because we have drifted so far away from that experience in most of our daily interactions. AI is already contributing to both problems, and it has the potential to make them much worse. A significant proportion of social media posts and likes are now made by bots, shaping opinions, driving the visibility of ideas, and crowding out real human interactions. We can also already form intimate relationships with AI models, with companies springing up to provide bots that can be partners, friends, and much else besides. As these trends accelerate, there is a very real danger that relationships with artificial entities will undermine our ability to form deep and authentic relationships with other humans.

Now, again, we can blame the algorithms, and we can blame the designers of apps, chatbots, and social media, for creating things that tap into our compulsions and addictions. And that blame is justified. But, again, we cannot stop there. We are complicit in the reshaping of our world, and so we must actively detach from the drive toward superficial and shallow connections.

Convenience

AI makes life easier. In its proper place, increasing convenience is not just a valid use of AI, but an essential part of what makes this technology so powerful and appealing. But we must be careful that we don't overdo it.

Let's begin with this simple observation: If Tenzing Norgay and Edmund Hillary had wanted to find the most convenient way to get to the top of Everest, they would have been better off taking a helicopter. But that type of journey was not what they were pursuing. Without presuming to read their minds or know their hearts, we can plausibly suppose that they were seeking, among other things, to find fulfillment in overcoming a difficult challenge. This willingness to not just engage with but to seek out challenges, and the personal and collective growth that results from this kind of behavior, is in our view one of humanity's noblest qualities. It is important that we do not outsource all our challenges to AI, because we will lose something very important if we adopt a life of perfect ease. Here are two examples of the kind of thing we have in mind.

First, AI is already remarkably good at writing. Pretty soon, it will be able to write novels and screenplays that are of such high quality that they will be better than most human outputs. If the point of writing novels and screenplays was simply to produce the best possible product in the most convenient way, most human beings would soon conclude that they should simply stop writing them. This would be a historic tragedy because it would mean that human beings would lose one of our most fundamental avenues for self-expression, self-discovery, and personal transcendence, a source of fulfilment, grandeur, and beauty that humans have benefited from for millennia.

The second example is in the realm of personal relationships. AI is probably already much better than most human beings at writing love letters. In the foreseeable future, it will be much better than most of us at not just declarations of love but also the difficult conversations that arise in any intimate relationship. But again, to ask AI to step in and conduct our deepest personal conversations would be first a tragedy and eventually a collective disaster. As we cede more and more of the activities and interactions in which we discover and create meaning to AI, so we will lose more and more of the qualities that make human beings valuable.

Devote

By detaching ourselves from distraction, division, shallow relationships, and convenience, we have begun clearing ground. But on its own, this is not enough. We need to use the newly liberated energy to make the right things grow in this newly cleared space. Having detached ourselves from some of the more harmful aspects and manifestations of humanity, we now turn to devoting ourselves to the better angels of our nature.

Freedom

We believe that human beings have the capacity for freedom, and we believe that this capacity is one of the finest parts of our nature. Therefore, we also believe that we should devote ourselves to exercising and nourishing this capacity. But what *is* it to be free?

Consider the man who is addicted to smoking. He lives in a country in which it is legal for him to smoke and he has enough money to buy cigarettes and still live comfortably. And so, every day he smokes, one cigarette after the next. In one sense, this man smokes freely—he chooses every morning to buy his packet of cigarettes, and he chooses to light each one up. No one is making him do any of this. But is he truly free?

We think not. He is acting in the grip of addiction—he smokes under a sort of compulsion to smoke. Even if he doesn't realize it, in an important sense he is not free at all, because he is acting under desires that he cannot control. To use the terms the Greek philosopher Plato used, he is not the master of his chariot but the slave of the horses that pull it along.

Addiction is an extreme case, and many of us are, thankfully, not addicts. But this should not lead to the conclusion that we are therefore free. Consider the desires many of us have for material objects—the new iPhone, a new car, a fancy house, fashionable clothes. Desires multiplying on desires, a never-ending cascade of want. Do we control these desires, or do they control us?

AI will be—indeed, already is—an incredibly powerful tool for generating and manipulating desires. Personalized marketing, personalized recommendations, chatbots that make us fall in love with them …. If we wish to avoid becoming slaves to the desires that AI will foist upon us, we must first learn how to distinguish our true desires from those we are manipulated into holding. Then, we must use this knowledge to take control of our desires, deciding which we accede to and which we do not. This is the freedom we need to devote ourselves to cultivating, because this freedom is the foundation for all true human action.

Connection

"All true life is encounter," said the Jewish philosopher-theologian-mystic Martin Buber. Buber is referring here to something quite specific, namely a kind of encounter that he called "I-Thou." This is the type of encounter in which two people are fully present to each other and in which they do not want anything from each other. They are simply meeting, fully aware, fully connected. For Buber, such encounters provide our route to finding God, because this unmediated experience of something beyond ourselves just is an encounter with God.

We do not have to subscribe to Buber's theology to see the importance of such encounters. I-Thou encounters express one of the ideals of human connection, because they are one of the highest possibilities for human beings—to have an I-Thou encounter with someone is to love them in a very profound way. We may have no more than a handful of such encounters in our entire life. By drawing attention to them, Buber is giving us an ideal that is important to hold on to. He is pointing to the possibilities of human connection, possibilities that go far beyond our usual ways of relating to each other. These possibilities are particularly important to retain in the coming age of AI.

Why? For many reasons, some of which we have already canvassed in this book. AI is already reducing opportunities for human encounters. For example, automation is increasingly finding traction in the restaurant industry.[4] In some restaurants—a few for now but the trend is accelerating—the food is cooked by robots and the customer simply enters their choice into a screen and then waits for the machine to deliver the finished product. The automation of service roles like these reduces the opportunity for human beings to connect. There is no longer a person to talk to or joke with as you order or wait for your food. It may sound like a small thing, and by itself it is a small thing, but imagine a world where all these small things add up, where most of the usual opportunities for small human interactions are no longer present—that is suddenly a very big thing. In parallel, the misinformation, polarization, and division that AI threatens to turbocharge increases the risk that we will begin to see many human beings as somehow bad or evil or in any case "on the wrong side." Instead of attempting to relate to them as human beings, we will increasingly be inclined to see them as enemies.

We are social creatures. And if we are to flourish, if we are to have even the slightest chance of living up to the best parts of ourselves, we must devote ourselves to connection.

Service

"Greed is good," Gordon Gekko tells us in the film *Wall Street*.[5] When the movie was released in 1987, the words were provocative to most viewers and shocking to many. Nowadays, the phrase, and the attitude it encapsulates, has become a commonplace. Politicians selling out their constituents for donations, tech lords chasing clicks and damn the consequences for mental health and community, crypto bros constructing ever fancier Ponzi schemes at the expense of the ordinary investor on Main Street ... we can barely even summon up outrage because these things have become so normal. Look after Number One and hang all the rest—that could be the epitaph for our age.

Perhaps, then, we are swimming against the current when we say this, but we say it anyway: Life is not about each of us acting separately, trying to maximize our wealth or opportunities or anything else. We are all in this together. We depend on each other. We have duties and responsibilities to each other. As the English poet John Donne wrote:

No man is an island,
Entire of itself.
Each is a piece of the continent,
A part of the main.
If a clod be washed away by the sea,
Europe is the less.
As well as if a promontory were.
As well as if a manor of thine own
Or of thine friend's were.
Each man's death diminishes me,
For I am involved in mankind.
Therefore, send not to know
For whom the bell tolls,
It tolls for thee.

Human beings are at their best when they are living the profound truth that John Donne expresses. We are at our best when we serve. It truly is more blessed to give than it is to receive. AI creates unparalleled opportunities for the acquisition and consolidation of wealth and power. But what are we going to do with those rewards? Are we going to use them to deepen inequality and increase division? Or will we use the bounty of AI to make the world a better place for everyone, and especially for those who are struggling?

Love

"Now these three remain," writes St. Paul in his Epistle to the Corinthians (NIV).[6] "Faith, hope, and love. But the greatest of these is love." And even in secular terms Paul is right. The greatest of these, the greatest of the human capacities, absolutely the best part of our nature, is our ability to love.

We can see love as the capstone of the first three domains of value to which we have suggested we should devote ourselves. Freedom is required to love, because love is only love when it is freely given rather than compelled. Connection is a movement of love, a movement toward the other that opens up the space where love can exist. And service is an act of love, an act that expresses love whether or not that love is felt.

Love is the capstone, but at the same time, love also goes beyond freedom, service, and connection, and that is why we mention it explicitly here. There is no point making an argument for the importance of love and for devoting ourselves to developing this part of our humanity. So, we won't. Instead, we will merely offer a few observations that may be helpful.

First: The ancient Stoics, or at least one of them named Hierocles, suggested that we should visualize the ethical goal in life in terms of an ever-expanding moral circle. To be in the circle is to be a being worthy of moral consideration. And moral progress, he argued, consists of the expansion of the circle to include increasingly distant groups of beings: from family to village to region to nation to all of humanity. This idea transfers to love. We may start off feeling love only for those very close to us (and hopefully also for ourselves). But Hierocles's image suggests that we should actively devote ourselves to increasing the radius of our love; eventually, we might even include future generations, animals, and nature itself within our circle.

Second: Being *in love* is easy, but *loving* is hard. Loving others requires consistent action and consistent attitudes over time, even at times when we are tired or angry or hurting or scared. In our efforts to devote ourselves to loving, we must expect these difficulties, and we must develop the fortitude to patiently endure them.

Third: A loving attitude is a fundamentally optimistic attitude, because it sees the world as worthy of love. So, no matter what we may see in the world, no matter how often we may be disappointed or disillusioned, we must retain something of this fundamental spirit. The world is worthy of love, and the highest expression of our humanity is to give it this love.

As we move into an era in which artificial agents surround us and take up more and more of our time, we can reground ourselves and return to our essential humanity in the active cultivation of love. If we let this foundationally human quality diminish and slip away, it is not clear that the world that remains will be worth saving.

Conclusion

"It is my contention," wrote the German philosopher Hans Jonas, "that the *nature of human action* has changed, and, since ethics is concerned with action, it should follow that the changed nature of human action calls for a change in ethics as well."[7] Jonas's argument went as follows.

In ancient times, human action was limited in its spatial and temporal effects, which is a fancy way of saying that human beings had the power to affect things that were close to them in space and time, and that this power got weaker as things got farther away. Further, even for the things that were close to human beings in space and time, the powers that human beings had were relatively limited because the technologies available for interacting with those things were limited. Even if they had wanted to, human beings in 2500 BC would not have been able to destroy the Amazonian rainforests or reclaim swamps and build skyscrapers on the new land.

Both those things are now untrue, says Jonas. Human beings have an increased power to affect the world, and this increased power stretches out much further in space and time. The most obvious example is perhaps human-induced climate change. Through our actions now, we contribute to events that will affect people living on different continents to us and people living in different centuries to us.

Jonas then says that the ethics we have was built for a world in which human action was limited in its power and range, and that this ethics is no longer fit for purpose because the nature of human action has changed. Finally, he starts the work of developing a new ethics that will better reflect the nature and conditions of human life as it currently is.

Jonas was writing in the 1970s, reflecting on the incredible changes humans and human technology had undergone in the last few centuries. But his point is even sharper today as we stand on the cusp of an era in which AI will be a dominant force. AI will change the nature of human action and the nature of human relationships. It will change what we feel, think, and do. Ultimately, it will change who we are. We need an ethics that is sensitive to these transformations, a vision of value that evolves along with humanity's own evolution. At the same time, this ethics and this vision must also provide a guide that will help humanity grow and develop as we enter this new era.

To build this ethics, to develop this vision—this is a collective enterprise. We have written this book, and this final chapter in particular, as a contribution to that collective task. We neither believe nor intend it to be the last word. Rather, we hope that it inspires many more words, many more thoughts. We hope that it will be part of humanity's journey toward realizing its potential for transcendence. We have offered a variety of frameworks and tools that we hope will help on that journey. But we want to end with something that transcends all practical tools.

St. Augustine, that great philosopher and architect of Christianity, wrote: "Love, and do as you please." The point is that if we have the right attitude in place, then we can do anything we please with AI, and it will turn out well. And if we don't, then all the frameworks and guardrails and conceptual models in the world are useless.

And the right attitude, we suggest, is simply this—a loving one. Love for ourselves, for others, for the world in the broadest possible sense. If we can love in this way, then we may do as we please. If we approach AI with flexibility and humility, if we approach it in the spirit of service, if we detach from what harms and devote ourselves to what heals—well, to quote the English writer Rudyard Kipling, ours is the earth and everything that's in it.

INDEX

INDEX

INDEX

TRANSCEND

NOTES

CHAPTER 1

1   Silva, H. E. C. D. et al. (2023). The use of artificial intelligence tools in cancer detection compared to the traditional diagnostic imaging methods: An overview of the systematic reviews. *Plos one*, 18(10), p. e0292063; Heaven, W. D. (2022). The big new idea for making self-driving cars that go anywhere. *MIT Technology Review*, 27 May. Available from: https://www.technologyreview.com/2022/05/27/1052826/ai-reinforcement-learning-self-driving-cars-autonomous-vehicles-wayve-waabi-cruise/ [Accessed 17 October 2024]; Chaudhri, I. (2023). *The disappearing computer—and a world where you can take AI everywhere.* Available from: https://www.ted.com/talks/imran_chaudhri_the_disappearing_computer_and_a_world_where_you_can_take_ai_everywhere? [Accessed 17 October 2024]

2   1 Corinthians 13:11, Holy Bible, King James Version.

3   Plato, *Gorgias* 485c-d.

4   Keynes, J. M. (1936). *The General Theory of Employment, Interest, and Money.* London: Macmillan and Co.

5   Brook, P. (2017). *The Shifting Point: Forty Years of Theatrical Exploration, 1946–87.* Bloomsbury Publishing.

6   In the course of writing this book, Microsoft changed the name of their commercial LLM from Bard to Gemini.

CHAPTER 2

1   Piper, K. (2022). AI experts are increasingly afraid of what they're creating, *Vox*, 28 November. Available from: https://www.vox.com/the-highlight/23447596/artificial-intelligence-agi-openai-gpt3-existential-risk-human-extinction [Accessed 15 October 2024];
Egan, M. (2023). Exclusive: 42% of CEOs say AI could destroy humanity in five to ten years, *CNN Business*, 14 June. Available from: https://edition.cnn.com/2023/06/14/business/artificial-intelligence-ceos-warning/index.html [Accessed 15 October 2024];
Andreessen, M. (2023). Why AI Will Save the World. Available from: https://a16z.com/ai-will-save-the-world/ [Accessed 15 October 2024];
Suleyman, M. (2023). How the AI Revolution Will Reshape the World, *Time*, September 1. Available from https://time.com/6310115/ai-revolution-reshape-the-world/ [Accessed 15 October 2024];

Klein, E. (2023). This Changes Everything, *New York Times*, March 12. Available from: https://www.nytimes.com/2023/03/12/opinion/chatbots-artificial-intelligence-future-weirdness.html [Accessed 15 October 2024];

Kushner, D. (2023). How A.I. Could Reincarnate Your Dead Grandparents—or Wipe Out Your Kids, *Rolling Stone*, September 4. Available from: https://www.rollingstone.com/culture/culture-features/ai-bots-destroy-humanity-immortality-1234816682/ [Accessed 15 October 2024];

Vallance, C. (2023). Artificial intelligence could lead to extinction, experts warn, *BBC*, 30 May. Available from: https://www.bbc.com/news/uk-65746524 [Accessed 15 October 2024];

Ho Tran, T. (2023). Advanced AI Is Scary—but It Could Help Save the Planet, *Daily Beast*, 22 April. Available from: https://www.thedailybeast.com/advanced-ai-is-scarybut-it-could-help-save-the-planet [Accessed 15 October 2024]

2   *Scholem*, G. (1972). "Golem" in Skolnik, F. and Berenbaum, M. (eds.), *Encyclopedia Judaica, Volume 7*. Jerusalem: Keter Publishing House.

3   Santayana, G., 2011. *The life of reason: Introduction and reason in common sense* (Vol. 1). MIT Press.

4   An alternative date that is popular with historians as the start of the AI era is 1956, when a now-famous conference on artificial intelligence was held at Dartmouth College.

5   Turing, A. M. (1950). Computing machinery and intelligence. *Mind*, 59, pp. 433–460.

6   Suleyman, M. (2023). *The Coming Wave: Technology, Power, and the Twenty-First Century's Greatest Dilemma*. Crown.

7   Executive Office of the President, National Science and Technology Council Committee on Technology. (2016). *Preparing for the future of artificial intelligence*. Available from: https://obamawhitehouse.archives.gov/sites/default/files/whitehouse_files/microsites/ostp/NSTC/preparing_for_the_future_of_ai.pdf [Accessed 11 October 2024].

8   Dworkin, R. (1986). *Law's Empire*. Cambridge, Mass.: Harvard University Press, p. 70.

9   This is not just a matter of principle; it is already happening in practice. For instance, AI's data processing capabilities already vastly outstrip those of their human creators.

10 Fradkov, A. L. (2020). Early history of machine learning. *IFAC-PapersOnLine*, 53(2), pp. 1385–1390.

11 Bommasani, R., Hudson, D. A., Adeli, E., Altman, R., Arora, S., von Arx, S., Bernstein, M. S., Bohg, J., Bosselut, A., Brunskill, E. and Brynjolfsson, E. (2021). On the opportunities and risks of foundation models. *arXiv preprint arXiv:2108.07258*.

12 Weizenbaum, J. (1976). *Computer Power and Human Reason: From Judgment to Calculation*. New York/San Francisco: W. H. Freeman and Company, pp. 6–7.

13 Altman, S. (2022). 5 December. Available from: https://x.com/sama/status/1599669571795185665 [Accessed: 15 October 2024]

14 Gardizy, A. and Ma, W. (2023). Microsoft Readies AI Chip as Machine Learning Costs Surge, *The Information*, April 18. Available from: https://www.theinformation.com/articles/microsoft-readies-ai-chip-as-machine-learning-costs-surge [Accessed 15 October 2024].

15 Hagey, K. and Fitch, A. (2024). Sam Altman Seeks Trillions of Dollars to Reshape Business of Chips and AI, February 8. Available from: https://www.wsj.com/tech/ai/sam-altman-seeks-trillions-of-dollars-to-reshape-business-of-chips-and-ai-89ab3db0 [Accessed 15 October 2024]

16 For example, a group of Microsoft researchers argued in 2023 that they saw sparks of artificial general intelligence in ChatGPT. Microsoft happens also to own a significant amount of stock in OpenAI, the company behind ChatGPT. See Bubeck, S., Chandrasekaran, V., Eldan, R., Gehrke, J., Horvitz, E., Kamar, E., Lee, P., Lee, Y.T., Li, Y., Lundberg, S., and Nori, H. (2023). Sparks of artificial general intelligence: Early experiments with gpt-4. *arXiv preprint arXiv:2303.12712*.

17 Hutson, M. (2024). Two-faced AI language models learn to hide deception. *Nature*, 23 January. Available from: https://www.nature.com/articles/d41586-024-00189-3 [Accessed 15 October 2024]. Note that the study has not yet been peer-reviewed.

18 Hubinger, E., Denison, C., Mu, J., Lambert, M., Tong, M., MacDiarmid, M., Lanham, T., Ziegler, D.M., Maxwell, T., Cheng, N., and Jermyn, A., 2024. Sleeper agents: Training deceptive LLMs that persist through safety training. arXiv preprint arXiv:2401.05566.

CHAPTER 3

1 Aristotle, *Rhetoric*, III.10, 1410b14f.

2 Ars staff. (2016). Tay, the neo-Nazi millennial chatbot, gets autopsied. Ars Technica, 25 March. Available from: https://arstechnica.com/information-technology/2016/03/tay-the-neo-nazi-millennial-chatbot-gets-autopsied/. [Accessed 15 October 2024]

3 Pelley, S. (2023). Is artificial intelligence advancing too quickly? What AI leaders at Google say. *CBS News*, April 16. Available from: https://www.cbsnews.com/news/google-artificial-intelligence-future-60-minutes-transcript-2023-04-16/ [Accessed 15 October 2024]

4 Sloan, K. (2023). Bar exam score shows AI can keep up with "human lawyers," researchers say. *Reuters*, March 15. Available from: https://www.reuters.com/technology/bar-exam-score-shows-ai-can-keep-up-with-human-lawyers-researchers-say-2023-03-15/ [Accessed 15 October 2024]

5   Hoque, F. and Baer, D. (2014). *Everything Connects: How to Transform and Lead in the Age of Creativity, Innovation, and Sustainability.* McGraw Hill Professional.

CHAPTER 4

1   *The Guardian.* (2024). Microsoft's AI chatbot will "recall" everything you do on its new PCs. 21 May. Available from: https://www.theguardian.com/technology/article/2024/may/20/microsoft-chatbot-assistant-pc [Accessed 15 October 2024]
2   Suzuki, S. (2020). *Zen mind, beginner's mind.* Shambhala Publications.
3   Harari, Y. N. (2014). *Sapiens: A brief history of humankind.* Harvill Secker.
4   Huizinga, J. (1980). *Homo Ludens: a Study of the Play Element in Culture.* London: Trowbridge & Esher.

CHAPTER 5

1   Verma, P. and De Vynck, G. (2023). ChatGPT took their jobs. Now they walk dogs and fix air conditioners. June 2. Available from: https://www.washingtonpost.com/technology/2023/06/02/ai-taking-jobs/ [Accessed 16 October 2024]
2   Aron, I. (2023). "I fear for the future of our jobs": Meet the people already replaced by AI. June 1. Available from: https://inews.co.uk/inews-lifestyle/ai-people-who-lost-work-fear-future-jobs-2376994 [Accessed 16 October 2024]
3   Thorbecke, C. (2023). AI is already linked to layoffs in the industry that created it. July 4. Available from: https://edition.cnn.com/2023/07/04/tech/ai-tech-layoffs/index.html [Accessed 16 October 2024]
4   Sjoding, M. W., Dickson, R. P., Iwashyna, T. J., Gay, S. E., and Valley, T. S. (2020). Racial bias in pulse oximetry measurement. *New England Journal of Medicine*, 383(25), pp. 2477–2478. Available from: https://www.nejm.org/doi/full/10.1056/NEJMc2029240.
5   IBM. Watson, "Jeopardy!" champion. Available from: https://www.ibm.com/history/watson-jeopardy [Accessed 15 October 2024]
6   Jie, Z., Zhiying, Z., and Li, L., 2021. A meta-analysis of Watson for Oncology in clinical application. *Scientific reports*, 11(1), p. 5792. Available from: https://www.nature.com/articles/s41598-021-84973-5
7   All quotes in this paragraph come from Ross, C. and Swetlitz, I. (2018). IBM's Watson supercomputer recommended "unsafe and incorrect" cancer treatments, internal documents, July 25. Available from: https://www.statnews.com/2018/07/25/ibm-watson-recommended-unsafe-incorrect-treatments [Accessed 15 October 2024]
8   See Dooley, B. and Ueno, H. (2022). This Man Married a Fictional Character. He'd Like You to Hear Him Out. *New York Times*, 29 April. Available from: https://www.nytimes.com/2022/04/24/business/akihiko-kondo-fictional-character-relationships.html [Accessed 16 October 2024]; and also Limon,

R. (2024). Widowed by computer death, or why it is dangerous for AI to talk like Scarlett Johannson. *El País.* June 15. Available from: https://english. elpais.com/technology/2024-06-15/widowed-by-computer-death-or-why-it-is-dangerous-for-ai-to-talk-like-scarlett-johansson.html [Accessed 16 October 2024]

9   See for example, Cazzaniga, M., Jaumotte, M. F., Li, L., Melina, M. G., Panton, A. J., Pizzinelli, C., Rockall, E. J., and Tavares, M. M. M. (2024). *Gen-AI: Artificial intelligence and the future of work.* International Monetary Fund. Available from: https://www.imf.org/en/Publications/Staff-Discussion-Notes/Issues/2024/01/14/Gen-AI-Artificial-Intelligence-and-the-Future-of-Work-542379

10 As we argued earlier, this ability to choose what one values and to ascribe meaning for oneself is one of the things that makes humanity special and worth preserving.

11 Weinstein, N. D. (1989). Optimistic biases about personal risks. *Science*, 246(4935), pp. 1232–1233.

CHAPTER 6

1   Norman, D. (2013). *The Design of Everyday Things: Revised and expanded edition.* Basic Books.

2   Hoque, F., 2023. *Reinvent: Navigating Business Transformation in a Hyperdigital Era.* Greenleaf Book Group, pp. 198–209.

3   For group intelligence, learning, and goal alignment as the three key factors behind collaboration, see Beyerlein, M. (1998). The future depends on collaboration. *Team Performance Management: An International Journal* 4(4).

4   Brandenburger, A. M. and Nalebuff, B. J. (2011). *Co-opetition.* Random House.

5   Hoque, F. (2022). *Lift: Fostering the Leader in You Amid Revolutionary Global Change.* Greenleaf Book Group.

6   Seneca, *Letters* 44.7, transl. R. Gummere.

7   Taleb, N. N. (2013). "Antifragility" as a mathematical idea. *Nature* 494(7438), pp. 430–430.

8   What follows is a purely hypothetical application of the OPEN framework by a fictional CEO at Nike. The authors have no connection with Nike, nor do the views and attitudes in our example represent those of the real Nike senior executive team.

9   This case study abstracts much of the complexity of the decision-making process within a large corporation. For the sake of brevity and accessibility, we put the reader ("you") in the driver's seat as the single source of authority for the development and management of the AI program. Of course, in reality many of the functions we centralize in a single figure would be spread out across the company.

10 Witte, R. (2019). With new Fit technology, Nike calls itself a tech company. *TechCrunch*, 9 May. Available from: https://techcrunch.com/2019/05/09/with-new-fit-technology-nike-calls-itself-a-tech-company/ [Accessed 16 October 2024]

11 Güemes-Castorena, D. and Ruiz-Monroy, B. C. (2020). Ambidexterity in the supply chain: studying the apparel industry. *International Journal of Agile Systems and Management* 13(2), pp. 130–158.

CHAPTER 7

1 Deutsch, C. H. (2008). At Kodak, Some Old Things Are New Again. *New York Times*, May 2. Available from: http://www.nytimes.com/2008/05/02/technology/02kodak.html [Accessed 16 October 2024]

2 UK. National Cyber Security Centre. (2024). *NCSC Assessment*: The near-term impact of AI on the cyber threat. Available from: https://www.ncsc.gov.uk/report/impact-of-ai-on-cyber-threat [Accessed 16 October 2024]

3 Yeats, W. B. (1921). "The Second Coming." *The Collected Poems of WB Keats*, pp. 210–11.

4 We only provide an outline sketch of this methodology here. For a more detailed discussion, see Hoque, F. (2023). *Reinvent: Navigating Business Transformation in a Hyperdigital Era*. Greenleaf Book Group.

5 Hoque, F. (2023). *Reinvent: Navigating Business Transformation in a Hyperdigital Era*. Greenleaf Book Group, p. 213.

6 Dastin, J. (2018). Insight—Amazon scraps secret AI recruiting tool that showed bias against women. *Reuters*, 11 October. Available from: https://www.reuters.com/article/world/insight-amazon-scraps-secret-ai-recruiting-tool-that-showed-bias-against-women-idUSKCN1MK0AG/ [Accessed 16 October 2024]

7 Reid, H. (2023). IKEA bets on remote interior design as AI changes sales strategy. *Reuters*, 13 June. Available from: https://www.reuters.com/technology/ikea-bets-remote-interior-design-ai-changes-sales-strategy-2023-06-13/ [Accessed 16 October 2024]

8 Smith, M. L., Erwin, J., and Diaferio, S. (2005). Role & responsibility charting (RACI). In *Project Management Forum (PMForum)* (Vol. 5).

9 Kahneman, D. (2011). *Thinking, Fast and Slow*. Farrar, Straus and Giroux.

10 *Oroville Mercury-Register*. (1987). "Biggs has plans for Tyson." August 19. Available from: https://www.newspapers.com/article/record-search-light/132118457/ [Accessed October 16 2024]. Over the years, Tyson's line has evolved in the popular consciousness into something punchier (pun very much intended): "Everyone has a plan until they get punched in the mouth."

11 As with the previous case study, what follows is a purely hypothetical application of the CARE framework by a fictional CEO at Nike. The authors have no connection with Nike; nor do the views and attitudes in our example represent those of the real Nike senior executive team.

12 This case study abstracts much of the complexity of the decision-making process within a large corporation. For the sake of brevity and accessibility, we put the reader ("you") in the driver's seat as the single source of authority for the development and management of the AI program. Of course, in reality many of the functions we centralize in a single figure would be spread out across the company.

13 Young, S. D. (2024). Advancing governance, innovation, and risk management for agency use of artificial intelligence. *Official Memorandum*. Available from: https://www.whitehouse.gov/wp-content/uploads/2024/03/M-24-10-Advancing-Governance-Innovation-and-Risk-Management-for-Agency-Use-of-Artificial-Intelligence.pdf [Accessed 16 October 2024]

CHAPTER 8

1 National Science and Technology Council, Networking and Information Technology Research and Development Subcommittee. (2016). *National Artificial intelligence Research and Development Strategic Plan*. Available from: https://www.nitrd.gov/pubs/national_ai_rd_strategic_plan.pdf [Accessed 16 October 2024]

2 Santiso, C. (2022). *Artificial intelligence in the public sector: An engine for innovation in government...if we get it right!* OECD Official Website, 6 July. Available from: https://oecd-opsi.org/blog/ai-an-engine-for-innovation/ [Accessed 17 October 2024]

3 Farrell, M. and Copeland, R. (2024). "Saudi Arabia Plans $40 Billion Push Into Artificial Intelligence." *New York Times*, March 19. Available from: https://www.nytimes.com/2024/03/19/business/saudi-arabia-investment-artificial-intelligence.html [Accessed 16 October 2024]

4 Nellis, S. and Cherney, M. A. (2024). "AI chip manufacturing subsidy leaves US officials with tough choices." *Reuters*, March 6. Available from: https://www.reuters.com/world/us/us-officials-face-tough-choices-subsidizing-ai-chip-manufacturing-2024-03-06/ [Accessed 16 October 2024]

5 "Regulation (EU) 2023/1781 of the European Parliament and of the Council." (2023). Available from: https://eur-lex.europa.eu/legal-content/EN/TXT/?uri=uriserv:OJ.L_.2023.229.01.0001.01.ENG [Accessed 16 October 2024]

6 OECD. (2024). *OECD Digital Economy Outlook 2024 (Volume 1): Embracing the Technology Frontier*. OECD Publishing, Paris, https://doi.org/10.1787/a1689dc5-en. Available from: https://www.oecd.org/en/publications/2024/05/oecd-digital-economy-outlook-2024-volume-1_d30a04c9.html [Accessed 16 October 2024]

7 Luong, N. and Konaev, M. (2023). "In & Out of China: Financial Support for AI Development." *Center for Security and Emerging Technology Blog, Georgetown University*. Available from: https://cset.georgetown.edu/article/

in-out-of-china-financial-support-for-ai-development/ [Accessed 16 October 2024]

8   Luong and Konaev, "In & Out of China."

9   Shubham, S. (2024). "Government announces India AI mission: What it is and more." *The Times of India*, March 8. Available from: https://timesofin-dia.indiatimes.com/gadgets-news/government-announces-india-ai-mission-what-it-is-and-more/articleshow/108322391.cms [Accessed 16 October 2024]

10   Carrasco, M., Habib, C., Felden, F., Sargeant, R., Mills, S., Shenton, S. and Dando, G., 2023. *Generative AI for the Public Sector: From Opportunities to Value.* Boston Consulting Group Report. Available from: https://www.bcg.com/publications/2023/unlocking-genai-opportunities-in-the-government [Accessible 17 October 2024]

11   New York State Department of Labor Website. (2022). *The New York State Department of Labor Receives Two National Awards for Technological Advancements that Helped Thousands of New Yorkers*, July 15. Available from: https://dol.ny.gov/news/new-york-state-department-labor-receives-two-nation-al-awards-technological-advancements-helped. [Accessed 17 October 2024]

12   Wisconsin Department of Workforce Development. (2020). *DWD Clears Wisconsin Unemployment Claims Backlog*, 30 December. Available from: https://dwd.wisconsin.gov/press/2020/201230-unemployment-claim-back-log-cleared.htm [Accessed 12 August 2024]

13   Govtech Singapore. *Activate public-facing chatbots and serve citizens better with VICA.* Available from: https://www.tech.gov.sg/products-and-services/vica/ [Accessed 17 October 2024]

14   Vica Singapore. *Meet AlphabotSG, your virtual assistant to find government services and information easily.* Available from: https://alphabotsg.vica.gov.sg/ [Accessed 17 October 2024]

15   Two seminal and highly influential works on our obligations to future genera-tions are: Parfit, D. (1984). *Reasons and Persons.* Oxford: Clarendon Press; and Jonas, H. (1984). *The Imperative of Responsibility: In Search of an Ethics for the Technological Age.* Chicago: University of Chicago Press.

16   Santiso, C. (2022). *Artificial intelligence in the public sector: An engine for inno-vation in government...if we get it right!* OECD Official Website, 6 July. Avail-able from: https://oecd-opsi.org/blog/ai-an-engine-for-innovation/ [Accessed 17 October 2024]

17   Samuelson, P. A. 1948. Consumption theory in terms of revealed preference, *Economica* 15(60), pp. 243–253.

18   Hoque, F. 2023. *Reinvent: Navigating Business Transformation in a Hyperdigi-tal Era.* Greenleaf Book Group, p. 196.

19   We are naming these tools for purely illustrative purposes. We are not recom-mending them.

20 Lerner, M. (2020). Government tech projects fail by default. It doesn't have to be this way. *Harvard Kennedy School Perspectives on Public Purpose*, October 21. Available from: https://www.belfercenter.org/publication/government-tech-projects-fail-default-it-doesnt-have-be-way [Accessed 17 October 2024]

21 YouGov. (2024). *US public attitudes towards Artificial Intelligence (AI)*. Available from: https://business.yougov.com/content/49938-us-artificial-intelligence-report-2024 [Accessed 17 October 2024]

22 What follows is a purely hypothetical application of the OPEN framework by a fictional senior innovation officer at the EDA. The authors have no connection with the EDA, nor do the views and attitudes in our example represent those of the real EDA leadership team.

23 US Department of Commerce. *About Commerce*. Available from: https://www.commerce.gov/about [Accessed 17 October 2024]

24 US Department of Commerce. *Economic Development Administration*. Available from: https://www.commerce.gov/bureaus-and-offices/eda [Accessed 17 October 2024]

25 This case study abstracts much of the complexity of the decision-making process within a government agency. For the sake of brevity and accessibility, we put the reader ("you") in the driver's seat as the single source of authority for the development and management of the AI program. Of course, in reality many of the functions we centralize in a single figure would be spread out across the agency.

26 US Economic Development Administration. *Tulsa Hub for Equitable & Trustworthy Autonomy (THETA)*. Available from: https://www.eda.gov/funding/programs/regional-technology-and-innovation-hubs/2023/Tulsa-Hub-for-Equitable-Trustworthy-Autonomy [Accessed 17 October 2024]

CHAPTER 9

1 Hinton, G. (2023). *I left so that I could talk about the dangers of AI*. Twitter (now X), May 1. Available from: https://x.com/geoffreyhinton/status/1652993570721210372 [Accessed 17 October 2024]

2 Egan, M. (2024). AI could pose "extinction-level" threat to humans and the US must intervene, State Dept.-commissioned report warns. *CNN Business*, March 12. Available from: https://edition.cnn.com/2024/03/12/business/artificial-intelligence-ai-report-extinction/index.html [Accessed 17 October 2024]

3 Korn, J. (2023). Why the "Godfather of AI" decided he had to "blow the whistle" on the technology. *CNN*, May 3. Available from: https://edition.cnn.com/2023/05/02/tech/hinton-tapper-wozniak-ai-fears/index.html [Accessed 17 October 2024]

4 See, for example, Suleyman, M. (2023). *The Coming Wave: Technology, Power, and the Twenty-First Century's Greatest Dilemma*. Crown.

5   Congressional Research Service. (2024). *Defense Primer: U.S. Policy on Lethal Autonomous Weapon Systems.* Available from: https://crsreports.congress.gov/product/pdf/IF/IF11150 [Accessed 17 October 2024]

6   US Department of Homeland Security. (2021). *Increasing Threats of Deepfake Identities.* Available from: https://www.dhs.gov/sites/default/files/publications/increasing_threats_of_deepfake_identities_0.pdf [Accessed 17 October 2024]

7   The World Economic Forum identifies misinformation and disinformation as the single greatest threat to global stability between 2024 and 2026. See World Economic Forum. (2024). *The Global Risks Report 2024.* Available from: https://www3.weforum.org/docs/WEF_The_Global_Risks_Report_2024.pdf [Accessed 17 October 2024]

8   All quotes in this paragraph are taken from: *The Economist.* (2023). Yuval Noah Harari argues that AI has hacked the operating system of human civilisation. Available from: https://www.economist.com/by-invitation/2023/04/28/yuval-noah-harari-argues-that-ai-has-hacked-the-operating-system-of-human-civilisation [Accessed 17 October 2024]

9   US White House. (2023). *Executive Order on the Safe, Secure, and Trustworthy Development and Use of Artificial Intelligence.* Available from: https://www.whitehouse.gov/briefing-room/presidential-actions/2023/10/30/executive-order-on-the-safe-secure-and-trustworthy-development-and-use-of-artificial-intelligence/ [Accessed 17 October 2024]

10   National Institute of Standards and Technology, US Department of Commerce. (2024). *Artificial Intelligence Risk Management Framework: Generative Artificial Intelligence Profile.* Available from: https://nvlpubs.nist.gov/nistpubs/ai/NIST.AI.600-1.pdf [Accessed 17 October 2024]. The NIST framework has been a useful resource for developing the CARE framework.

11   US Library of Congress. (2023). *China: Generative AI Measures Finalized,* July 10. Available from: https://www.loc.gov/item/global-legal-monitor/2023-07-18/china-generative-ai-measures-finalized/ [Accessed 17 October 2024]

12   Blumenthal, R. and Hawley, J. (2023). *Bipartisan Framework for U.S. AI Act.* Available from: https://www.blumenthal.senate.gov/imo/media/doc/09072023bipartisanaiframework.pdf [Accessed 17 October 2024]

13   IBM Institute for Business Value. (2023). *Augmented work for an automated, AI-driven world.* Available from: https://www.ibm.com/downloads/cas/NGAW'MXAK [Accessed 17 October 2024]

14   Davenport, C. et al. (2024). Here's What the Court's Chevron Ruling Could Mean in Everyday Terms, *New York Times,* June 28. Available from: https://www.nytimes.com/2024/06/28/us/politics/chevron-deference-decision-meaning.html [Accessed 17 October 2024]

15   Suleyman, M. (2023). *The Coming Wave*. London: Bodley Head, pp. 208–210.

16   Browne, R. (2024). Tech giants pledge AI safety commitments—including a "kill switch" if they can't mitigate risks. *CNBC*, May 21. Available from: https://www.cnbc.com/2024/05/21/tech-giants-pledge-ai-safety-commitments-including-a-kill-switch.html [Accessed 17 October 2024]

17   Department for Science, Innovation & Technology, U.K. (2024). *Frontier AI Safety Commitments, AI Seoul Summit 2024*. Available from: https://www.gov.uk/government/publications/frontier-ai-safety-commitments-ai-seoul-summit-2024/frontier-ai-safety-commitments-ai-seoul-summit-2024#fn:1 [Accessed 17 October 2024]

18   Sastry, G. et al. 2024. Computing Power and the Governance of Artificial Intelligence. *arXiv preprint arXiv:2402.08797*.

19   What follows is a purely hypothetical application of the CARE framework by a fictional senior innovation officer at the EDA. The authors have no connection with the EDA; nor do the views and attitudes in our example represent those of the real EDA leadership team.

20   This case study abstracts much of the complexity of the decision-making process within a government agency. For the sake of brevity and accessibility, we put the reader ("you") in the driver's seat as the single source of authority for the development and management of the AI program. Of course, in reality many of the functions we centralize in a single figure would be spread out across the agency.

CHAPTER 10

1   Mark 3:25, Holy Bible, King James Version.

2   Lincoln, A. (1858). House Divided speech. June 6, Springfield, Illinois. Available from: https://housedivided.dickinson.edu/sites/teagle/texts/lincoln-house-divided-speech-1858/ [Accessed 17 October 2024]

3   Dunbar, R. I. (1992). Neocortex size as a constraint on group size in primates. *Journal of Human Evolution*, 22(6), pp. 469–493.

4   There are by now too many examples of this to list all of them. But to give a little flavor, see, for example, Luna, N. (2019). Food truck powered by advanced robotics lands in L.A., *Nation's Restaurant News*, 14 October. Available from: https://www.nrn.com/technology/food-truck-powered-advanced-robotics-lands-la [Accessed 17 October 2024]; Hang, K. (2024). The Robots Are Coming for Chinese Food Next, Eater Los Angeles, 27 June. Available from:https://la.eater.com/2024/6/27/24187466/tigawok-sawtelle-wok-robot-machine-cooking-restaurant-opening-los-angeles [Accessed 17 October 2024]; and Fioresi, D. (2024). World's first AI-powered restaurant soon opening doors in Pasadena. CBS News, 6 January. Available from: https://www.cbsnews.com/losangeles/news/worlds-first-ai-powered-restaurant-soon-opening-doors-in-pasadena/ [Accessed 17 October 2024]

5   Well, actually he said, "Greed, for lack of a better word, is good," but that's not as snappy as the phrase that's lodged in the collective consciousness.
6   1 Corinthians 13:13, Holy Bible, New International Version.
·7   Jonas, H. (1984). *The Imperative of Responsibility: In Search of an Ethics for the Technological Age*. Chicago: University of Chicago Press, p. 1.

ACKNOWLEDGMENTS

TRANSCEND represents more than just a meeting of ideas—it stands as a testament to the power of collaboration, resilience, and the pursuit of something greater than ourselves. This book explores how AI can empower humanity to transcend its limits while protecting what is most precious about the human experience. It is the culmination of the efforts, wisdom, and inspiration of many people, and I am eternally grateful for what I have learned from all of them.

To my family and closest friends, you are the foundation of all that I strive to achieve. Your love, support, and unwavering belief in me fuel every step of my journey.

Rian, you are the true inspiration behind this book. Your battle with multiple myeloma, fought with such grace, courage, and resilience, has revealed the boundless potential of the human spirit. You are a beacon of hope, reminding us all that no challenge is too great to overcome. The possibility that AI might one day unlock cures for diseases like cancer is a driving force behind this work.

To my extraordinary research, editorial, design, production, publishing, marketing, and public relations teams—your expertise and dedication have been nothing short of world-class. You brought this vision to life with professionalism, creativity, and passion. I cannot thank you enough for transforming this idea into a reality.

I am deeply thankful to the cross-industry customers, partners, team members, leaders, and academics who have embraced and applied my methods, processes, and platforms. Your commitment to innovation and sustainable success has driven me to continuously push against boundaries, refining pragmatic solutions that address complex problems. I am honored to travel with you on these journeys, learning, growing, and serving together.

To the thought leaders and visionary thinkers who provided invaluable feedback and reviews, your wisdom has inspired new ideas and has sparked deeper exploration of the ground that lies at the intersection of leadership, technology, and mindfulness. You have challenged me to think bigger, connect in ways I hadn't imagined, and push beyond the ordinary. Your contributions were instrumental in shaping the heart of *TRANSCEND*.

To my readers, thank you for your curiosity and engagement. Your ongoing interest in the ways human values and technology connect with and reflect each other has motivated me to write this book. I hope *TRANSCEND* serves as a guide and a source of inspiration as we navigate this evolving landscape together.

Finally, to the creators, innovators, and visionaries who are shaping the future of humanity with empathy and integrity—this book is dedicated to you. You are the architects of tomorrow, building a future in which technology enhances, rather than diminishes, our humanity. Together, we can unlock the limitless potential of the future.

Thank you all.

Faisal Hoque, October 2024.

ABOUT THE AUTHOR

*F*aisal Hoque is recognized as one of the world's leading management thinkers and technologists. He is an entrepreneur, innovator, and best-selling author with close to thirty years of cross-industry success. Faisal is the founder of SHADOKA, NextChapter, and other companies. He also serves as a transformation and innovation partner for CACI, an $8 billion company focused on US national security.

As a founder and CEO of multiple companies, Faisal is a three-time winner of the Deloitte Technology Fast 50™ and Fast 500™ awards. He has developed more than twenty commercial platforms and worked with leadership at the US Departments of Defense and Homeland Security, GE, MasterCard, American Express, Home Depot, PepsiCo, IBM, Chase, and others. Faisal is a three-time *Wall Street Journal* bestselling author for his books *REINVENT* (#1), *Everything Connects* (#2), and *LIFT* (#1), with the latter two also reaching the *USA Today* bestseller list.

Faisal has authored ten award-winning books (published by Cambridge University Press, the *Financial Times*, HarperCollins Leadership, McGraw Hill, Fast Company Press, and others). His more than thirty awards include Axiom Gold, Nautilus, Foreword, Book Excellence, 2023 Thinkers50 Distinguished Achievement Awards Shortlist, and others in the fields of humanity, business, and technology. He volunteers for educational organizations around the world, including MIT's IDEAS Social Innovation program, and is a contributor at the Swiss business school IMD, Thinkers50, and the Project Management Institute (PMI).

Faisal has been named among the Top 100 Most Influential People in Technology by the editors of Ziff Davis Enterprise while Trust Across America-Trust Around the World (TAA-TAW) named him one of their

Top 100 Thought Leaders. His work has appeared in and on the *Wall Street Journal*, Fox, CBS, the *Financial Times*, *Fast Company*, *Business Insider*, *BusinessWeek*, *Forbes*, *Inc.*, and others.

Faisal frequently speaks at international conferences, business schools, corporate gatherings, and business summits. His talks focus on leadership, innovation, and transformation with a particular emphasis on long-term sustainable impact. His books, articles, and speeches offer guidance on how to overcome challenges and foster meaningful leadership in the age of AI and digital technologies. Inspired by his personal experiences, Faisal is also a passionate advocate for cancer research, raising awareness and supporting research efforts to combat the disease.

RESEARCH AND EDITORIAL TEAM

DR. PAUL SCADE

Paul is a bestselling and award-winning writer and editor with more than twenty years of research, writing, and editorial experience. His commercial writing work spans a wide range of genres, with an emphasis on thought leadership, organizational leadership, technology, and health care. Paul trained as an academic historian of philosophy and spent fifteen years teaching and researching at universities in Europe and the United States. His research on ancient philosophy has been published by the leading academic presses in the world, and he continues to work as a writing coach and editor for senior historians, philosophers, management thinkers, and scientists. Paul is an Honorary Fellow in the Faculty of Humanities and Social Sciences at the University of Liverpool.

DR. PRANAY SANKLECHA

Pranay was admitted to the University of Oxford at the age of fifteen, graduated at eighteen to become a commodities trader, and then returned to academia five years later to begin a research and teaching career as a philosopher. He now works as a philosophical consultant and a writer, researcher, and editor. Pranay's areas of expertise include intergenerational justice, with a particular focus on how changes in technology and society alter what it means to be human, and the practical application of philosophy to life and business. A passionate cricket fan, he has also written about the sport as a correspondent for ESPN.

MORE FROM THE AUTHOR

LEAD. INNOVATE. TRANSFORM.

At SHADOKA, we enable sustainable capabilities at the intersection of humanity, business, and technology by bringing together thought leadership, education, and digital platforms to reshape the future of work.

Our mission is to empower organizations to thrive in an ever-changing landscape by leveraging cutting-edge technologies, fostering innovation, and developing transformational leadership. What sets us apart is our unique blend of deep technological understanding, advanced management science, and a fundamentally human-centric approach.

For more information, visit SHADOKA.com.

NEXTCHAPTER®
HUMANITY. BUSINESS. TECHNOLOGY.

NextChapter breaks new ground in the fields of research and thought leadership by exploring the intersections of humanity, business, and technology. Our work informs industry leaders and helps organizations shape the future of business.

Our core focus areas include transformational leadership, where we explore innovative leadership models to inspire change; AI and digital innovation, investigating the impact of emerging technologies on business growth; organizational transformation, analyzing how businesses can stay agile and adaptive; and entrepreneurship and intrapreneurship, examining how both can drive continuous innovation within companies.

For more information, visit NextChapter.org.

PREVIOUS BOOKS

DIGITAL. BUSINESS. MANAGEMENT.
Transformation Requires Much More Than Technology

Transformation requires more than simply obtaining the latest technology, plugging it in, and sitting back to watch reinvention take place. To make the most of new technologies, organizations must change from top to bottom, adopting new mindsets, attitudes, and assumptions about how they operate, how they can grow, and even the very reason for their existence. *REINVENT* takes the reader on a journey rich with promise, explaining complex concepts in an accessible and understandable manner. This multi-award-winning and highly acclaimed *Wall Street Journal* #1 bestseller introduces readers to ideas, concepts, and a comprehensive practical framework that can help them reap the benefits of business and digital transformation.

MINDFULNESS. CREATIVITY. INNOVATION.
A Holistic Approach to Creating Long-Term Value

Part philosophical treatise, part business book, and part history, *Everything Connects* brings together the thought of East and West, from the wisdom of 2500-year-old philosophies and the interconnected insights of Leonardo da Vinci to the experience of transforming Fortune 100 companies. This multi-award-winning *Wall Street Journal* and *USA Today* bestseller draws lessons from this broad canvas of ideas to show how any business can harness creative thinking and a start-up attitude to adapt smoothly and easily to change. The lessons here don't just offer a quick fix for your next financial quarter; they show you how to succeed in the long run.

EMPATHY. KNOWLEDGE. EXECUTION.
Transformational Leaders Leverage Positive Change

This highly acclaimed *Wall Street Journal* (#1) and *USA Today* bestseller explores the intersection of transformational leadership, systemic thinking, and experiential learning—all of which are required to survive and thrive when facing the tsunami of disruptions that confront us today. *LIFT* proposes that "transformational" leaders—those who focus on people and long-term innovations and solutions—are the key to a prosperous future. In *LIFT*, Faisal Hoque shows his readers how to become transformational leaders in an ever-changing world through the convergence of empathy, execution, and knowledge.